Apple Watch 7 User Guide

Comprehensive Step-by-Step Apple Watch Series 7 User Manual for WatchOS 8

Daniel Dean

Contents

Set up and get started 9
    Get started 9
    Your Apple Watch 12
Your Apple Watch 13
    Apple Watch gestures 14
    Set up and pair your Apple Watch with iPhone 14
    The Apple Watch app 19
    Charge Apple Watch 20
    What's new in Apple Watch and watchOS 8 26
    Turn on and wake Apple Watch 33
    Lock or unlock Apple Watch 36
    Change language and orientation on Apple Watch 40
    Remove, change, and fasten Apple Watch bands 41
    Stay fit with Apple Watch 43
    Track important health information with Apple Watch 47
    Stay connected with Apple Watch 50
Set up Apple Watch for a family member 53
    Set up reminders on a family member's Apple Watch 59
    Upgrade reminders 59
    Get started with Schooltime on Apple Watch 60
    Play music on a managed Apple Watch 62
    See activity and health reports for family members 63
    Use Apple Cash Family on a family member's Apple Watch .. 65
Basics 66
    Apps on Apple Watch 66
    Open apps on Apple Watch 71
    Organize apps on Apple Watch 74
    Get more apps on Apple Watch 77

Tell time on Apple Watch 79

The Apple Watch status icons 79

Use Control Center on Apple Watch 82

Use Focus on Apple Watch 91

Adjust brightness, text size, sounds, and haptics on Apple Watch 95

See and respond to notifications on Apple Watch 98

Change notification settings on Apple Watch 101

Manage your Apple ID settings on Apple Watch 105

Use shortcuts on Apple Watch 107

Create an emergency Medical ID 108

Manage fall detection on Apple Watch 110

Set up Handwashing on Apple Watch 111

Connect Apple Watch to a Wi-Fi network 112

Connect Apple Watch to Bluetooth headphones or speakers 114

Hand off tasks from Apple Watch 117

Unlock your Mac with Apple Watch 117

Unlock your iPhone with Apple Watch 119

Use Apple Watch without its paired iPhone 120

Use Apple Watch with a cellular network 121

Siri 122

Use Siri on Apple Watch 122

Listen and respond to notifications with AirPods and Beats headphones on Apple Watch 125

Announce calls with Siri on Apple Watch 127

Apple Watch faces 127

Explore the Face Gallery on Apple Watch 127

Customize the watch face 129

Share Apple Watch faces 133

Apple Watch faces and their features 135

Apple Fitness+ 178

    Subscribe to Apple Fitness+ 178

    All about Apple Fitness+ 180

    Set up Apple Fitness+ on Apple TV 184

    Browse Apple Fitness+ workouts and Meditations 185

    Start an Apple Fitness+ workout 190

    Pause and resume an Apple Fitness+ workout 192

    End and review an Apple Fitness+ workout 193

    Work out together using SharePlay 193

    Change what's on the screen during an Apple Fitness+ workout 195

    Download an Apple Fitness+ workout on iPhone or iPad 197

APPS 198

    Activity 198

    Track daily activity with Apple Watch 198

    Share your activity from Apple Watch 204

    Add an alarm on Apple Watch 205

Audiobooks 210

    Add audiobooks to Apple Watch 210

    Play audiobooks on Apple Watch 210

    Measure blood oxygen levels on Apple Watch 213

    Use Calculator on Apple Watch 215

    Check and update your calendar on Apple Watch 217

    Use Camera Remote and timer on Apple Watch 220

    Use Compass on Apple Watch 222

    Use Cycle Tracking on Apple Watch 224

    Contacts 225

    Record an electrocardiogram with the ECG app on Apple Watch 228

Find People, Devices, and Items 229

Find People 229

View a friend's location with Apple Watch 229

Use Apple Watch to get directions or contact a friend 232

Find misplaced devices with Apple Watch 232

Find Items 236

Locate an AirTag or other item in Find Items 236

Mark an AirTag or other item as lost in Find Items on Apple Watch 239

Check your heart rate on Apple Watch 239

Home 244

Control your home with Apple Watch 244

Send and receive Intercom messages from Apple Watch 246

Remotely access your smart home accessories from Apple Watch 247

Mail 248

Read mail on Apple Watch 248

Write and reply to mail on Apple Watch 250

Manage mail on Apple Watch 253

Maps 256

Find places and explore with Apple Watch 256

Get directions on Apple Watch 260

Use Memoji on Apple Watch 263

Messages 265

Read messages on Apple Watch 265

Send messages from Apple Watch 268

Reply to messages on Apple Watch 274

Mindfulness 275

Use Apple Watch to practice mindfulness 275

Listen to guided Meditations on Apple Watch (Apple Fitness+ subscription required) 279

Music 280

Add music to Apple Watch 280

5

Remove music from Apple Watch 282
Play music on Apple Watch 283
Listen to radio on Apple Watch 287
Read news stories on Apple Watch 288

Noise 290
Measure noise levels with Apple Watch 290
Monitor your environmental noise exposure with Apple Watch 292
Use Now Playing on Apple Watch 293

Phone 295
Answer phone calls on Apple Watch 295
Make phone calls on Apple Watch 297
Make an emergency phone call on Apple Watch 299
Use Dual SIM iPhone with Apple Watch cellular models 302

Photos 304
Choose a photo album and manage storage on Apple Watch 304
View photos and Memories on Apple Watch 306

Podcasts 309
Add podcasts to Apple Watch 309
Play podcasts on Apple Watch 311
Set and respond to reminders on Apple Watch 313

Remote 315
Use Apple Watch to control music on a Mac or PC 315
Control Apple TV with Apple Watch 316
Track your sleep with Apple Watch 317
Track stocks on Apple Watch 322
Time events with a stopwatch on Apple Watch 324
Set timers on Apple Watch 326
Tips 328
Record and play voice memos on Apple Watch 330

Use Walkie-Talkie on Apple Watch 331
Wallet and Apple Pay 333
   About Wallet on Apple Watch 333
   Apple Pay on Apple Watch 334
   Set up Apple Pay on Apple Watch 334
   Make purchases with Apple Watch 337
   Send, receive, and request money with Apple Watch (U.S. only) 339
   Manage Apple Cash with Apple Watch (U.S. only) 342
   Add and use passes in Wallet on Apple Watch 343
   Use rewards cards on Apple Watch 345
   Pay with Apple Watch on Mac 346
   Use transit cards with Apple Watch 347
   Unlock your car, home, and hotel room with keys in Wallet on Apple Watch 348
   Use vaccination cards in Wallet on Apple Watch 349
   Check the weather on Apple Watch 350
Workout 353
   Work out with Apple Watch 353
   Start a workout on Apple Watch 354
   End and review your workout on Apple Watch 357
   Go for a swim with Apple Watch 358
   Use gym equipment with Apple Watch 359
   Adjust the workout settings on Apple Watch 361
   Use World Clock on Apple Watch to check the time in other locations 363
Accessibility and related settings 366
   Use VoiceOver on Apple Watch 366
   Set up Apple Watch using VoiceOver 368
   Apple Watch basics with VoiceOver 370
   Use AssistiveTouch on Apple Watch 371

Use a braille display with VoiceOver on Apple Watch 374

Use Zoom on Apple Watch 375

Tell time with haptic feedback on Apple Watch 376

Adjust text size and other visual settings on Apple Watch 377

Adjust motor skills settings on Apple Watch 379

Set up and use RTT on Apple Watch (cellular models only) 380

Accessibility audio settings on Apple Watch 382

The Accessibility Shortcut on Apple Watch 382

Restart, reset, restore, and update 383

Restart Apple Watch 383

Erase Apple Watch 384

Restore Apple Watch from a backup 385

Update Apple Watch software 386

If you forget your Apple Watch passcode 386

8

Set up and get started

Get started

It takes just a few minutes to get up and running with Apple Watch.

Pair Apple Watch with your iPhone

To set up your Apple Watch, put it on your wrist snugly, then press and hold the side button to turn it on. Bring your iPhone near your watch, then follow the onscreen instructions. To prepare an Apple Watch for a person in your family, tap Set Up for a Family Member.

Choose a watch face

Apple Watch comes with many attractive and useful watch faces. To switch to a different face, swipe left or right across the screen. To see even more available faces, touch and hold the display, swipe left until you see 　, tap the button, then scroll through the faces. Tap Add, customize the watch face if you choose to, then press the Digital Crown to use it.

Open an app

Your Apple Watch comes with a variety of apps for staying on top of your health, working out, and keeping in touch. To open an app, press the Digital Crown, then tap the app. To return to the Home Screen, press the Digital Crown again. You can download more apps from the App Store on Apple Watch.

Quickly change settings

Control Center gives you instant access to silent mode, Do Not Disturb, Wi-Fi, flashlight, and more—just like on iPhone. To open Control Center, touch and hold the bottom of the display, then swipe up.

Your Apple Watch

This guide helps you get started using Apple Watch Series 7 with watchOS 8.1.

Your Apple Watch

Apple Watch Series 7

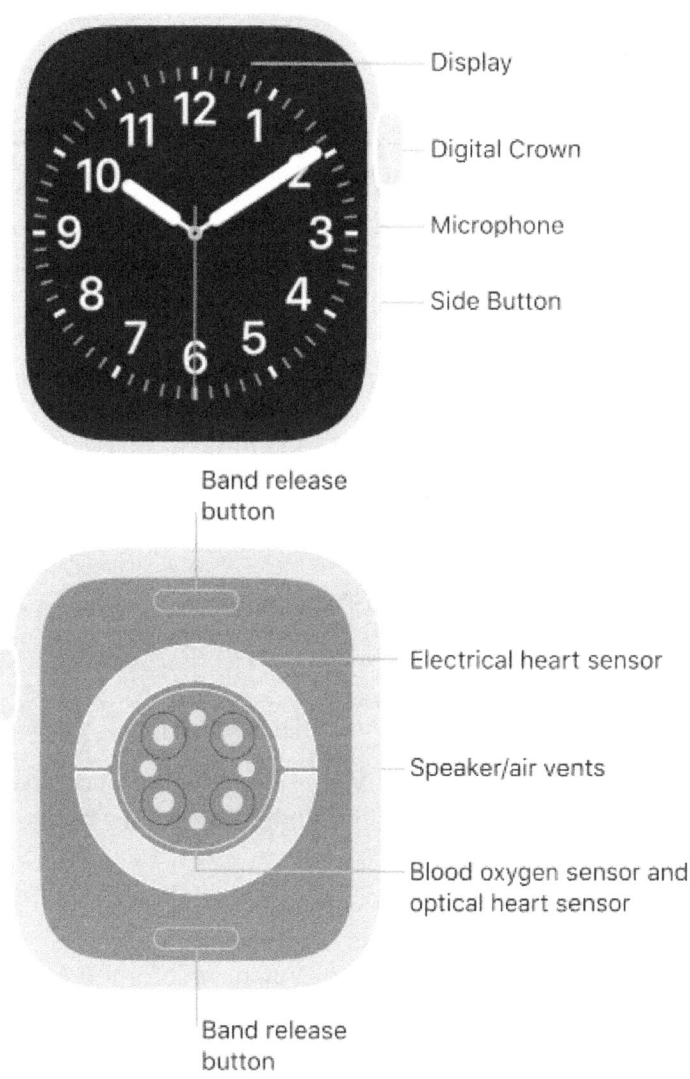

13

Apple Watch gestures

You use several basic gestures to interact with Apple Watch.

●	Tap: Touch one finger lightly on the screen.
◇	Swipe: Move one finger across the screen—up, down, left, or right.
✥	Drag: Move one finger across the screen without lifting.

Set up and pair your Apple Watch with iPhone

To use your Apple Watch with watchOS 8, you need to pair your Apple Watch with an iPhone 6s or later with iOS 15 or later. Setup assistants on your iPhone and Apple Watch work together to help you pair and set up your Apple Watch.

If you have difficulty seeing your Apple Watch or iPhone, VoiceOver or Zoom can help—even during setup.

Turn on, pair, and set up your Apple Watch

1. Put your Apple Watch on your wrist. Adjust the band or choose a band size so your Apple Watch fits closely but comfortably on your wrist.
2. To turn on your Apple Watch, press and hold the side button until you see the Apple logo.
3. Bring your iPhone near your Apple Watch, wait for the Apple Watch pairing screen to appear on your iPhone, then tap Continue.
   Or open the Apple Watch app on your iPhone, then tap Pair

New Watch.

4. Tap Set Up for Myself.
5. When prompted, position your iPhone so that your Apple Watch appears in the viewfinder in the Apple Watch app. This pairs the two devices.
6. Tap Set Up Apple Watch, then follow the instructions on your iPhone and Apple Watch to finish setup.

To learn more about your Apple Watch while it's syncing, tap Get to Know Your Watch. You can learn what's new, view Apple Watch tips, and read this user guide, right on your iPhone. After your Apple Watch is set up, you can find this information by opening the Apple Watch app on your iPhone, then tapping Discover.

Activate cellular service

You can activate cellular service on your Apple Watch during setup. If you don't wish to, you can activate it later in the Apple Watch app on your iPhone.

Your iPhone and Apple Watch must use the same cellular carrier. However, if you set up an Apple Watch for someone in your Family Sharing group, that watch can use a cellular carrier different from the one used on the iPhone you manage it with.

Cellular service not available in all regions.

Trouble pairing?

- If you see a watch face when you're trying to pair: Your Apple Watch is already paired to an iPhone. You need to first erase all Apple Watch content and reset settings.
- If the camera doesn't start the pairing process: Tap Pair Apple Watch Manually at the bottom of the iPhone screen, and follow the onscreen instructions.
- If Apple Watch isn't pairing with iPhone: See the Apple Support article If your Apple Watch isn't connected or paired with your iPhone.

Unpair Apple Watch

1. Open the Apple Watch app on your iPhone.
2. Tap My Watch, then tap All Watches at the top of the screen.
3. Tap ⓘ next to the Apple Watch you want to unpair, then tap Unpair Apple Watch.

Pair more than one Apple Watch

You can pair another Apple Watch in the same way you paired your first one. Bring your iPhone near your Apple Watch, wait for the Apple Watch pairing screen to appear on your iPhone, then tap Pair. Or follow these steps:

1. Open the Apple Watch app on your iPhone.
2. Tap My Watch, then tap All Watches at the top of the screen.
3. Tap Add Watch, then follow the onscreen instructions.

Quickly switch to a different Apple Watch

Your iPhone detects the paired Apple Watch you're wearing and automatically connects to it. Just put on a different Apple Watch and raise your wrist.
You can also choose an Apple Watch manually:

1. Open the Apple Watch app on your iPhone.
2. Tap My Watch, then tap All Watches at the top of the screen.

3. Turn off Auto Switch.

To see if your Apple Watch is connected to your iPhone, touch and hold the bottom of the watch screen, swipe up to open Control Center, then look for the Connected status icon .

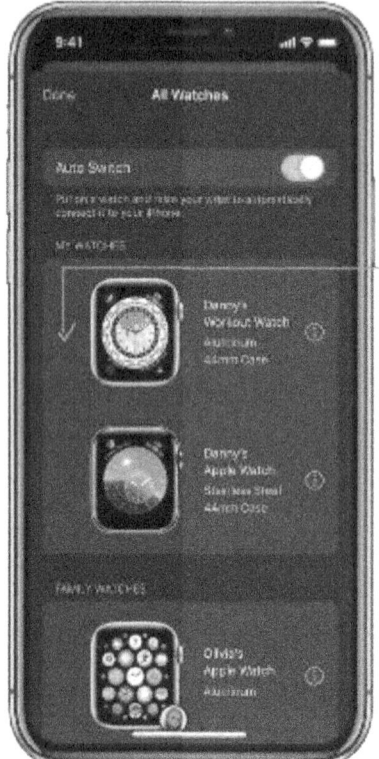

The active Apple Watch.

Pair Apple Watch to a new iPhone

If your Apple Watch is paired to your old iPhone and you now want to pair it with your new iPhone, follow these steps:
1. Use iCloud Backup to back up the iPhone currently paired to your Apple Watch.
2. Set up your new iPhone. On the Apps & Data screen, choose to restore from an iCloud backup, then select the latest backup.
3. Continue iPhone setup and, when prompted, choose to use your Apple Watch with your new iPhone.

When iPhone setup completes, your Apple Watch prompts you to pair it to the new iPhone. Tap OK on your Apple Watch, then enter its passcode.

Transfer an existing cellular plan to a new Apple Watch

You can transfer your existing cellular plan from your Apple Watch with cellular to another Apple Watch with cellular by following these steps:
1. While wearing your Apple Watch, open the Apple Watch app on your iPhone.
2. Tap My Watch, tap Cellular, then tap ⓘ next to your cellular plan.
3. Tap Remove [name of carrier] Plan, then confirm your choice.
   You may need to contact your carrier to remove this Apple Watch from your cellular plan.
4. Remove your old watch, put on your other Apple Watch with cellular, tap My Watch, then tap Cellular.
   Follow the instructions to activate your watch for cellular.

The Apple Watch app

Use the Apple Watch app on your iPhone to customize watch faces, adjust settings and notifications, configure the Dock, install apps, and more.

Open the Apple Watch app

1. On your iPhone, tap the Apple Watch app icon.
2. Tap My Watch to see the settings for your Apple Watch.

If you have more than one Apple Watch paired with your iPhone, you see the settings for your active Apple Watch.

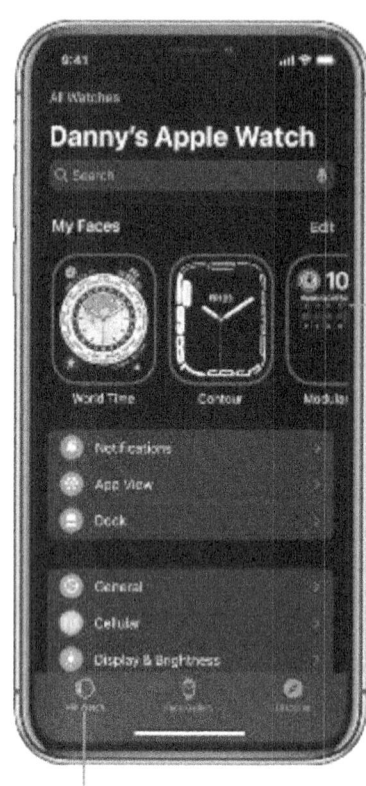

Swipe to see your watch face collection.

Settings for Apple Watch.

Learn more about Apple Watch

The Discover tab in the Apple Watch app includes links to Apple Watch tips, a helpful overview of your Apple Watch, and this user guide, all viewable on iPhone.

Charge Apple Watch

Set up the charger

1. In a well-ventilated area, place your charger or charging cable on a flat surface.
   Your Apple Watch comes with the Apple Watch Magnetic Fast Charger to USB-C Cable (Apple Watch Series 7 only)

or the Apple Watch Magnetic Charging Cable (earlier models). You can also use a MagSafe Duo Charger or Apple Watch Magnetic Charging Dock (sold separately).
2. Plug the charging cable into the power adapter (sold separately).
3. Plug the adapter into a power outlet.

Note: Fast charging is not available in all regions.

Begin charging Apple Watch

Place the Apple Watch Magnetic Fast Charger to USB-C cable (included with Apple Watch Series 7) or Apple Watch Magnetic Charging Cable (included with earlier models) on the back of your Apple Watch. The concave end of the charging cable magnetically snaps to the back of your Apple Watch and aligns it properly.
You hear a chime when charging begins (unless your Apple Watch is in silent mode) and see a charging symbol ⚡ on the watch face. The symbol is red when Apple Watch needs power and turns green when Apple Watch is charging.
You can charge your Apple Watch in a flat position with its band open, or on its side.

- If you're using the Apple Watch Magnetic Charging Dock or MagSafe Duo Charger: Lay your Apple Watch on the dock.
- If your battery is very low: You may see an image of the Apple Watch Magnetic Fast Charger to USB-C Cable or Apple Watch Magnetic Charging Cable and the low battery symbol ⚡ on the screen.

Apple Watch Series 7

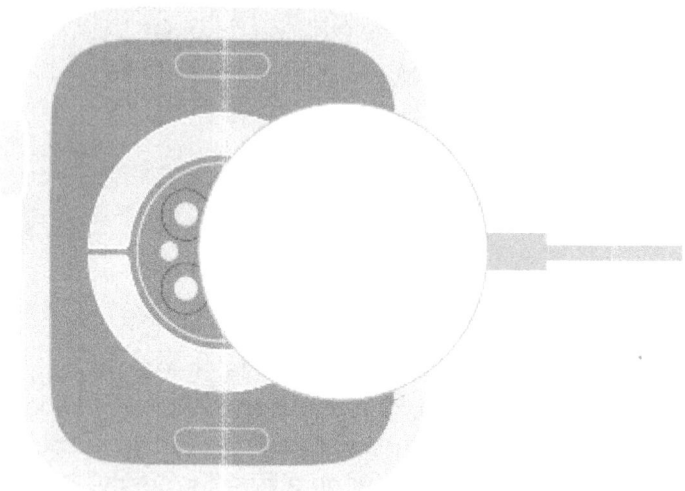

Check remaining power

To see remaining power, touch and hold the bottom of the screen, then swipe up to open Control Center. To more quickly check the remaining power, add a battery complication to the watch face.

View the percentage of remaining battery life.

Prevent apps from refreshing in the background

When you switch to a new app, the app you were using doesn't remain open or take up system resources, but it may still "refresh"—check for updates and new content—in the background.
Refreshing apps in the background can use power. To maximize battery life, you can turn this option off.

1. Open the Settings app on your Apple Watch.
2. Go to General > Background App Refresh, then turn off Background App Refresh to turn off refresh for all your apps, or turn off refresh for individual apps.

Note: Apps with complications on the current watch face will continue to refresh, even when their background app refresh setting is off.

Save power when the battery is low

You can put your Apple Watch in Power Reserve mode to stretch the remaining battery power. Your Apple Watch still displays the time, but you can't use apps.

1. Touch and hold the bottom of the screen, then swipe up to open Control Center.
2. Tap the battery percentage, then drag the Power Reserve slider to the right.

Tip: If you have battery-powered devices such as AirPods connected to your Apple Watch through Bluetooth, their remaining charge appears on this screen.
When battery charge drops to 10 percent or lower, your Apple Watch alerts you and gives you the opportunity to enter Power Reserve mode.

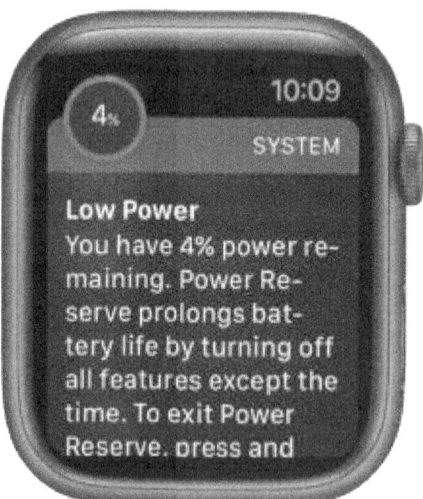

When your Apple Watch is almost out of power, it enters Power Reserve mode automatically.

Return to normal power mode

Restart your Apple Watch—press and hold the side button until the Apple logo appears.
The battery must have at least 10 percent charge for your Apple Watch to restart.

Check time since the last charge

1. Open the Settings app on your Apple Watch.
2. Tap Battery.
   The Battery screen shows the remaining battery percentage, a graph that details the recent history of the battery charge, and information about when the battery was last charged.

Check battery health

You can find out the capacity of your Apple Watch battery relative to when it was new.

1. Open the Settings app on your Apple Watch.
2. Tap Battery, then tap Battery Health.

Apple Watch alerts you if battery capacity is significantly reduced, allowing you to check your service options.

Use optimized battery charging

To reduce battery aging, Apple Watch uses on-device machine learning to learn your daily charging routines so it can wait to finish charging past 80 percent until you need to use it.

1. Open the Settings app on your Apple Watch.
2. Tap Battery, then tap Battery Health.
3. Turn on Optimized Battery Charging.

What's new in Apple Watch and watchOS 8

The largest and most advanced display, most durable Apple Watch, and fast charging (Apple Watch Series 7) The latest Apple Watch features more screen area, with smaller borders and a refractive edge effect. With the included USB-C cable, Apple Watch Series 7 charges faster than any previous Apple Watch model.

Note: Fast charging is not available in all regions.

Explore new watch faces Switch things up with new watch faces for Apple Watch—World Time, which makes it easy to see the time across the globe, Portraits, which brings your favorite portrait photos front and center, and, on Apple Watch Series 7, Contour and Modular Duo.

Edit on the fly To correct errors in text, use the Digital Crown to scroll precisely to the spot you want to edit.

Scribble and dictate, all on one screen In Mail and Messages it's easier than ever to make your point by seamlessly switching from Scribble to dictation and back again.

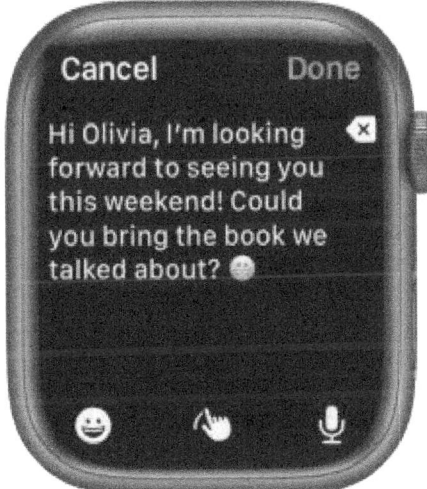

QWERTY and QuickPath keyboard Enter text with the full QWERTY keyboard. Just tap each character or use QuickPath to swipe between letters without lifting your finger.

Enjoy a mindful moment The new Reflect feature in the Mindfulness app helps you establish a meditation practice by focusing on a short, thought-provoking theme. With an Apple Fitness+ subscription, listen to guided Meditations right on Apple Watch.

Try new workouts Strengthen your core with the new Pilates workout, and clear your mind and reduce stress with Tai Chi.

See your respiratory rate as you sleep Your Apple Watch can track your respiratory rate when you're sleeping. Knowing your sleep respiratory rate can give you greater insight into your overall health.

Keep keys on Apple Watch Store your home, car, and hotel key in the Wallet app on your watch, so you're never without it.

Store and present your vaccination card (watchOS 8.1) Add a vaccination record in the Health app on your iPhone, add it to the Wallet app, and double-click the side button on Apple Watch to present your card when you need to show proof of vaccination.

Better control your home In watchOS 8, the Home app has been redesigned to make it easier than ever to control the smart devices in your home by highlighting the accessories you're most likely to use based on the time of day.

Locate misplaced devices and items In addition to finding your friends, you can now locate your missing Apple devices and AirTags with the new Find Devices and Find Items apps on Apple Watch.

Rediscover significant people, places, and events Photo highlights from your Memories and Featured Photos now automatically sync to your watch, serving up something new every day.

Stay focused Focus helps you stay in the moment when you need to concentrate, allowing only the notifications you want. Choose from preset Focus suggestions like working or exercising, or sync a custom Focus you've created on your iPhone, iPad, or Mac.

Navigate your watch with AssistiveTouch People who have limb differences can use Apple Watch and its built- in motion sensors to answer calls, control an onscreen pointer, and even launch a menu of actions—all through hand gestures.

Make contact Use the new Contacts app to quickly browse, add, or edit contacts right on your Apple Watch.

Create multiple timers When making a multicourse meal, timing is everything. In the Timers app, start multiple timers as you begin cooking and use Siri to give each one a label.

Check the volume In watchOS 8 you can see real- time headphone audio levels in Control Center when you're listening to media.

Turn on and wake Apple Watch

Turn your Apple Watch on and off

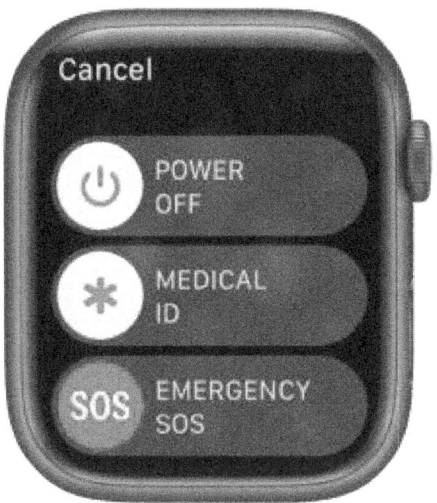

- Turn on: If your Apple Watch is off, press and hold the side button until the Apple logo appears (you might see a black screen for a short time first).
  The watch face appears when Apple Watch is on.
- Turn off: Normally, you'll leave your Apple Watch on all of the time, but if you need to turn it off, press and hold the side button until the sliders appear, then drag the Power Off slider to the right.

Tip: You can't turn off your Apple Watch while it's charging. To turn off your Apple Watch, first disconnect it from the charger.

Always On

Always On lets Apple Watch display the watch face and time, even when your wrist is down. When you raise your wrist, Apple Watch functions fully.

1. Open the Settings app on your Apple Watch.
2. Tap Display & Brightness, then tap Always On.
3. Turn on Always On, then tap the following options to configure them:
    - Show Complication Data: Choose the complications that show data when your wrist is down.
    - Show Notifications: Choose the notifications that are visible when your wrist is down.
    - Show Apps: Choose the apps that are visible when your wrist is down.

Wake the Apple Watch display

By default, you can wake the Apple Watch display in these ways:
- Raise your wrist. Your Apple Watch sleeps again when you lower your wrist.
- Tap the display or press the Digital Crown.
- Turn the Digital Crown upward.

If you don't want your Apple Watch to wake when you raise your wrist or turn the Digital Crown, open the Settings app on your Apple Watch, go to Display & Brightness, then configure Wake on Wrist Raise and Raise On Crown Up.

Tip: To temporarily prevent your Apple Watch from waking when you raise your wrist, use theater mode.

If your Apple Watch doesn't wake when you raise your wrist, make sure you selected the proper wrist and watch orientation. If your Apple Watch doesn't wake when you tap the display or press or turn the Digital Crown, it may need charging.

Return to the clock face

You can choose how long before Apple Watch returns to the clock face from an open app.

1. Open the Settings app on your Apple Watch.
2. Go to General > Return to Clock, then scroll down and choose when you want your Apple Watch to return to the clock face: Always, After 2 minutes, or After 1 hour.
3. You can also return to the clock face by pressing the Digital Crown.

By default, the setting you select applies to all apps, but you can choose a custom time for each app. To do so, tap an app on this screen, tap Custom, then choose a setting.

Wake to your last activity

For some apps, you can set Apple Watch to return you to where you were before it went to sleep. These apps include Audiobooks, Maps, Mindfulness, Music, Now Playing, Podcasts, Stopwatch, Timers, Voice Memos, Walkie-Talkie, and Workout.

1. Open the Settings app on your Apple Watch.
2. Go to General > Return to Clock, scroll down and tap an app, then turn on Return to App.

To return to the clock face, just stop what you're doing in the app—for example, stop a podcast, end a route in Maps, or cancel a timer. You can also open the Apple Watch app on your iPhone, tap My Watch, then go to General > Return to Clock.

Keep the Apple Watch display on longer

You can keep the display on longer when you tap to wake your Apple Watch.

1. Open the Settings app ⚙ on your Apple Watch.
2. Tap Display & Brightness, tap Wake Duration, then tap Wake for 70 Seconds.

Lock or unlock Apple Watch

Unlock Apple Watch

You can unlock Apple Watch manually, by entering the passcode, or set it to unlock automatically when you unlock your iPhone.

- Enter the passcode: Wake Apple Watch, enter the watch passcode, then tap OK.
- Unlock Apple Watch when you unlock your iPhone: Open the Settings app ⚙ on your Apple Watch, tap Passcode, then turn on Unlock with iPhone.
  You can also open the Apple Watch app on your iPhone, tap My Watch, tap Passcode, then turn on Unlock with iPhone. Your iPhone must be within normal Bluetooth range (about 33 feet or 10 meters) of your Apple Watch to unlock it. If Bluetooth is off on Apple Watch, enter the passcode on Apple Watch to unlock it.

Tip: Your Apple Watch passcode can be different from your iPhone passcode—in fact, it's better to use different passcodes.

Change your passcode

You can change the passcode you created when you first set up your Apple Watch by following these steps:

1. Open the Settings app on your Apple Watch.
2. Tap Passcode, then tap Change Passcode and follow the onscreen prompts.

You can also open the Apple Watch app on your iPhone, tap My Watch, tap Passcode, then tap Change Passcode and follow the onscreen prompts.

Tip: To use a passcode longer than four digits, open the Settings app on your Apple Watch, tap Passcode, then turn off Simple Passcode.

Turn off the passcode

1. Open the Settings app on your Apple Watch.
2. Tap Passcode, then tap Turn Passcode Off.

You can also open the Apple Watch app on your iPhone, tap My Watch, tap Passcode, then tap Turn Passcode Off.

Note: If you disable your passcode, you can't use Apple Pay on your Apple Watch.

Lock automatically

By default, your Apple Watch locks automatically when you're not wearing it. To change the wrist detection setting, do the following.

1. Open the Settings app on your Apple Watch.
2. Tap Passcode, then turn Wrist Detection on or off.

Turning off wrist detection affects these Apple Watch features:
- When you use Apple Pay on your Apple Watch, you'll be prompted to enter your passcode when you double-click the side button to authorize the payment.
- Some Activity measurements are unavailable.
- Heart rate tracking and notifications are turned off.
- Apple Watch will no longer automatically lock and unlock.
- Apple Watch SE and Apple Watch Series 4 and later won't automatically make an emergency call even after it has detected a hard impact fall.

Lock manually

1. Touch and hold the bottom of the screen, then swipe up to open Control Center.
2. Tap 🔒.

Note: To manually lock your Apple Watch, you must turn off wrist detection. (Open the Settings app ⚙ on your Apple Watch, tap Passcode, then turn off Wrist Detection.)
You must enter your passcode the next time you try to use your Apple Watch.
You can also lock your screen to avoid accidental taps during a workout. While using the Workout app 🏃 on your Apple Watch, just swipe right, then tap Lock. When you start a swimming workout, your Apple Watch automatically locks the screen with Water Lock.

If you forget your password

If you forget your password, you must erase your Apple Watch. You can do so in these ways:

- Unpair your Apple Watch from your iPhone to erase your Apple Watch settings and passcode, then pair again.
- Reset your Apple Watch and pair it again with your iPhone.

Erase Apple Watch after 10 unlock attempts

To protect your information if your watch is lost or stolen, you can set Apple Watch to erase its data after 10 consecutive attempts to unlock it using the wrong password.

1. Open the Settings app ⚙ on your Apple Watch.
2. Tap Passcode, then turn on Erase Data.

Change language and orientation on Apple Watch

Choose language or region

1. Open the Apple Watch app on your iPhone.
2. Tap My Watch, go to General > Language & Region, tap Custom, then tap Watch Language.

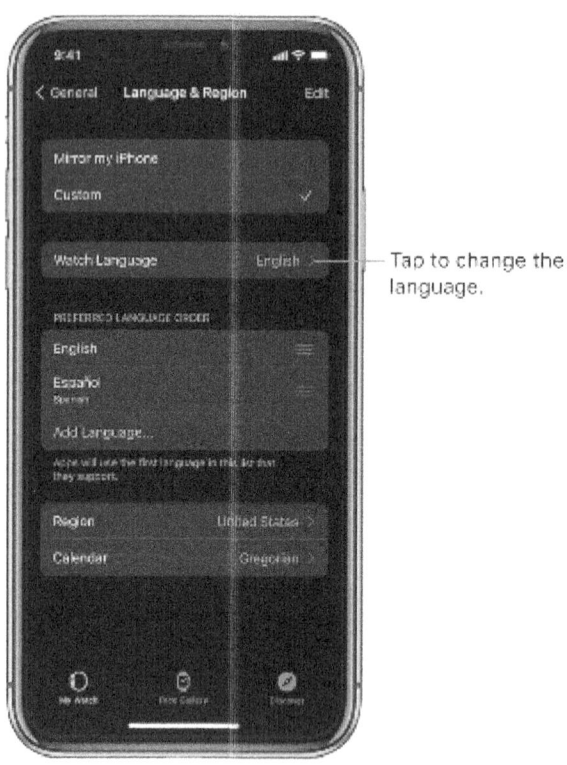

Tap to change the language.

Switch wrists or Digital Crown orientation

If you want to move your Apple Watch to your other wrist or prefer the Digital Crown on the other side, adjust your orientation settings so that raising your wrist wakes your Apple Watch, and turning the Digital Crown moves things in the direction you expect.

1. Open the Settings app  on your Apple Watch.
2. Go to General > Orientation.

You can also open the Apple Watch app on your iPhone, tap My Watch, then go to General > Watch Orientation.

Remove, change, and fasten Apple Watch bands

Follow these general instructions for removing, changing, and fastening bands.

Make sure that you use a band that corresponds to your Apple Watch case size. You can use a band that's designed for Apple Watch (1st generation) or Apple Watch Series 1, 2, and 3 with Apple Watch Series 4, Apple Watch Series 5, Apple Watch SE, Apple Watch Series 6, and Apple Watch Series 7, as long as the sizes are compatible. Bands for 38mm, 40mm, and 41mm cases work with each other, and bands for 42mm, 44mm, and 45mm cases work with each other.

Most bands designed for Apple Watch Series 4, Apple Watch Series 5, Apple Watch SE, Apple Watch Series 6, and Apple Watch Series 7 work with any previous version of Apple Watch. The Solo Loop and Braided Solo Loop bands are designed specifically for Apple

Watch Series 4, Apple Watch Series 5, Apple Watch SE, Apple Watch Series 6, and Apple Watch Series 7. Bands designed for early Apple Watch models also work with Apple Watch Series 4, Apple Watch Series 5, Apple Watch SE, Apple Watch Series 6, and Apple Watch Series 7.

Remove and change bands

1. Press the band release button on your Apple Watch.
2. Slide the band across to remove it, then slide the new band in.

Never force a band into the slot. If you're having trouble removing or inserting a band, press the band release button again.

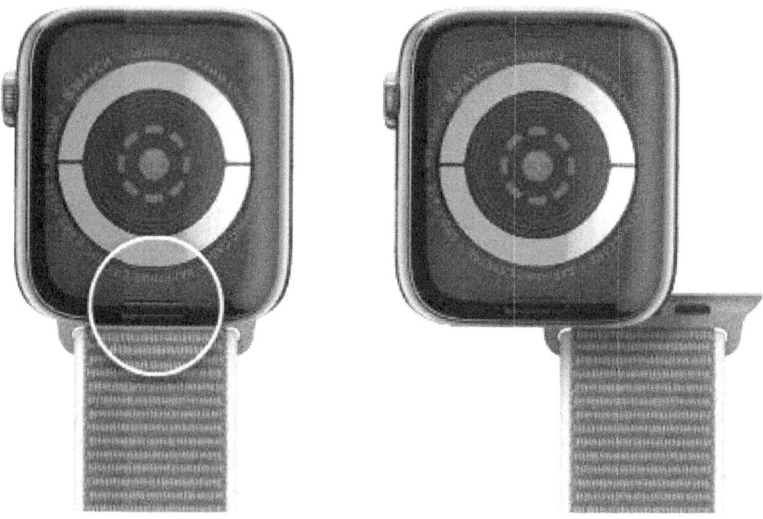

Fasten a band

For optimal performance, your Apple Watch should fit closely on your wrist.

For best results, the back of your Apple Watch needs skin contact for features like wrist detection, haptic notifications, and the heart rate sensor. Wearing your Apple Watch with the right fit—not too tight, not too loose, and with room for your skin to breathe—keeps

42

you comfortable and lets the sensors do their job. In addition, the sensors work only when you wear your Apple Watch on the top of your wrist.

Stay fit with Apple Watch

Apple Watch can track your activity and workouts, and encourage you to lead a more active life through gentle reminders and friendly competitions.

Close each ring

Your Apple Watch tracks how much you move, how often you stand up, and how long you exercise each day. Set goals in the Activity app ⦿, then check your progress throughout the day. Scroll down for more details like your total steps and distance. Apple Watch lets you know when you've completed a goal.

Start a workout

Open the Workout app 🏃, then tap the type of workout you want—something active like a run or swim, or maybe a more contemplative yoga or Tai Chi workout. Your stats appear on one screen so, during your workout, you can check your progress with a glance. If you forget to start a workout before a walking, running, or swimming workout, don't worry—Apple Watch suggests that you open the Workout app and gives you credit for the exercise you've already done.

Focus on your fitness

In watchOS 8, you can filter out distractions with the new Focus feature. Before beginning an intense workout, create a Fitness focus on your iPhone, then turn it on to stay in the moment, allowing only the notifications you really want.

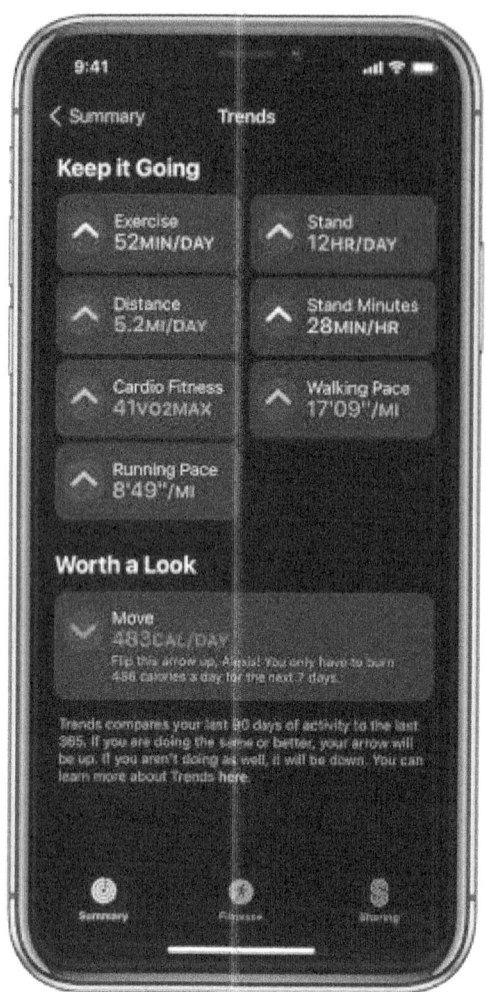

How are you doing?

Your recent activity statistics look great, but how do they compare to last year? The Trends feature can tell you. Open the Fitness app on your iPhone, tap the Summary tab, and swipe up to see where your activity metrics are headed so you can keep it going or turn it around.

Track important health information with Apple Watch

Your Apple Watch can help you meet your sleep goals, track important information related to your heart, check your blood oxygen levels, and encourage you to wash your hands.

Prioritize your sleep

Apple Watch can help you create a sleep schedule, track your sleep, measure your respiratory rate during sleep, then report your sleep trends over time. To get started, open the Health app on iPhone and create a sleep schedule. Then wear your watch to bed and Apple Watch does the rest.

Get heart health notifications

You can enable notifications from the Heart Rate app on your Apple Watch to alert you to high or low heart rates. The irregular heart rhythm notification on the Apple Watch can also alert you if an irregular rhythm suggestive of Atrial fibrillation is identified. Open the Apple Watch app on your iPhone, go to My Watch, then tap Heart. Turn on High Heart Rate or Low Heart Rate, then set a heart rate threshold, also turn on irregular rhythm notifications.

Take a moment to reflect

Tend to your mental well-being. The new Reflect feature in the Mindfulness app includes written prompts and soothing, energetic animation that guide you to be more present and mindful.

Wash your hands thoroughly

Turn on Handwashing in the Apple Watch app on iPhone, and your Apple Watch encourages you to keep going for 20 seconds, the time recommended by global health organizations. Your watch can also notify you if you haven't washed your hands within a few minutes of returning home.

Track your menstrual cycle

Use the Cycle Tracking app to log daily information about your menstrual cycle. The app uses that information to provide period and fertility window predictions. The app can also use heart rate data from Apple Watch to improve predictions.

Stay connected with Apple Watch

Apple Watch makes it easy to communicate with friends, family, and coworkers, even when your iPhone isn't with you.

Send a message, right from your wrist

Quickly respond to a message with Siri. When Apple Watch is connected to Wi-Fi or cellular, just raise your wrist and say, "Tell Julie I'll be there in five minutes." Or touch and hold the message to give your friend a thumbs up with a Tapback reply.

Make a call

Use Siri to help you make a quick call. With an Apple Watch with a cellular or Wi-Fi connection, raise your wrist and say "Call Mom." If you have a Wi-Fi connection, a simple "FaceTime Mom" does the trick.

Announce your departure

Meeting a friend? Apple Watch can let them know you're on your way. Open the Find People app and tap your friend. Scroll up, tap Notify [your friend's name], then choose to notify your friend when you leave your location.

Care to share?

In watchOS 8 you can share any photo on your Apple Watch—a favorite photo you've synced from iPhone or one of several images from a Memory. Just select a photo, tap 📤, then share via Messages or Mail.

Set up Apple Watch for a family member

Set up a family member's Apple Watch

You can set up and manage Apple Watch for someone who doesn't have their own iPhone—your school-aged child or parent, for example. To do so, you must be the family organizer or parent/guardian in your Family Sharing group.
The iPhone you use to initially pair and set up the Apple Watch must be within normal Bluetooth range (about 33 feet or 10 meters) of the Apple Watch to manage settings and update the software. The

person you set up Apple Watch for must be part of your Family (Your family member's watch doesn't have to use the same cellular carrier as the iPhone you manage it with.)

Using the Apple Watch app and Screen Time on your iPhone, you can manage the following:

- Communications limits
- A schedule for time away from the screen
- Schooltime—a feature that limits certain Apple Watch features during school hours
- Mail and calendar settings for iCloud and Gmail accounts
- Restriction settings for explicit content, purchases, and privacy

In addition, you can view Activity, Health, and Location information for the managed Apple Watch based on how it's set up.

Note: An Apple Watch set up for a family member is limited in some of its interactions with the iPhone used to set it up. For example, you can't unlock a paired iPhone from an Apple Watch you set up for a family member, nor can you hand off tasks from the managed Apple Watch to the iPhone. If you delete an app from an Apple Watch set up for a family member, it's not also removed from the iPhone used to set it up.

Set up your family member's Apple Watch

Setting up an Apple Watch for a family member is similar to setting up a watch for yourself. Before you pair and set up a watch for your family member, erase the watch to ensure that it doesn't have any content.

1. Have your family member put on their Apple Watch. Adjust the band or choose a band size so the Apple Watch fits closely but comfortably on their wrist.
2. To turn on Apple Watch, press and hold the side button until the Apple logo appears.
3. Bring your iPhone near the Apple Watch, wait for the Apple Watch pairing screen to appear on your iPhone, then tap Continue.

    Or open the Apple Watch app on your iPhone, tap All

Watches, then tap Pair New Watch.

4. Tap Set Up for a Family Member, then tap Continue on the next screen.
5. When prompted, position your iPhone so that the Apple Watch appears in the viewfinder in the Apple Watch app. This pairs the two devices.
6. Tap Set Up Apple Watch. Follow the instructions on your iPhone and Apple Watch to finish setup.

Manage a family member's Apple Watch

1. Open the Apple Watch app on the iPhone used to manage the watch.
2. Tap All Watches, tap a watch under Family Watches, then tap Done.

When you tap My Watch for a managed watch, you see a variety of settings, including the following:

Setting	Options
General	Check for updates, change language and region, and reset Apple Watch.
Cellular	Set up cellular if you haven't.
Accessibility	Configure accessibility settings.
Emergency SOS	Turn on or off the option to hold the side button to call emergency services, and add and change emergency contacts.
Schooltime	Set up a Schooltime schedule.

Screen Time	Manage parental controls, get insights about your family member's screen time, and set limits.
Activity	Manage a fitness experience made for younger users.
App Store	Allow automatic downloads and updates.
Contacts	Choose trusted contacts.
Handwashing	Manage restrictions, and turn the handwashing timer on or off.
Health	Add or edit health details and Medical ID, view the health data (with the proper permissions and settings) of the person who uses the managed Apple Watch, request to share health data, and choose to stop receiving health data.
Heart	View the heart data (with the proper permissions and settings) of the person who uses the managed Apple Watch, including heart rate, heart rate variability, resting heart rate, and walking heart rate average.
Mail & Calendar	Add a family member's Gmail account and turn Gmail mail, contacts, and calendars on or off. Also choose how often Apple Watch fetches calendar updates.
Messages	Choose dictation options, and edit smart replies.
Noise	Turn Environmental Sound Measurements on or off, and set the noise threshold.
Photos	Select a photo album from the iPhone used to manage the watch, and choose the number of photos Apple Watch can display.

Tips	Choose notifications settings.
Wallet & Apple Pay	Set up Apple Cash and Express Transit cards.
Workout	Choose a workout view.

Set up Screen Time

Use Screen Time to configure controls for a family member's Apple Watch. With Screen Time you can schedule time away from the screen, and limit both contacts and the apps your family member can use to communicate with those contacts. You can also impose limits on iTunes Store and app purchases, explicit content, and location information.

To set up Screen Time, follow these steps:
1. Open the Apple Watch app on the iPhone used to manage the watch.
2. Tap All Watches, then tap the watch under Family Watches.
3. Tap Done, tap Screen Time, tap Screen Time Settings, then tap Turn On Screen Time.
4. Select settings for Downtime, App Limits, and Content & Privacy Restrictions.
5. Create a Screen Time passcode.

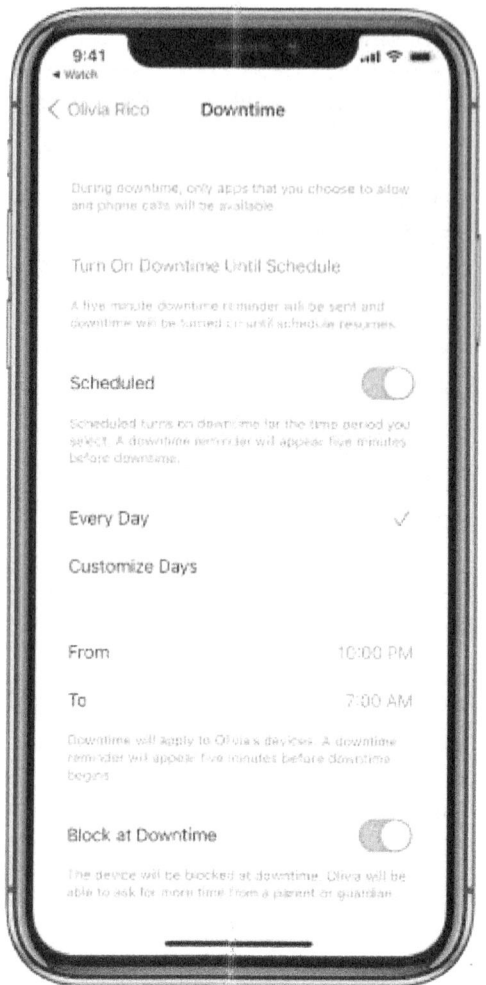

On this screen you can also see a Screen Time activity report for your family member's watch.

Alternatively, you can open the Settings app on your iPhone, tap Screen Time, tap your family member's name under the Family heading, then choose a setting.

Set up reminders on a family member's Apple Watch

Upgrade reminders

On a managed Apple Watch, you need to upgrade your iCloud reminders to take advantage of additional Siri interactions, have the ability to create all-day reminders (reminders set to a specific day, but not a specific time), and join lists shared by others. If you haven't yet upgraded your reminders, do the following:

1. Open the Settings app on the managed Apple Watch.
2. Tap Reminders, then tap Upgrade.

Set a notification time for all-day reminders

1. Open the Settings app on the managed Apple Watch.
2. Tap Reminders, turn on Today Notification to show the time, then tap the time.
3. Enter the time you want notifications to appear, then tap Set.

Choose a default list

On a managed Apple Watch, reminders created outside a specific list appear in the default list.

1. Open the Settings app on the managed Apple Watch.
2. Tap Reminders, then tap the current default list setting.
3. Tap the list you want to be the default list.

Get started with Schooltime on Apple Watch

Schooltime limits Apple Watch features during school hours, allowing a family member to focus.

Set up Schooltime

1. Open the Apple Watch app on the iPhone used to manage the watch.
2. Tap All Watches, then tap the watch under Family Watches.
3. Tap Done, then tap Schooltime.
4. Turn on Schooltime, then tap Edit Schedule.
5. Choose the days and times you want Schooltime to be active on the watch.
6. Tap Add Time if you want to set up multiple schedules during a day—from 8:00 a.m. to noon and then 1:00 p.m. to 3:00 p.m., for example.

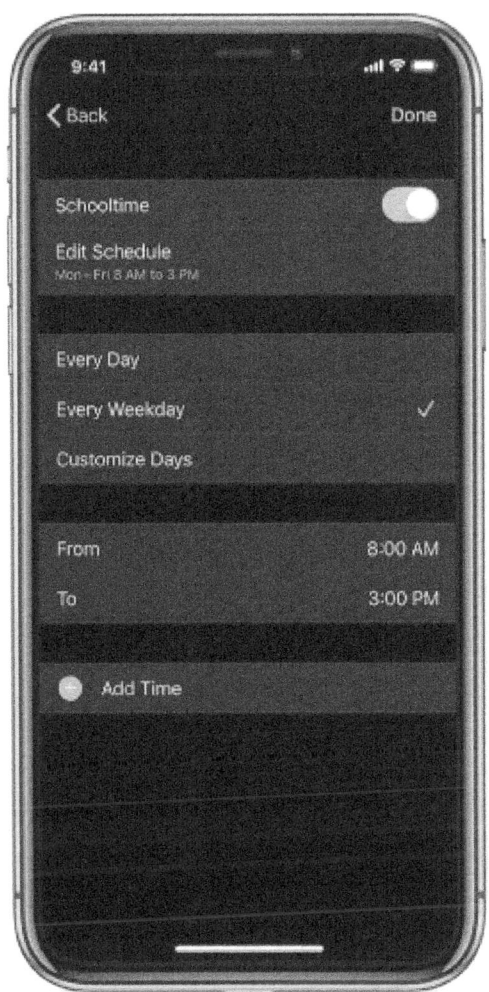

Exit Schooltime

Your family member can temporarily exit Schooltime—to check their activity rings, for example.
Tap the display, turn the Digital Crown, then tap Exit.
If you exit Schooltime during scheduled hours, the Schooltime watch face returns when you lower your wrist. During non-scheduled

hours, Schooltime remains inactive until the next scheduled start time, or until you tap in Control Center.

See when Schooltime was unlocked

When your family member exits Schooltime, you receive a report that tells you the time they exited and for how long. To see the report, follow these steps:
1. Open the Apple Watch app on the iPhone used to manage the watch.
2. Tap All Watches, then tap the watch under Family Watches.
3. Tap Done, then tap Schooltime.
4. Swipe up to see reports for the days, times, and durations Schooltime was unlocked.
   The report also appears on the Apple Watch. To see it, open the Settings app on the Apple Watch, then tap Schooltime.

Schooltime turns on again when the display goes to sleep.
Tip: When Schooltime isn't active, your family member can turn it on—for example, if they've joined an after-school study group that falls outside scheduled hours and don't want to be distracted. Just touch and hold the bottom of the screen, swipe up, and tap in Control Center. To exit Schooltime, turn the Digital Crown. Schooltime will turn on again when it's scheduled or turned on in Control Center.

Play music on a managed Apple Watch

If you're part of a Family Sharing group that has an Apple Music family subscription, you can listen to Apple Music on your managed Apple Watch as long as you have a Wi-Fi or cellular connection.

1. Open the Music app on your managed Apple Watch, then do any of the following.
    - Tap Library to browse music saved on Apple Watch.
    - Tap Listen Now to see music chosen for you based on your listening habits.
    - Tap Search, then type (Apple Watch Series 7 only), dictate, or scribble an artist, album, or playlist.
      Note: Scribble is not available in all languages.
    - Tap a playlist created for kids and teens by Apple Music editors.
    - Tap albums or playlists you've added to Apple Watch.
2. Use the music controls in the Music app and Now Playing app to play and choose music.

See activity and health reports for family members

After setting up daily activity goals, you can see how active your family member was each day. With your family member's permission, you can also view their health information.

Set up activity goals for a family member

For children with a managed Apple Watch, move goals are based on move minutes instead of active calories. The exercise goal focuses on minutes of brisk activity (such as running, jumping, and playing), and outdoor run, walk, and cycle workouts are tailored to children under 13.
If you manage an Apple Watch for a family member, you can change from an under-13 to over-13 fitness experience, regardless of the family member's actual age.
1. On the iPhone used to manage the watch, open the Apple Watch app.
2. Tap All Watches, then tap the watch under Family Watches.

3. Tap Done, tap Activity, then turn "Under 13 years old" off or on.

The family member can also do this on their Apple Watch by opening the Settings app ⚙ on their Apple Watch, tapping Activity, then turning "Under 13 years old" on or off.

See an activity report

1. After setting up activity goals for your family member, open the Health app on your iPhone.
2. Tap Sharing, then tap the name of your family member under Sharing With You.
3. Tap Activity.
4. Tap the timeline to see how active your family member was up to that time of day.

You can view activity information by day, week, month, or year.

See health information

If your family member has allowed you to, you can see additional information about their activity as well as body measurement, hearing health, and heart rate information.

1. Open the Health app on your iPhone, then tap Sharing.
2. Tap the name of your family member under Sharing With You.
3. Tap Health Categories, then tap a category.

Add health details and Medical ID

If you didn't enter your family member's health details during setup, follow these steps:

1. Open the Apple Watch app on the iPhone used to manage the watch.
2. Tap All Watches, then tap the watch under Family Watches.
3. Tap Done, tap Health, then do any of the following.
    - Tap Health Details to enter or edit information such as birthdate, height, and weight.

- Tap Medical ID to add emergency contacts and more.

You can see health details and Medical ID on the iPhone used to manage the Apple Watch and on the watch.

- On your iPhone: Open the Health app, tap Sharing, tap your family member's name, then tap Profile.

- On the managed Apple Watch: Open the Settings app on the Apple Watch, then tap Health.

Use Apple Cash Family on a family member's Apple Watch

If you're the organizer for a Family Sharing group, you can set up Apple Cash for the children and teens in your family group so they can make purchases, and send and receive money in Messages. You can even limit who your child can send money to, get notified when they make transactions, and lock their account.

Note: Apple Cash isn't available in all regions.

Set up Apple Cash Family

To set up Apple Cash Family, you must be the family organizer.

1. On your iPhone, go to Settings > [your name] > Family Sharing.
2. Tap Apple Cash, then do one of the following:
    - If there isn't a child in your family group: Tap Create an Account for a Child, then follow the onscreen instructions.
    - If there is a child in your family group: Tap Set Up Apple Cash, tap the child's name, then follow the onscreen instructions.

In the U.S., your family member can send, receive, and request money and use Apple Pay for purchases.

Manage Apple Cash on a family member's Apple Watch

1. Open the Wallet app on the iPhone used to manage the watch.
2. Tap your Apple Cash card, then tap ●●●.
3. Swipe up, then tap a name under Family.
4. Set up the following options:
    - Choose who your family member can send money to.
    - Choose to be notified when your family member makes a transaction.
5. Tap Send Money to open the Messages app and send money with Apple Pay.
6. Tap Lock Apple Cash to prevent the family member from making payments with Apple Pay or sending and receiving money in the Messages app.

To see a family member's transactions, tap Transactions on this screen, or open the Wallet app on your iPhone, then tap your Apple Cash card. Your family member's transactions appear under Latest Transactions and when you tap Transactions in [year].

Basics

Apps on Apple Watch

Your Apple Watch comes with a collection of helpful apps. They include:

App icon	App name
🌐	World Clock

🏃	Workout
☁	Weather
👛	Wallet
📻	Walkie-Talkie (not available in all regions)
🎙	Voice Memos
💡	Tips
⏲	Timers
⏱	Stopwatch
📈	Stocks
🛏	Sleep
🔀	Shortcuts

⚙	Settings
▶	Remote
⦿	Reminders
🎙	Podcasts
🌸	Photos
📞	Phone
🎵	Now Playing
👂	Noise
N	News (not available in all regions)
🎵	Music
✿	Mindfulness

◯	Messages
😊	Memoji
🧭	Maps
✉	Mail
🏠	Home
♡	Heart Rate
👥	Find People
⦁⦁	Find Items
💻	Find Devices
⩘	ECG (not available in all regions)
⋯	Cycle Tracking

![]	Contacts
![]	Compass
![]	Camera Remote
![]	Calendar
![]	Calculator
![]	Blood Oxygen (not available in all regions)
![]	Audiobooks
![]	App Store
![]	Alarms
![]	Activity

Open apps on Apple Watch

The Home Screen lets you open any app on your Apple Watch. The Dock gives you quick access to the apps you use the most. You can add up to 10 apps to the Dock to keep your favorites handy.

Display your apps on a grid or in a list

The Home Screen can display apps in a grid or list view. To choose one, follow these steps:
1. Touch and hold the Home Screen.
2. Choose Grid View or List View.

Open apps from the Home Screen

How you open an app depends on which view you choose.

- Grid view: Tap the app icon. If you're already looking at the Home Screen, you can turn the Digital Crown to open the app that's in the center of the display.

From the watch face, press to see the Home Screen.

Tap to open an app.

- *List view:* Turn the Digital Crown, then tap an app.

Turn the Digital Crown to browse the apps.

Tap to open an app.

To return to the Home Screen from an app, press the Digital Crown once, then press it again to switch to the watch face (or, in grid view, tap ⌄ on the Home Screen).
To quickly open the last app you used while viewing another app or the watch face, double-click the Digital Crown.

Open an app from the Dock

1. Press the side button, then turn the Digital Crown to scroll through the apps in the Dock.
2. Tap an app to open it.

Turn the Digital Crown to see more apps. Tap one to open it.

Choose which apps appear in the Dock

You can choose to show the most recently used apps in the Dock or up to 10 of your favorite apps.

- See recently used apps: Open the Apple Watch app on your iPhone, tap My Watch, tap Dock, then tap Recents. The most recently used app appears at the top of the Dock with other apps below, in the order they were last opened.

    You can also open the Settings app on your Apple Watch, tap Dock, then tap Recents.

- See your favorite apps: Open the Apple Watch app on your iPhone, tap My Watch, then tap Dock. Select Favorites, tap Edit, then tap next to the apps you want to add. Drag to adjust their order.

- Remove an app from the Dock: Press the side button, then turn the Digital Crown to the app you want to remove. Swipe left on the app, then tap X.

Swipe left on an app, then tap the X.

- Switch from the Dock to the Home Screen: Scroll to the bottom of the Dock, then tap All Apps.

Tip: You can also add the apps you use most as complications to your watch face.

Organize apps on Apple Watch

Rearrange your apps in grid view

1. On your Apple Watch, press the Digital Crown to go to the Home Screen.
   If the screen is in list view, touch and hold the Home Screen, then tap Grid View. Or open the Settings app on your Apple Watch, tap App View, then tap Grid View.
2. Touch and hold an app, then tap Edit Apps.
3. Drag the app to a new location.

4. Press the Digital Crown when you're done.

Touch and hold an app, then drag to a new location.

Or open the Apple Watch app on your iPhone, tap My Watch, tap App View, then tap Arrangement. Touch and hold an app icon, then drag it to a new location.

Note: In list view, apps are always arranged in alphabetical order.

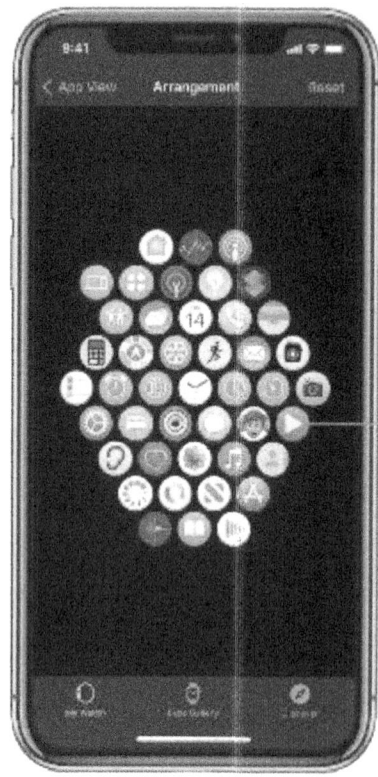

Touch and hold, then drag to move apps around.

Remove an app from Apple Watch

Touch and hold the Home Screen, tap Edit Apps, then tap the X to remove the app from your Apple Watch. It remains on your paired iPhone, unless you delete it there, too.

In list view, you can also swipe the app left, then tap 🗑 to remove it from your Apple Watch.
Note: Not all apps can be removed from your Apple Watch.

Adjust app settings

1. Open the Apple Watch app on your iPhone.
2. Tap My Watch, then scroll down to see apps you installed.
3. Tap an app to change its settings.

Some restrictions you set on your iPhone in Settings > Screen Time > Content & Privacy Restrictions affect your Apple Watch also. For example, if you disable Camera on your iPhone, the Camera Remote icon is removed from the Apple Watch Home Screen.

Check storage used by apps

You can learn how the storage space is being used on your Apple Watch—the total amount of storage used, the amount remaining, and how much storage each app uses.

1. Open the Settings app on your Apple Watch.
2. Go to General > Storage.

You can also open the Apple Watch app on your iPhone, tap My Watch, then go to General > Storage.

Get more apps on Apple Watch

Your Apple Watch includes apps for a variety of communication, health, fitness, and timekeeping tasks. You can also choose to install third-party apps you have on your iPhone, and get new apps from the App Store, either on Apple Watch or from your iPhone. All your apps are on a single Home Screen.
Note: To automatically download the companion iOS version of an app you've added to your Apple Watch, go to Settings on your Apple Watch, tap App Store, then turn on Automatic Downloads. To get the most recent versions of your Apple Watch apps, make sure Automatic Updates is also turned on.

Get apps from the App Store on Apple Watch

1. Open the App Store app on your Apple Watch.
2. Turn the Digital Crown to browse featured apps.
Tap a category or tap See All below a collection to see more apps.

3. To get a free app, tap Get. To buy an app, tap the price.

 If you see ☁︎ instead of a price, you've already purchased the app and you can download it again without a charge. Some apps require that you also have the iOS version of the app on your iPhone.

To find a specific app, tap the Search field at the top of the screen, then type, or use dictation or Scribble to enter the name of the app. You can also browse trending categories of apps by tapping a category.

Note: When using Apple Watch with cellular, cellular data charges may apply. Scribble is not available in all languages.

Install apps you already have on iPhone

By default, apps on your iPhone that have a watchOS app available are automatically installed and appear on the Home Screen. To instead choose to install specific apps, follow these steps:
1. Open the Apple Watch app on your iPhone.
2. Tap My Watch, tap General, then turn off Automatic App Install.

3. Tap My Watch, then scroll down to Available Apps.
4. Tap Install next to the apps you want to install.

Tell time on Apple Watch

There are several ways to tell time with your Apple Watch.

- Raise your wrist: The time appears on the watch face, in the clock in grid view, and in the top-right corner of most apps.

- Hear the time: Open the Settings app on your Apple Watch, tap Clock, then turn on Speak Time. Hold two fingers on the watch face to hear the time.
  Apple Watch can also play chimes on the hour. In the Settings app on Apple Watch, tap Clock, then turn on Chimes. Tap Sounds to choose Bells or Birds.

- Feel the time: To feel the time tapped out on your wrist when Apple Watch is in silent mode, open the Settings app on your Apple Watch, tap Clock, tap Taptic Time, turn on Taptic Time, then choose an option.
  Note: If Taptic Time is disabled, Apple Watch might be set to always speak the time. To be able to use Taptic Time, first go to Settings > Clock, then turn on Control With Silent Mode under Speak Time.

- Use Siri: Raise your wrist and say "What time is it?"

The Apple Watch status icons

Status icons at the top of the screen give you information about your Apple Watch.

Status icon	What it means

79

	You've made yourself available to be reached on Walkie-Talkie. Tap the icon to open the Walkie-Talkie app.
	Maps is providing directions. Tap the icon to open the Maps app.
	A phone call is in progress. Tap the icon to open the Phone app.
	Audio is playing on Apple Watch. Tap the icon to open Now Playing.
	Apple Watch is connected to a cellular network. The number of green bars indicates signal strength.
	The microphone is on.
	There's wireless activity or an active process happening.
	Apple Watch is connected to a known Wi-Fi network.
	An app on Apple Watch is using location services.
	Apple Watch is connected to its paired iPhone.
	Apple Watch has lost the connection with its paired iPhone. This happens when Apple Watch isn't close

		enough to iPhone, or when airplane mode is enabled on iPhone.
	✕	Apple Watch with cellular has lost the connection to a cellular network.
		You have a workout in progress.
	🎭	Theater mode is turned on. Apple Watch is silenced and its display won't light up when you raise your wrist.
	✈	Airplane mode is turned on. Wireless is turned off but non-wireless features are still available.
		Work Focus is turned on.
		Sleep Focus is turned on.
		Personal Focus is turned on.
	🚀	Gaming Focus is turned on.
	🌙	Do Not Disturb is turned on. Calls and alerts won't sound or light up the screen, but alarms are still in effect.
	💧	Water Lock is on, and the screen doesn't respond to taps. Turn the Digital Crown to unlock.

	Apple Watch is locked. Tap to enter the passcode and unlock.
	Apple Watch battery is low.
	Apple Watch is charging.
	You have an unread notification. Swipe down on the watch face to read it.

Use Control Center on Apple Watch

Control Center gives you an easy way to check your battery, silence your watch, choose a Focus, turn your Apple Watch into a flashlight, put your Apple Watch in airplane mode, turn on theater mode, and more.

Open or close Control Center

- Open Control Center: From the watch face, swipe up. From other screens, touch and hold the bottom of the screen, then swipe up.
  Note: You can't open Control Center from the Home Screen on your Apple Watch. Instead, press the Digital Crown to go to the watch face or open an app, then open Control Center.

- Close Control Center: Swipe down from the top of the screen, or press the Digital Crown.

Apple Watch    Apple Watch with Cellular

Touch and hold the bottom, then swipe up to open Control Center.

Icon	Description
	Turn Announce Notifications on or off.
	Check headphone volume.
	Choose audio output.
	Turn on Water Lock.
	Turn on airplane mode.
	Turn on the flashlight.

83

	Turn off Work Focus.
	Turn off Sleep Focus.
	Turn off Personal Focus.
	Turn off Gaming Focus.
	Choose a Focus/Do Not Disturb.
	Make yourself available for Walkie-Talkie.
	Turn on theater mode.
	Lock your watch with a passcode.
	Silence Apple Watch.
100%	Check your battery percentage.
	Ping your iPhone.

🧘		Turn on Schooltime—managed Apple Watch models only.
📶		Disconnect from Wi-Fi.
📡		Turn cellular on or off—Apple Watch models with cellular only.

Check Control Center status

Icons at the top of Control Center give you information about the status of common settings on your Apple Watch. For example, a series of small icons may indicate that your Apple Watch is connected to your iPhone, Airplane mode is on, and your location has been requested by an app.

To get details, just tap the group of icons at the top of Control Center.

Rearrange Control Center

You can rearrange the buttons in Control Center by following these steps:
1. Touch and hold the bottom of the screen, then swipe up to open Control Center.
2. Scroll to the bottom of Control Center, then tap Edit.
3. Drag a button to a new location.
4. Tap Done when you're finished.

Remove Control Center buttons

You can remove the buttons in Control Center by following these steps:
1. Touch and hold the bottom of the screen, then swipe up to open Control Center.
2. Scroll to the bottom of Control Center, then tap Edit.
3. Tap in the corner of the button you want to remove.
4. Tap Done when you're finished.

To restore a button you've removed, open Control Center, tap Edit, then tap in the corner of the button you want to restore. Tap Done when you're finished.

Turn on airplane mode

Some airlines let you fly with your Apple Watch (and iPhone) turned on if you put them in airplane mode. By default, turning on airplane mode turns off Wi-Fi and cellular (on Apple Watch models with cellular) and keeps Bluetooth turned on. However, you can change which settings are turned on and off when you turn on airplane mode.

- Turn on airplane mode on Apple Watch: Touch and hold the bottom of the screen, swipe up to open Control Center, then tap .

Turn airplane mode on or off.

Ask Siri. Say something like: "Turn on airplane mode."

- Put both your Apple Watch and iPhone in airplane mode in one step: Open the Apple Watch app on your iPhone, tap My Watch, go to General > Airplane Mode, then turn on Mirror iPhone. When your iPhone and Apple Watch are within normal Bluetooth range of each other (about 33 feet or 10 meters), any time you switch to airplane mode on one device, the other switches to match.
- Change which settings are turned on or off in airplane mode:

  On Apple Watch, open the Settings app, tap Airplane Mode, then choose whether to turn Wi-Fi or Bluetooth on or off by default when you turn on airplane mode.
  To turn Wi-Fi or Bluetooth on or off while your Apple Watch is in airplane mode, open the Settings app, then tap Wi-Fi or Bluetooth.

When airplane mode is on, appears at the top of the screen. Note: Even with Mirror iPhone turned on, you must turn off airplane mode separately on your iPhone and Apple Watch.

87

Use the flashlight on Apple Watch

Use the flashlight to light a darkened door lock, alert others when you're out for an evening run, or light nearby objects while preserving your night vision.

- Turn on the flashlight: Touch and hold the bottom of the screen, swipe up to open Control Center, then tap . Swipe left to choose a mode—steady white light, flashing white light, or steady red light.
- Turn off the flashlight: Press the Digital Crown or side button, or swipe down from the top of the watch face.

Use theater mode on Apple Watch

Theater mode prevents the Apple Watch display from turning on when you raise your wrist, so it stays dark. It also turns on silent mode and makes your Walkie-Talkie status unavailable, but you still receive haptic notifications.

Touch and hold the bottom of the screen, swipe up to open Control Center, tap , then tap Theater Mode.

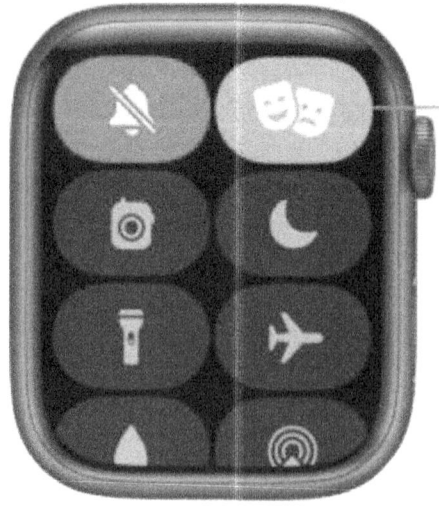

Turn theater mode on or off.

When theater mode is on, you see at the top of the screen.

To wake Apple Watch when theater mode is on, tap the display, press the Digital Crown or side button, or turn the Digital Crown.

Disconnect from Wi-Fi

You can temporarily disconnect from a Wi-Fi network and, on Apple Watch models with cellular, use an available cellular connection instead—right from Control Center.

Touch and hold the bottom of the screen, swipe up to open Control Center, then tap in Control Center.

Tap to disconnect from Wi-Fi.

Your Apple Watch temporarily disconnects from the Wi-Fi network. If you have an Apple Watch with cellular, the cellular connection activates if you have coverage. When you leave and later return to the place where you were connected to Wi-Fi, your Apple Watch automatically joins that network again unless you've forgotten it on your iPhone.

Tip: To quickly open Wi-Fi settings on your Apple Watch, touch and hold the Wi-Fi button in Control Center.

Turn on silent mode

Touch and hold the bottom of the screen, swipe up to open Control Center, then tap 🔔.

Note: If your Apple Watch is charging, alarms and timers will still sound even in silent mode.

You can also open the Apple Watch app on your iPhone, tap My Watch, tap Sounds & Haptics, then turn on silent mode.

Tip: When you get a notification, you can quickly mute your Apple Watch by resting the palm of your hand on the watch display for at least three seconds. You'll feel a tap to confirm that mute is on. Make sure you turn on Cover to Mute on your Apple Watch—open the Settings ⚙ app, tap Sounds & Haptics, then turn on Cover to Mute.

Locate your iPhone

Your Apple Watch can help you find your iPhone if it's nearby.
Touch and hold the bottom of the screen, swipe up to open Control Center, then tap 📱.
Your iPhone makes a tone so you can track it down.

90

Tip: In the dark? Touch and hold the Ping iPhone button and iPhone flashes as well.

If your iPhone isn't in range of your Apple Watch, try using Find My from iCloud.com.

Find your Apple Watch

If you lost your watch, use Find My to find it.
1. Open the Find My app on your iPhone.
2. Tap Devices, then tap your watch in the list.

You can play a sound on your watch, tap Directions to see directions to it in Maps, mark it as lost, or erase it.
You can also track your Apple Watch using Find My and iCloud.

Use Focus on Apple Watch

Focus helps you stay in the moment when you want to concentrate on an activity. Focus can reduce distractions—allowing only notifications you want to receive (ones that match your focus)—and lets other people and apps know you're busy.
You can choose from provided Focus options—for example, Driving, Personal, Sleep, and Work. Or you can create a custom Focus on your iPhone, choosing who is allowed to contact you, which apps

can send you notifications, and whether or not you receive time-sensitive notifications.
Note: To have your Focus settings shared across all your devices where you're signed in with the same Apple ID, go to Settings > Focus, scroll to the bottom of the screen, then turn on Share Across Devices.

Turn a Focus on or off

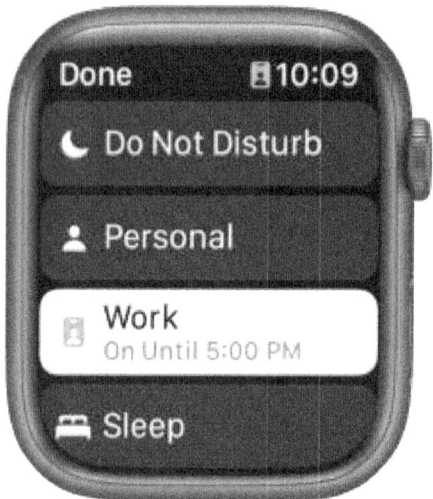

1. Touch and hold the bottom of the screen, then swipe up to open Control Center.
2. Touch and hold the current Focus button, then tap a Focus. If no Focus is on, Control Center shows the Do Not Disturb button .
3. Choose a Focus option—On, On for 1 hour, On until tomorrow morning, or On until I leave.

To turn off a Focus, just tap its button in Control Center.
When a Focus is active, its icon appears at the top of the watch face, next to the time in apps, and in Control Center.

Create your own Focus

1. On your iPhone, go to Settings  > Focus.

2. Tap +, choose a Focus, then follow the onscreen instructions.
   If you create a custom focus, you can choose a color and an icon to represent it, and enter a name for it.

Create a Focus schedule

On Apple Watch you can schedule when each Focus occurs—you can even choose to have a Focus start at different times of the day. For example, you could schedule the Work Focus to start at 9 AM and end at noon, Monday through Friday. From noon to 1 PM you may have no Focus or have a Personal Focus take over. Then, start Work Focus again from 1 PM until 5 PM, Monday through Thursday.

1. Open the Settings app on your Apple Watch.
2. Tap Focus, tap a Focus—Work, for example—then tap "Add new."
3. Tap the From and To fields and enter the times you want the Focus to begin and end.
4. Scroll up, then choose days when the Focus will be active.
5. Tap < in the top-left corner to save the Focus.
6. Repeat this process to add other events to the Focus.

Disable or delete a Focus schedule

To disable or delete a Focus schedule, do either of the following:

- Disable a Focus schedule: Open the Settings app on your Apple Watch, tap Focus, then tap a Focus. Tap a schedule, scroll down, then turn off Enabled.
  Turn on Enabled when you want the schedule to be active again.

- Delete a Focus schedule: Open the Settings app on your Apple Watch, tap Focus, then tap a Focus. Tap a schedule, scroll down, then tap Delete.

Adjust brightness, text size, sounds, and haptics on Apple Watch

Adjust brightness and text on Apple Watch

Open the Settings app ⚙ on your Apple Watch, then tap Display & Brightness to adjust the following:
- Brightness: Tap the Brightness controls to adjust, or tap the slider, then turn the Digital Crown.
- Text size: Tap Text Size, then tap the letters or turn the Digital Crown.
- Bold text: Turn on Bold Text.

You can also make these adjustments on your iPhone. Open the Apple Watch app on your iPhone, tap My Watch, tap Display & Brightness, then adjust brightness and text.

Adjust sound

1. Open the Settings app ⚙ on your Apple Watch.
2. Tap Sounds & Haptics.

3. Tap the volume controls under Alert Volume or tap the slider, then turn the Digital Crown to adjust.

Or, on your iPhone, open the Apple Watch app, tap Sounds & Haptics, then drag the Alert Volume slider.

You can also reduce loud sounds coming from headphones connected to your Apple Watch. In the Settings app, go to Sounds & Haptics > Headphone Safety, then turn on Reduce Loud Sounds.

Adjust haptic intensity

You can adjust the strength of the haptics—or wrist taps—Apple Watch uses for notifications and alerts.

1. Open the Settings app on your Apple Watch.
2. Tap Sounds & Haptics, then turn on Haptic Alerts.
3. Choose Default or Prominent.

Or, on your iPhone, open the Apple Watch app, tap My Watch, tap Sounds & Haptics, then choose Default or Prominent.

Turn Digital Crown haptics off or on

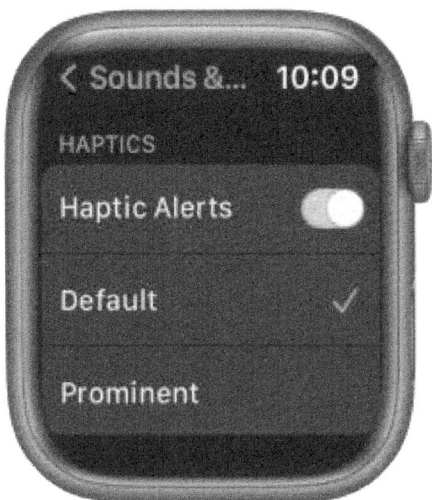

You feel clicks when you turn the Digital Crown to scroll. To turn these haptics off or on, follow these steps:

1. Open the Settings app on your Apple Watch.
2. Tap Sound & Haptics, then turn Crown Haptics off or on.

Or, on your iPhone, open the Apple Watch app, tap My Watch, tap Sounds & Haptics, then turn Crown Haptics off or on.

Use Taptic Time

When Apple Watch is in silent mode, it can tap out the time on your wrist with a series of distinct taps.

1. Open the Settings app ⚙ on your Apple Watch.
2. Tap Clock, scroll up, then tap Taptic Time.
3. Turn on Taptic Time, then choose a setting—Digits, Terse, or Morse Code.
    - Digits: Apple Watch long taps for every 10 hours, short taps for each following hour, long taps for every 10 minutes, then short taps for each following minute.
    - Terse: Apple Watch long taps for every five hours, short taps for the remaining hours, then long taps for each quarter hour.
    - Morse Code: Apple Watch taps each digit of the time in Morse code.

You can also configure Taptic Time on iPhone. Open the Apple Watch app on iPhone, tap My Watch, go to Clock > Taptic Time, then turn it on.

Note: If Taptic Time is disabled, Apple Watch might be set to always speak the time. To be able to use Taptic Time, first go to Settings ⚙ > Clock, then turn on Control With Silent Mode under Speak Time.

See and respond to notifications on Apple Watch

Apps can send notifications to keep you informed—meeting invitations, messages, noise alerts, and Activity reminders are just a few examples. Your Apple Watch can display notifications as they arrive, but if you don't read one right away, it's saved so you can check it later.

Respond to a notification when it arrives

1. If you hear or feel a notification, raise your wrist to view it.
2. Turn the Digital Crown to scroll to the bottom of the notification, then tap a button there.
   You can also tap the app icon in the notification to open the corresponding app.
   3. To clear a notification, swipe down on it. Or scroll to the bottom of the notification, then tap Dismiss.

See notifications you haven't responded to

If you don't respond to a notification when it arrives, it's saved in Notification Center. A red dot at the top of your watch face shows you have an unread notification. To view it, follow these steps:

1. From the watch face, swipe down to open Notification Center. From other screens, touch and hold the top of the screen, then swipe down.
   Note: You can't open Notification Center when viewing the Home Screen on your Apple Watch. Instead, press the Digital Crown to go to the watch face or open an app, then open Notification Center.
2. Swipe up or down or turn the Digital Crown to scroll the notifications list.

3. Tap the notification to read or respond to it.

To clear a notification from Notification Center without reading it, swipe it to the left, then tap X. To clear all notifications, scroll to the top of the screen, then tap Clear All.

If you use group notifications, tap a group to open it, then tap a notification.

Tip: To keep the red dot from appearing on the watch face, open the Settings app on your Apple Watch, tap Notifications, then turn off Notifications Indicator.

Swipe down to view unread notifications.

Silence all notifications on Apple Watch

Touch and hold the bottom of the screen, swipe up to open Control Center, then tap .

You still feel a tap when a notification arrives. To prevent sound and taps, follow these steps:

1. Touch and hold the bottom of the screen, then swipe up to open Control Center.

2. Tap or the active Focus.

3. Tap Do Not Disturb, then choose an option—On, On for 1 hour, On until tomorrow morning, or On until I leave.

Tip: When you get a notification, you can quickly mute your Apple Watch by resting the palm of your hand on the watch display for at least three seconds. You'll feel a tap to confirm that mute is on.

Make sure you turn on Cover to Mute—open the Settings app on your Apple Watch, tap Sounds & Haptics, then turn on Cover to Mute.

Change notification settings on Apple Watch

By default, the notification settings for the apps on an Apple Watch that you set up for yourself mirror the settings on your iPhone. But you can customize how some apps display notifications.

Note: Mirrored settings don't apply to an Apple Watch you manage for a family member.

Choose how apps send notifications

1. Open the Apple Watch app on your iPhone.
2. Tap My Watch, then tap Notifications.
3. Tap the app (for example, Messages), tap Custom, then choose an option. Options may include:
    - Allow Notifications: The app displays notifications in Notification Center.
    - Send to Notification Center: Notifications are sent directly to Notification Center without your Apple Watch making a sound or displaying the notification.
    - Notifications Off: The app sends no notifications.
4. Notification grouping: Choose how notifications for the app are grouped. Options include:
    - Off: Notifications aren't grouped.
    - Automatically: Your Apple Watch uses information from the app to create separate groups. For example, News notifications are grouped by the channels you follow—CNN, Washington Post, and People.

- By App: All the app's notifications are grouped.

Tip: Some apps let you choose the specific kind of notifications you receive. For example, for Calendar, you can allow notifications only for certain things, like when you get an invitation or someone changes a shared calendar. For Mail, you can choose which email accounts are allowed to send notifications.

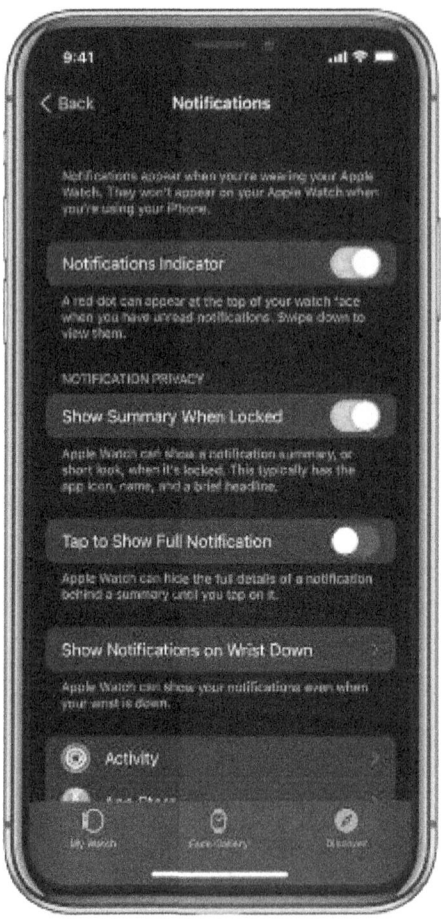

Change notification settings directly on Apple Watch

You can manage other notifications preferences directly on your Apple Watch by swiping left on a notification and tapping ●●● . Options may include:

- Mute 1 hour or Mute for Today: For the next hour or for the rest of the day, notifications are sent directly to Notification Center without your Apple Watch making a sound or displaying the notification. To see and hear these notification alerts again, swipe left on a notification, tap ●●● , then tap Unmute.
- Add to Summary: Future notifications from the app appear in the Notification Summary on your iPhone.
  To have the app once again notify you immediately, open the Settings app on your iPhone, tap Notifications, tap the app, then tap Immediate Delivery.
- Turn off Time Sensitive: Time-sensitive notifications are always delivered immediately, even if you're using a Focus that delays most notifications. However, if you want to prevent this app from delivering even time-sensitive notifications immediately, tap this option.
- Turn off: The app sends no notifications. To reenable notifications from the app, open the Apple Watch app on your iPhone, tap My Watch, tap Notifications, tap the app you want to adjust, then tap Allow Notifications.

Show notifications on the lock screen

You can choose how notifications appear on the lock screen of your Apple Watch.

1. Open the Settings app on your Apple Watch.
2. Tap Notifications.
3. Choose the following options:
    - Show Summary When Locked: With this option on, your Apple Watch shows a notification summary—or short look—when it's locked. The summary includes the notifying app's name and icon along with a brief headline.
    - Tap to Show Full Notification: When you raise your wrist to see a notification, you see a quick summary, then full details a few seconds later. For example, when a message arrives, you see who it's from first, then the message appears. Turn on this option to stop the full notification from appearing unless you tap it.
    - Show Notifications on Wrist Down: By default, notifications don't appear on your Apple Watch when your wrist is down. Turn on this option to make

notifications appear, even when your Apple Watch is turned away from you.

Manage your Apple ID settings on Apple Watch

In watchOS 8 you can view and edit information associated with your Apple ID. You can add and edit your contact information, change your password, add a trusted phone number, and more.

Edit contact information

1. Open the Settings app on your Apple Watch.
2. Tap [your user name].
3. Tap Name, Phone Numbers, or Email, then do any of the following:
    - Edit your name: Tap your name, then tap First, Middle, or Last.
    - View, edit, and add contact information: Tap a phone number under Reachable At. You can add an email address or phone number by tapping Add Email or Phone Number. To remove an email address, tap it, then tap Remove Email Address.
    - Change your birthday: Tap Birthday, then enter a new date.
    - Get announcements, recommendations, or the Apple News newsletter: Under Subscriptions, you can turn on Announcements; recommendations for apps, music, TV, and more; or opt in to the Apple News Newsletter.

Manage Apple ID password and security

1. Open the Settings app  on your Apple Watch.
2. Tap [your user name].

3. Tap Password & Security, then do any of the following:
   - Change your Apple ID password: Tap Change Password, then follow the onscreen instructions.
   - Change "Sign in with Apple" settings for an app or website: Tap Apps Using Your Apple ID, then choose an app. Tap Stop Using Apple ID to disassociate your Apple ID from the app. (You may be asked to create a new account the next time you try to sign in with the app.)
   - Edit or add a trusted phone number: Tap your current trusted phone number, verify when prompted, then tap Remove Phone Number—if you have only one trusted number, you must enter a new one before you can delete the current number. To add an additional trusted phone number, tap Add a Trusted Phone Number.
   - Get a verification code to sign in on another device or at iCloud.com: Tap Get Verification Code.

View and manage subscriptions

1. Open the Settings app on your Apple Watch.
2. Tap [your user name].
3. Tap Subscriptions, then tap a subscription to see information about it—its cost and length, for example.
4. Tap Cancel to cancel your subscription.
   Note: Some subscriptions must be canceled on your iPhone.

View and manage your devices

1. Open the Settings app 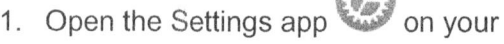 on your Apple Watch.
2. Tap [your user name].
3. Scroll down, then tap a device to display information about it.
4. Tap Remove from Account if you don't recognize the device.

Use shortcuts on Apple Watch

The Shortcuts app on Apple Watch lets you trigger tasks with just a tap. With the shortcuts you create on your iPhone, you can quickly get directions home, create a top 25 playlist, and more. You can run shortcuts from the Shortcuts app or add them as complications to your watch face.

Note: Not all shortcuts on iPhone are compatible with Apple Watch.

Run a shortcut

1. Open the Shortcuts app on your Apple Watch.
2. Tap a shortcut.

Add a shortcut complication

1. Touch and hold the watch face, then tap Edit.
2. Swipe left to the Complications screen, then tap a complication.
3. Scroll to Shortcuts, then choose a shortcut.

Add more shortcuts to Apple Watch

1. Open the Shortcuts app on your iPhone.
2. Tap ••• in the top-right corner of a shortcut.
3. Tap the settings icon on the shortcut screen, then turn on Show on Apple Watch.

Create an emergency Medical ID

A Medical ID provides information about you that may be important in an emergency, like allergies and medical conditions. Your Apple Watch can display this information so that it's available for someone attending to you in an emergency.

Tip: Having an emergency Medical ID that includes your date of birth is particularly important for those who are 55 and older. Apple Watch includes fall detection, which is turned on if you are 55 and older (and can also be turned on for those who are 18 years and older).

Set up your Medical ID

1. Open the Health app on your iPhone.
2. Tap your profile picture at the top right, then tap Medical ID.
3. Tap Get Started, then enter your information.

View your Medical ID on Apple Watch

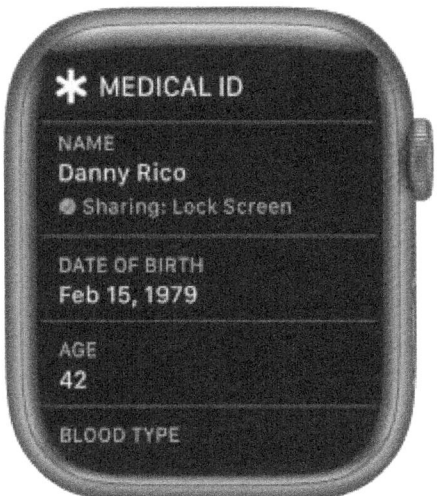

1. On your Apple Watch, hold the side button until the sliders appear.
2. Drag the Medical ID slider to the right.

If you don't see your Medical ID when you hold the side button on your Apple Watch, open the Apple Watch app on your iPhone, tap My Watch, tap Health, tap Medical ID, tap Edit, then turn on Show When Locked. To hide your Medical ID when your Apple Watch is locked, turn off Show When Locked.

Tip: Add emergency contacts to your Medical ID, and your Apple Watch alerts them if it makes an Emergency SOS call to emergency services.

Manage fall detection on Apple Watch

With fall detection enabled, if Apple Watch SE or Apple Watch Series 4 or later detects a hard fall, it can help connect you to emergency services and send a message to your emergency contacts. If Apple Watch detects a hard fall and that you have been immobile for about a minute, it will tap your wrist, sound an alarm, and then attempt to call emergency services.

If the birthdate you enter when setting up your Apple Watch (or adding it to the Health app on iPhone) indicates that you're 55 or older, fall detection is turned on automatically. If you're between age 18 and 55, you can turn on fall detection manually by doing the following:

1. Open the Settings app on your Apple Watch.
2. Go to SOS > Fall Detection, then turn on Fall Detection. You can also open the Apple Watch app on your iPhone, tap My Watch, tap Emergency SOS, then turn on Fall Detection. Note: If you turn off wrist detection, Apple Watch won't automatically attempt to call emergency services even after it has detected a hard impact fall.

3. Choose "Always on" to have fall detection on at all times, or "Only on during workouts" to have fall detection on only when you've started a workout.
   If you're between age 18 and 55, and setting up a new Apple Watch with watchOS 8.1, fall detection during workouts is turned on automatically. If you upgrade your existing Apple Watch from an earlier version of watchOS, you must turn on the feature to detect hard falls only during workouts.

Note: Apple Watch cannot detect all falls. The more physically active you are, the more likely you are to trigger fall detection due to high-impact activity that can appear to be a fall.

Set up Handwashing on Apple Watch

Your Apple Watch can detect when you start washing and encourage you to keep going for 20 seconds, the time recommended by global health organizations. Your Apple Watch can also notify you if you haven't washed your hands within a few minutes of returning home.

Turn on Handwashing

1. Open the Settings app ⚙ on your Apple Watch.
2. Tap Handwashing, then turn on Handwashing Timer.

When Apple Watch detects that you've started washing your hands, it starts a 20-second timer. If you stop washing in fewer than 20 seconds, you're encouraged to finish the job.

Receive Handwashing notifications

Apple Watch can remind you to wash your hands shortly after returning home.

1. Open the Settings app on your Apple Watch.
2. Tap Handwashing, then turn on Handwashing Reminders.

Note: On an Apple Watch set up for a family member, you can also turn on handwashing reminders. Open the Settings app on the managed Apple Watch, tap Handwashing, turn on Handwashing Timer, then turn on Handwashing Reminders.

To receive handwashing reminders, you must set a home address in your My Card in the Contacts app on iPhone.

To see a report of your average handwashing times, open the Health app on your iPhone, go to Browse > Other Data, then tap Handwashing.

Connect Apple Watch to a Wi-Fi network

By connecting your Apple Watch to a Wi-Fi network, you can continue to use many of its features, even when you don't have your iPhone with you.

Choose a Wi-Fi network

1. Touch and hold the bottom of the screen, then swipe up to open Control Center.
2. Touch and hold 📶, then tap the name of an available Wi-Fi network.
   Wi-Fi networks compatible with Apple Watch are 802.11b/g/n 2.4GHz.
3. If the network requires a password, do one of the following:
   - Use the QWERTY keyboard on Apple Watch to enter the password.
   - Use your finger to scribble the password characters on the screen. Use the Digital Crown to choose uppercase or lowercase characters.
   - Tap 🔑, then choose a password from the list.
   - Use the keyboard on your iPhone to enter the password.
4. Tap Join.

Use a private network address on Apple Watch

To help protect your privacy, your Apple Watch uses a unique private network address, called a media access control (MAC) address, on each Wi-Fi network it joins. If a network can't use a private address (for example, to provide parental controls or to identify your Apple Watch as authorized to join), you can stop using a private address for that network.

1. Touch and hold the bottom of the screen, then swipe up to open Control Center.
2. Touch and hold 📶, then tap the name of the network you joined.
3. Turn off Private Address.

Important: For better privacy, leave Private Address turned on for all networks that support it. Using a private address helps reduce tracking of your Apple Watch across different Wi-Fi networks.

113

Forget a network

1. Touch and hold the bottom of the screen, then swipe up to open Control Center.
2. Touch and hold 📶 , then tap the name of the network you joined.
3. Tap Forget This Network.

If you rejoin that network at a later time, you must reenter its password if it requires one.

Connect Apple Watch to Bluetooth headphones or speakers

Play audio from Apple Watch on Bluetooth headphones or speakers without your iPhone nearby.
Tip: If you have AirPods that you set up with your iPhone, they're ready to use with your Apple Watch—just press play.

Pair Bluetooth headphones or speakers

You need Bluetooth headphones or speakers to listen to most audio on your Apple Watch (Siri, phone calls, voicemail, and voice memos play through the speaker on Apple Watch). Follow the instructions that came with the headphones or speakers to put them in discovery mode. When the Bluetooth device is ready, follow these steps:

1. Open the Settings app ⚙️ on your Apple Watch, then tap Bluetooth.
2. Tap the device when it appears.

You can also tap 📡 on the play screens of the Audiobooks, Music, Now Playing, and Podcasts apps to open the Bluetooth setting.

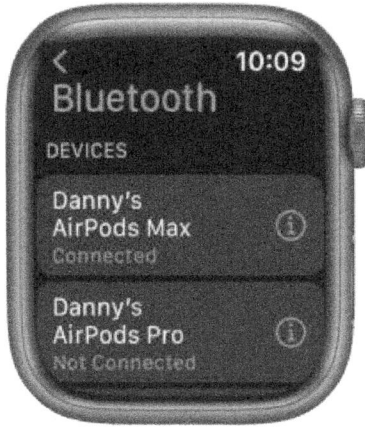

Choose an audio output

1. Touch and hold the bottom of the screen, then swipe up to open Control Center.
2. Tap , then choose the device you want to use.

Monitor your headphone volume

1. Touch and hold the bottom of the screen, then swipe up to open Control Center.
2. Tap Edit, then tap next to the Headphone button to add it.
3. While listening to headphones paired to your Apple Watch, open Control Center, then tap .
   A meter shows the current headphone volume.

Reduce loud sounds

Apple Watch can limit the loudness of your headphone audio to a set decibel level.

1. Open the Settings app on your Apple Watch.
2. Go to Sounds & Haptics > Headphone Safety, then tap Reduce Loud Sounds.
3. Turn on Reduce Loud Sounds, then set a level.

View loud headphone audio notifications

If you listen to loud audio through your headphones for long enough that it could affect your hearing, Apple Watch sends you a headphone notification and automatically turns down the volume to a more moderate level to protect your hearing.

To view details about headphone notifications on your iPhone, open the Health app, tap Browse, tap Hearing, tap Headphone Notifications, then tap a notification.

Hand off tasks from Apple Watch

Handoff lets you move from one device to another without losing focus on what you're doing. For example, even though you can reply to email using the Mail app on your Apple Watch, you might want to switch to your iPhone so you can reply using the onscreen keyboard. Handoff is available on an Apple Watch you set up for yourself, but not an Apple Watch you set up for a family member. Follow these steps to use Handoff.
1. Unlock your iPhone.
2. On an iPhone with Face ID, swipe up from the bottom edge and pause to show the App Switcher. (On an iPhone with a Home button, double-click the Home button to show the App Switcher.)
3. Tap the button that appears at the bottom of the screen to open the same item on your iPhone.

Tip: If you don't see a button in App Switcher, make sure Handoff is turned on for your iPhone in Settings > General > AirPlay & Handoff. Handoff is on by default. To disable it, open the Apple Watch app on your iPhone, tap My Watch, tap General, then turn off Enable Handoff.

Handoff works with Activity, Alarm, Calendar, Home, Mail, Maps, Messages, Music, News, Phone, Podcasts, Reminders, Settings, Siri, Stocks, Stopwatch, Timers, Wallet, Weather, and World Clock. For Handoff to work, your Apple Watch must be connected to your paired iPhone.

If you have a Mac with OS X 10.10 or later installed, you can also hand off from your Apple Watch to your Mac.

Unlock your Mac with Apple Watch

If you have a Mac (mid-2013 or later) with macOS 10.13 or later, your Apple Watch can instantly unlock your Mac when it wakes from sleep. You need to be signed in to iCloud using the same Apple ID on both your Mac and Apple Watch.

Tip: To find the model year of your Mac, click the Apple menu in the top-left corner of your computer screen, then choose About This Mac. The year your Mac was made is listed next to the model—for example, "MacBook Pro (15-inch, 2018)."

Turn on Auto Unlock

1. Make sure that your devices are set up as follows:
    - Your Mac has Wi-Fi and Bluetooth turned on.
    - Your Mac and Apple Watch are signed in to iCloud with the same Apple ID, and your Apple ID is using two-factor authentication.
    - Your Apple Watch is using a passcode.
2. On your Mac, choose Apple menu > System Preferences.
3. Click Security & Privacy, then click General.
4. Select "Use Apple Watch to unlock apps and your Mac" or "Allow your Apple Watch to unlock your Mac."
    If you have more than one Apple Watch, select the watch you want to use to unlock your apps and Mac.

If you don't have two-factor authentication turned on for your Apple ID, follow the onscreen instructions, then try selecting the checkbox again.

Unlock your Mac

While wearing your watch, just wake up your Mac—no need to type in your password.

Tip: Make sure your Apple Watch is on your wrist and unlocked and you're near your Mac.

Unlock your iPhone with Apple Watch

When you're wearing your Apple Watch, you can use it to securely unlock iPhone (models with Face ID) when you're wearing a face mask.

To allow Apple Watch to unlock your iPhone, do the following:

1. On iPhone, go to Settings > Face ID & Passcode, then enter your passcode.
2. Scroll down, then turn on Apple Watch (below Unlock With Apple Watch).
   If you have more than one watch, turn on the setting for each one.
3. To unlock your iPhone when you're wearing a face mask, make sure you're wearing your Apple Watch, wake your iPhone, then glance at its screen.
   Apple Watch taps your wrist to let you know that your iPhone has been unlocked.

Note: To unlock your iPhone, your Apple Watch must have a passcode, be unlocked and on your wrist, and be close to your iPhone.

Use Apple Watch without its paired iPhone

Use your Apple Watch without your iPhone nearby

With Apple Watch with cellular and an activated cellular plan, you can stay connected even when away from your iPhone. For all other models of Apple Watch, there are still things you can do even when you are away from your iPhone and not connected to Wi-Fi.

Note: Apple Watch has a built-in GPS that allows you to get more accurate distance and speed information during an outdoor workout without your paired iPhone. The always-on altimeter in Apple Watch Series 7 is even more accurate, showing your current elevation in real time.

If your Apple Watch is connected to Wi-Fi

When your Apple Watch is connected to a Wi-Fi network, you can still do the following (even if your iPhone is turned off):
- Get apps from the App Store
- Send and receive messages with the Messages app
- Make calls on Apple Watch (make phone calls if you have Wi-Fi calling enabled or want to make a FaceTime audio call and you're within range of a Wi-Fi network)
- Use Walkie-Talkie
- Stream music, podcasts, and audiobooks to your Apple Watch
- Add music to Apple Watch
- Check current weather conditions
- Track your stocks
- Control your home with your Apple Watch
- Use third-party apps that support Wi-Fi connectivity

- Your Apple Watch uses Bluetooth® wireless technology to connect to its paired iPhone and uses the iPhone for many wireless functions. Your Apple Watch can configure Wi-Fi networks on its own, and also connect to Wi-Fi networks you've set up or connected to using the paired iPhone.

Use Apple Watch with a cellular network

With Apple Watch with cellular and a cellular connection to the same carrier used by your iPhone, you can make calls, reply to messages, use Walkie-Talkie, stream music and podcasts, receive notifications, and more, even when you don't have your iPhone or a Wi-Fi connection.
Note: Cellular service not available in all areas or with all carriers.

Add Apple Watch to your cellular plan

You can activate cellular service on your Apple Watch by following the instructions during the initial setup. To activate service later, follow these steps:
1. Open the Apple Watch app on your iPhone.
2. Tap My Watch, then tap Cellular.

Turn cellular off or on

Your Apple Watch with cellular uses the best network connection available to it—your iPhone when it's nearby, a Wi-Fi network that you've connected to previously on your iPhone, or a cellular connection. You can turn cellular off—to save battery power, for example. Just follow these steps:
1. Touch and hold the bottom of the screen, then swipe up to open Control Center.
2. Tap ((¶)), then turn Cellular off or on.

The Cellular button turns green when your Apple Watch has a cellular connection and your iPhone isn't nearby.

Note: Turning on cellular for extended periods uses more battery power (see the Apple Watch General Battery Information website for more information). Also, some apps may not update without a connection to your iPhone.

Check cellular signal strength

Try one of the following when connected to a cellular network:
- Use the Explorer watch face, which uses green dots to show cellular signal strength. Four dots is a good connection. One dot is poor.
- Open Control Center. The green bars at the top show the cellular connection status.
- Add the Cellular complication to the watch face.

Check cellular data usage

1. Open the Apple Watch app on your iPhone.
2. Tap My Watch, then tap Cellular.

Siri

Use Siri on Apple Watch

Useful Siri commands

You can use Siri to perform tasks and get answers right on your Apple Watch. For example, use Siri to translate what you say into another language, identify a song and provide an instant Shazam result, or, after you ask a general question, display the first few search results along with a brief excerpt from each page. Just tap Open Page to view the page on Apple Watch. Try using Siri to do things that usually take you a couple of steps.

Siri is not available in all regions and languages.

Ask Siri. Say something like:
- "How do you say 'How are you?' in Chinese?"
- "Start a 30-minute outdoor run"
- "Tell Kathleen I'm almost finished"
- "Open the Sleep app"
- "What song is this?"
- "What causes rainbows?"
- "What's my update?"
- "What kinds of things can I ask you?"

How to use Siri

To make a Siri request, do any of the following:
- Raise your wrist and speak into your Apple Watch.
  To turn off the Raise To Speak feature, open the Settings app  on your Apple Watch, tap Siri, then turn off Raise to Speak.
- Say "Hey Siri" followed by your request.

  To turn off "Hey Siri," open the Settings app on your Apple Watch, tap Siri, then turn off Listen for "Hey Siri."

- Tap the Siri button on the Siri watch face.
- Press and hold the Digital Crown until you see the listening indicator, then speak your request.
  To turn off the Press Digital Crown feature, open the Settings app ⚙ on your Apple Watch, tap Siri, then turn off Press Digital Crown.

Tip: After you activate Siri, you can lower your wrist. You'll feel a tap when there's a response.

To reply to a question from Siri or to continue the conversation, hold down the Digital Crown and speak.

Siri can speak responses to you, as it does on iOS, iPadOS, and macOS.
Note: To use Siri, Apple Watch must be connected to the internet. Cellular charges may apply.

Change voice feedback settings

Siri can speak responses on your Apple Watch. Open the Settings app ⚙ on your Apple Watch, tap Siri, then choose from the following:

- Always On: Siri speaks responses, even when your Apple Watch is in silent mode.
- Control With Silent Mode: Siri responses are silenced when your Apple Watch is set to silent mode.
- Headphones Only: Siri only speaks responses when your Apple Watch is connected to Bluetooth headphones.

To change the language and voice used for Siri, open the Settings app ⚙ on your Apple Watch, tap Siri, then tap Language or Siri Voice. When you tap Siri Voice you can change the variety and gender of the voice.
Note: The option to change Siri Voice is not available in all languages.

Delete Siri history

When you use Siri or dictation, your requests are stored for six months on Apple servers to help improve Siri responses to you. Your requests are associated with a random identifier, not with your Apple ID or email address. You can delete these interactions from the server at any time.

1. Open the Settings app on your Apple Watch.
2. Tap Siri, tap Siri History, then tap Delete Siri History.

Listen and respond to notifications with AirPods and Beats headphones on Apple Watch

Siri can read out notifications from many apps without having to unlock your iPhone when you're using supported AirPods and Beats headphones. Siri avoids interrupting you and listens after reading notifications so you can reply without saying "Hey Siri."

Turn on Announce Notifications

1. Put your paired headphones in or on your ears, depending on the kind of headphones you have.
2. Pair them with Apple Watch.
3. Open the Settings app on your Apple Watch.
4. Go to Siri > Announce Notifications, then turn on Announce Notifications.

You can also open the Settings app on your iPhone, go to Notifications > Announce Notifications, then turn on Announce Notifications.

Choose apps for notifications

You can choose the apps that are allowed to announce notifications.

1. Put your paired headphones in or on your ears, depending on the kind of headphones you have.
2. Open the Settings app ⚙ on your Apple Watch.
3. Go to Siri > Announce Notifications, scroll up, then tap the apps you want audio notifications from.

Temporarily turn off Announce Notifications

1. Touch and hold the bottom of the screen, then swipe up to open Control Center.
2. Tap 🔔.

Tap 🔔 again to turn it on.
Note: The Announce Notifications button is disabled when you remove AirPods.

Reply to a message

Say something like "Reply that's great news."
Siri repeats what you said, then asks for confirmation before sending your reply. (To send replies without waiting for confirmation, open the Settings app ⚙ on your Apple Watch, go to Siri > Announce Notifications, then turn on Reply without Confirmation.)

Stop Siri from reading a notification

You can do any of the following:
- Say something like "Stop" or "Cancel."
- Press the Digital Crown (AirPods Max).
  Note: While listening to a notification, you can turn the Digital Crown to change the volume.
- Press either Force Sensor (AirPods Pro).
- Double-tap either of your AirPods (2nd generation).
- Remove one of your AirPods (AirPods Pro and AirPods 2nd generation).

If you didn't turn on Announce Notifications when you set up your AirPods, open the Settings app ⚙ on your Apple Watch, go to Siri > Announce Notifications, then turn on Announce Notifications.

Announce calls with Siri on Apple Watch

With Announce Calls, Siri identifies incoming phone calls and FaceTime calls, which you can accept or decline using your voice. Announce Calls also works with supported third-party apps.

1. Open the Settings app ⚙ on your Apple Watch.
2. Tap Siri, then turn on Announce Calls.
3. When a call comes in, the caller is identified and you're asked if you want to answer the call. Say "yes" to accept the call or "no" to decline it.

Apple Watch faces

Explore the Face Gallery on Apple Watch

The Face Gallery in the Apple Watch app is the easiest way to see all of the available watch faces. When you find one that looks interesting, you can customize it, choose complications, then add the face to your collection—all from the gallery.

Open the Face Gallery

Open the Apple Watch app on your iPhone, then tap Face Gallery.

Tap a face to customize it and add it to your collection.

Choose features for a face

In the Face Gallery, tap a face, then tap a feature such as color or style.
As you play around with different options, the face at the top changes so you can make sure the design is just right.

Add complications in the Face Gallery

1. In the Face Gallery, tap a face, then tap a complication position, such as Top Left, Top Right, or Bottom.
2. Swipe to see which complications are available for that position, then tap the one you want.
3. If you decide you don't want a complication in that position, scroll to the top of the list and tap Off.

Add a face

1. After you customize a face in the Face Gallery, tap Add.

Customize the watch face

Personalize your Apple Watch face so it looks the way you want and provides the functions you need. Choose a design, adjust colors and features, then add it to your collection. Switch faces at any time to see the right timekeeping tools—or to shake things up.
The Face Gallery in the Apple Watch app is the easiest way to see all of the available watch faces, customize one, and add it to your collection. But, if your iPhone isn't handy, you can customize the face right on your watch.

Choose a different watch face

- Swipe edge to edge across the watch face to see other faces in your collection.
- To see all available watch faces, touch and hold the watch face, swipe to the one you want, then tap it.

Swipe left or right to see other watch faces.

Add features to your watch face.

Add complications to the watch face

You can add special features—called complications—to some watch faces, so you can instantly check things like stock prices, the weather report, or information from other apps you installed.

1. With the watch face showing, touch and hold the display, then tap Edit.
2. Swipe left all the way to the end.
   If a face offers complications, they're shown on the last screen.
3. Tap a complication to select it, then turn the Digital Crown to choose a new one—Activity or Heart Rate, for example.

4. When you're finished, press the Digital Crown to save your changes, then tap the face to switch to it.

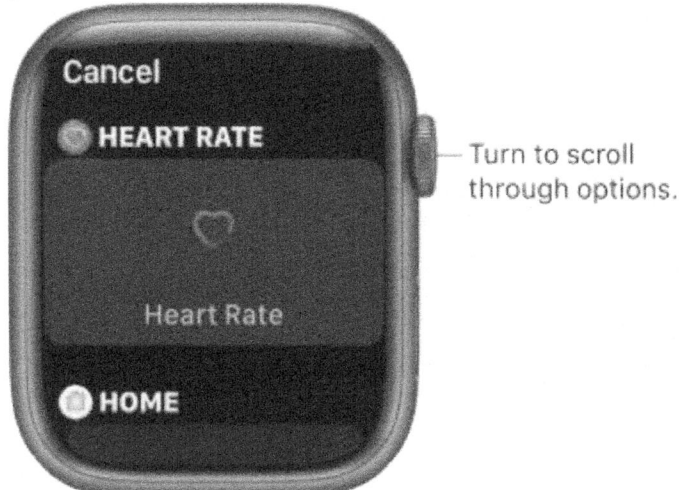

Turn to scroll through options.

Some apps you get from the App Store also include complications.

Add a watch face to your collection

Create your own collection of custom faces—even variations of the same design.
1. With the current watch face showing, touch and hold the display.
2. Swipe left all the way to the end, then tap the New button (+).
3. Turn the Digital Crown to browse watch faces, then tap Add.
Tip: Tap a collection such as New in watchOS to browse a specific category of watch faces.

After you add it, you can customize the watch face.

131

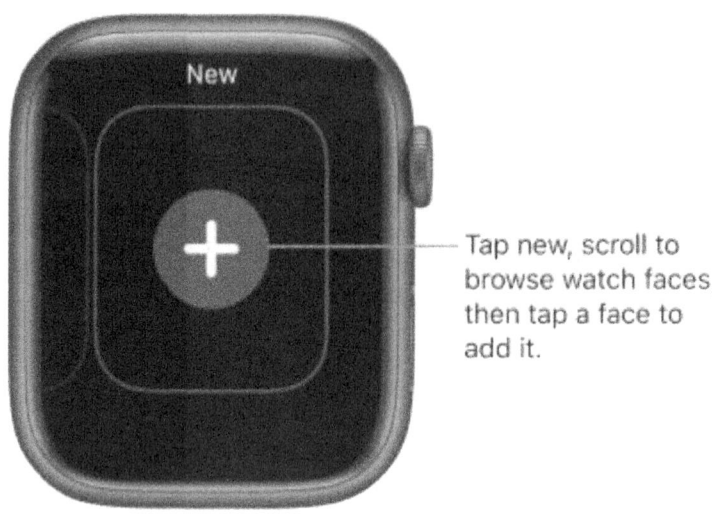

Tap new, scroll to browse watch faces, then tap a face to add it.

View your collection

You can see all your watch faces at a glance.
1. Open the Apple Watch app on your iPhone.
2. Tap My Watch, then swipe through your collection below My Faces.

To rearrange the order of your collection, tap Edit, then drag next to a watch face up or down.

Delete a face from your collection

1. With the current watch face showing, touch and hold the display.
2. Swipe to the face you don't want, then swipe it up and tap Remove.

Or, on your iPhone, open the Apple Watch app, tap My Watch, then tap Edit in the My Faces area. Tap next to the watch faces you want to delete, then tap Remove.

You can always add the watch face again later.

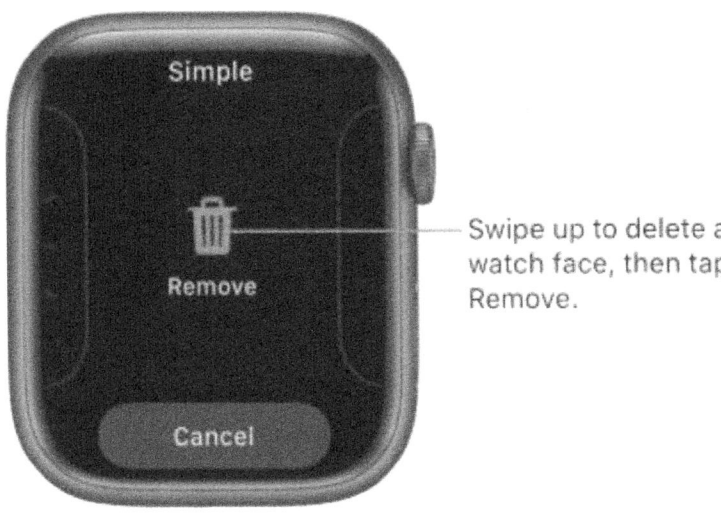

Swipe up to delete a watch face, then tap Remove.

Set the watch ahead

1. Open the Settings app  on your Apple Watch.
2. Tap Clock.
3. Tap +0 min, then turn the Digital Crown to set the watch ahead by as much as 59 minutes.

This setting changes only the time shown on the watch face—it doesn't affect alarms, times in notifications, or any other times (such as World Clock).

Share Apple Watch faces

You can share watch faces with friends. Shared faces can include the complications included in watchOS as well as those created by third parties.

Note: The recipient of the watch face must also have an Apple Watch with watchOS 7 or later.

Share a watch face

1. On Apple Watch, show the watch face you want to share.

2. Touch and hold the display, then tap ⬆️.
3. Tap the name of the watch face, then tap "Don't include" for any complications that you don't want to share.
4. Tap a recipient, or tap Messages or Mail.
If you tap Messages or Mail, add a contact, subject (Mail), and message.
5. Tap Send.

You can also open the Apple Watch app, tap a watch face from your collection or Face Gallery, tap ⬆️, then choose a sharing option.

Receive a watch face

You can receive shared watch faces sent to you in Messages or Mail, or by clicking a link online.
1. Open a text, email, or link that contains a shared watch face.
2. Tap the shared watch face, then tap Add.

If you receive a watch face with a complication from a third-party app, tap the price of the app or Get to download the app from the App Store. You can also tap Continue Without This App to get the watch face without the third-party complication.

Apple Watch faces and their features

Your Apple Watch comes with a variety of watch faces, most of which you can customize.

Look for software updates; the set of watch faces that follows might differ from what you see on your Apple Watch. Not all watch faces available in all regions or on all models.

Activity Analog

This watch face shows your Activity progress, superimposed over a traditional analog clock. You can choose to see your Activity rings in the familiar stacked design or as subdials.

- Customizable features: Color • Style (Rings or Subdials)
- Available complications: Activity • Alarms • Astronomy (Moon Phase) • Audiobooks • Blood Oxygen • Calculator • Calendar (Today's Date, Your Schedule) • Camera Remote • Compass (Compass, Compass/Elevation, Elevation) • Contacts • Controls (Battery, Cellular) • ECG • Find Devices • Find Items • Find People • Heart Rate • Home • Mail • Maps (Maps, Nearby Transit) • Messages • Mindfulness • Music • News • Noise (Sound Levels) • Now Playing • Phone •

Podcasts • Reminders • Shortcuts • Sleep • Stocks • Stopwatch • Timer • Tips • Voice Memos • Walkie-Talkie • Weather • Workout • World Clock (Sunrise/Sunset)

Activity Digital

With large, uniform fonts, this watch face shows the time in a digital format, along with your Activity progress.

- Customizable features: Color • Seconds time
- Available complications: Activity • Alarms • Astronomy (Moon Phase) • Audiobooks • Blood Oxygen • Calculator • Calendar (Today's Date, Your Schedule) • Camera Remote • Compass (Compass, Compass/Elevation, Elevation) • Contacts • Controls (Battery, Cellular) • Cycle Tracking • ECG • Find Devices • Find Items • Find People • Heart Rate • Home • Mail • Maps (Maps, Nearby Transit) • Messages • Mindfulness • Music • News • Noise (Sound Levels) • Now Playing • Phone • Podcasts • Reminders • Remote • Shortcuts • Sleep • Stocks • Stopwatch • Timer • Tips • Voice Memos • Walkie-Talkie • Weather • Workout • World Clock (Sunrise/Sunset)

Artist

This visually engaging face algorithmically changes every time you tap the display, and there are millions of combinations.

Astronomy

This watch face shows a continuously updating 3D model of the earth, moon, or solar system.

Turn to move forward or back in time.

- Customizable features: View (Earth, Moon, or Solar System)

- Available complications: Activity • Alarms • Astronomy (Moon Phase) • Audiobooks • Calendar (Today's Date, Your Schedule) • Compass (Compass, Compass/Elevation, Elevation) • Contacts • Controls (Battery) • Heart Rate • Messages • Music • News • Noise (Sound Levels) • Now Playing • Podcasts • Reminders • Shortcuts • Stocks • Stopwatch • Timer • Weather • Workout • World Clock (Sunrise/Sunset)

Tip: When you add the Moon complication to a corner of a watch face that includes it, you can see the time of the next moonrise or moonset. For example, 11:44 PM, 12H 4M indicates that, at your location, the moon will set below the horizon at 11:44 in the evening, which is 12 hours and 4 minutes from the current time.

Breathe

This watch face encourages you to relax and breathe mindfully. Just tap the display to begin.

- Customizable features: Style (Classic, Calm, and Focus)
- Available complications: Activity • Alarms • Astronomy (Moon Phase) • Audiobooks • Blood Oxygen • Calculator • Calendar (Today's Date, Your Schedule) • Camera Remote • Compass (Compass, Elevation) • Contacts • Controls (Battery, Cellular) • Cycle Tracking • ECG • Find Devices •

Find Items • Find People • Heart Rate • Home • Mail • Maps (Maps, Nearby Transit) • Messages • Mindfulness • Music • News • Noise (Sound Levels) • Now Playing • Phone • Podcasts • Reminders • Remote • Shortcuts • Sleep • Stocks • Stopwatch • Timer • Tips • Voice Memos • Walkie-Talkie • Weather • Workout • World Clock (Sunrise/Sunset)

California

- Customizable features: Color • Numerals (Pills, Roman, California, Arabic, Arabic Indic, and Devanagari) • Dial (Full Screen or Circular)
- Available complications: Activity • Alarms • Astronomy (Earth, Moon, Moon Phase, Solar, Solar System) • Audiobooks • Blood Oxygen • Calculator • Calendar (Today's Date, Your Schedule) • Camera Remote • Compass (Compass, Elevation) • Contacts • Controls (Battery, Cellular) • Cycle Tracking • ECG • Find Devices • Find Items • Find People • Heart Rate • Home • Mail • Maps (Maps, Nearby Transit) • Messages • Mindfulness • Monogram • Music • News • Noise (Sound Levels) • Now Playing • Phone • Podcasts • Reminders • Remote • Shortcuts • Sleep • Stocks • Stopwatch • Time (Analog Seconds, Analog Time,

Digital Seconds, Digital Time) • Timer • Tips • Voice Memos • Walkie-Talkie • Weather • Workout • World Clock (Sunrise/Sunset)

Chronograph

This watch face measures time in precise increments, like a classic analog stopwatch. It includes a stopwatch that can be activated right from the face.

- Customizable features: Color • Timescale
- Available complications: Activity • Alarms • Astronomy (Moon Phase) • Audiobooks • Blood Oxygen • Calculator • Calendar (Today's Date, Your Schedule) • Camera Remote • Compass (Compass, Elevation) • Contacts • Controls (Battery, Cellular) • Cycle Tracking • ECG • Find Devices • Find Items • Find People • Heart Rate • Home • Mail • Maps (Maps, Nearby Transit) • Messages • Mindfulness • Music • News • Noise (Sound Levels) • Now Playing • Phone • Podcasts • Reminders • Remote • Shortcuts • Sleep • Stocks • Stopwatch • Timer • Tips • Voice Memos • Walkie-Talkie • Weather • Workout • World Clock (Sunrise/Sunset)

Chronograph Pro

Tap the bezel surrounding the main 12-hour dial on this watch face, and it transforms into a chronograph. Record time on scales of 60, 30, 6, or 3 seconds. Or select the tachymeter timescale to measure speed based on time travel over a fixed distance..

- Customizable features: Color • Timescale
- Available complications: Activity • Alarms • Astronomy (Moon) • Audiobooks • Blood Oxygen • Calculator • Calendar (Today's Date, Your Schedule) • Camera Remote • Compass (Compass, Elevation) • Contacts • Controls (Battery, Cellular) • Cycle Tracking • ECG • Find Devices • Find Items • Find People • Heart Rate • Home • Mail • Maps (Maps, Nearby Transit) • Messages • Mindfulness • Music • News • Noise (Sound Levels) • Phone • Podcasts • Reminders • Remote • Shortcuts • Sleep • Stocks • Stopwatch • Timer • Tips • Voice Memos • Walkie-Talkie • Weather • Workout • World Clock (Sunrise/Sunset)

Color

This watch face displays the time and any features you add in your choice of bright colors.

- Customizable features: Color • Style (Circular or Dial. Apple Watch includes a full-screen facet) • Monogram
- Available complications: Activity • Alarms • Astronomy (Moon Phase) • Audiobooks • Blood Oxygen • Calculator • Calendar (Today's Date, Your Schedule) • Camera Remote • Compass (Compass, Elevation) • Contacts • Controls (Battery, Cellular) • Cycle Tracking • ECG • Find Devices • Find Items • Find People • Heart Rate • Home • Mail • Maps (Maps, Nearby Transit) • Messages • Mindfulness • Music • News • Noise (Sound Levels) • Phone • Podcasts • Reminders • Remote • Shortcuts • Sleep • Stocks • Stopwatch • Timer • Tips • Voice Memos • Walkie-Talkie • Weather • Workout • World Clock (Sunrise/Sunset)

Contour

This watch face gradually changes to highlight the current hour. The numerals are a custom font designed to fit into the edge of the display and move seamlessly from one hour to the next.

- Customizable features: Color • Style (Regular or Rounded) • Dial Color
- Available complications: Activity • Alarms • Astronomy (Earth, Moon, Solar, Solar System) • Audiobooks • Blood Oxygen • Calculator • Calendar (Today's Date) • Camera Remote • Compass (Compass, Elevation) • Contacts • Controls (Battery, Cellular) • Cycle Tracking • ECG • Find Devices • Find Items • Find People • Heart Rate • Home • Mail • Maps (Maps, Nearby Transit) • Messages • Mindfulness • Monogram • Music • News • Noise (Sound Levels) • Phone • Podcasts • Reminders • Remote • Shortcuts • Sleep • Stocks • Stopwatch • Time (Analog Seconds, Analog Time, Digital Seconds, Digital Time) • Timer • Tips • Voice Memos • Walkie-Talkie • Weather • Workout • World Clock (Sunrise/Sunset)

Count Up

This watch face can be used to track elapsed time.

- Customizable features: Color
- Available complications: Activity • Alarms • Astronomy (Moon) • Audiobooks • Blood Oxygen • Calculator • Calendar (Today's Date, Your Schedule) • Camera Remote • Compass (Compass, Elevation) • Contacts • Controls (Battery, Cellular) • Cycle Tracking • ECG • Find Devices • Find Items • Find People • Heart Rate • Home • Mail • Maps (Maps, Nearby Transit) • Messages • Mindfulness • Monogram • Music • News • Noise (Sound Levels) • Phone • Podcasts • Reminders • Remote • Shortcuts • Sleep • Stocks • Stopwatch • Timer • Tips • Voice Memos • Walkie-Talkie • Weather • Workout • World Clock (Sunrise/Sunset)

To start timing, tap the main 12-hour dial to align the marker on the outer bezel with the minute hand, turn the Digital Crown to set the length of time, then tap Start. To return the face to its default state, tap the red elapsed time button.

Explorer

The Explorer watch face (available on Apple Watch with cellular) prominently features green dots, which indicate cellular signal strength.

- Customizable features: Color of the hands • Style
- Available complications: Activity • Alarms • Astronomy (Moon Phase) • Audiobooks • Blood Oxygen • Calculator • Calendar (Today's Date, Your Schedule) • Camera Remote • Compass (Compass, Compass/Elevation, Elevation) • Contacts • Controls (Battery, Cellular) • Cycle Tracking • ECG • Find Devices • Find Items • Find People • Heart Rate • Home • Mail • Maps (Maps, Nearby Transit) • Messages • Mindfulness • Monogram • Music • News • Noise (Sound Levels) • Now Playing • Phone • Podcasts • Reminders • Remote • Shortcuts • Sleep • Stocks • Stopwatch • Timer • Tips • Voice Memos • Walkie-Talkie • Weather • Workout • World Clock (Sunrise/Sunset)

Fire and Water

This watch face animates whenever you raise your wrist or tap the display.

- Customizable features: Color (Fire, Water, or Fire & Water) • Style (Apple Watch SE and Apple Watch Series 4 and later includes a full-screen facet)
- Available complications (Circular style only): Activity • Alarms • Astronomy (Moon Phase) • Audiobooks • Blood Oxygen • Calculator • Calendar (Today's Date, Your Schedule) • Camera Remote • Compass (Compass, Compass/Elevation, Elevation) • Contacts • Controls (Battery, Cellular) • Cycle Tracking • ECG • Find Devices • Find Items • Find People • Heart Rate • Home • Mail • Maps (Maps, Nearby Transit) • Messages • Mindfulness • Music • News • Noise (Sound Levels) • Now Playing • Phone • Podcasts • Reminders • Remote • Shortcuts • Sleep • Stocks • Stopwatch • Timer • Tips • Voice Memos • Walkie-Talkie • Weather • Workout • World Clock (Sunrise/Sunset)

GMT

This watch face has two dials: a 12-hour inner dial that displays local time, and a 24-hour outer dial that lets you track a second time zone.

- Customizable features: Color
- Available complications: Activity • Alarms • Astronomy (Moon) • Audiobooks • Blood Oxygen • Calculator • Calendar (Today's Date, Your Schedule) • Camera Remote • Compass (Compass, Elevation) • Contacts • Controls (Battery, Cellular) • Cycle Tracking • ECG • Find Devices • Find Items • Find People • Heart Rate • Home • Mail • Maps (Maps, Nearby Transit) • Messages • Mindfulness • Music • News • Noise (Sound Levels) • Phone • Podcasts • Reminders • Remote • Shortcuts • Sleep • Stocks • Stopwatch • Timer • Tips • Voice Memos • Walkie-Talkie • Weather • Workout • World Clock (Sunrise/Sunset)

To set a second time zone, tap the watch face, then turn the Digital Crown to choose a time zone. Tap to confirm your choice and return to the watch face. The red hand shows you the hour in the second time zone.

Gradient

This watch face features gradients that move with the time.

- Customizable features: Color • Style • Dial (Full Screen or Circular)
- Available complications: Activity • Alarms • Astronomy (Moon, Moon Phase) • Audiobooks • Blood Oxygen • Calculator • Calendar (Today's Date, Your Schedule) • Camera Remote • Compass (Compass, Compass/Elevation, Elevation) • Contacts • Controls (Battery, Cellular) • Cycle Tracking • ECG • Find Devices • Find Items • Find People • Heart Rate • Home • Mail • Maps (Maps, Nearby Transit) • Messages • Mindfulness • Music • News • Noise (Sound Levels) • Now Playing • Phone • Podcasts • Reminders • Remote • Shortcuts • Sleep • Stocks • Stopwatch • Timer • Tips • Voice Memos • Walkie-Talkie • Weather • Workout • World Clock (Sunrise/Sunset)

Infograph

Features up to eight rich, full-color complications and subdials.

- Customizable features: Color
- Available complications: Activity • Alarms • Astronomy (Earth, Moon, Solar, Solar System) • Audiobooks • Blood Oxygen • Calculator • Calendar (Today's Date, Your Schedule) • Camera Remote • Compass (Compass, Elevation) • Contacts • Controls (Battery, Cellular) • Cycle Tracking • ECG • Find Devices • Find Items • Find People • Heart Rate • Home • Mail • Maps (Maps, Nearby Transit) • Messages • Mindfulness • Monogram • Music • News • Noise (Sound Levels) • Phone • Podcasts • Reminders • Remote • Shortcuts • Sleep • Stocks • Stopwatch • Time (Digital Time) • Timer • Tips • Voice Memos • Walkie-Talkie • Weather • Workout • World Clock (Sunrise/Sunset)

Infograph Modular

Featuries up to six rich, full-color complications.

- Customizable features: Color
- Available complications: Activity • Alarms • Astronomy (Earth, Moon, Solar, Solar System) • Audiobooks • Blood Oxygen • Calculator • Calendar (Today's Date, Your Schedule) • Camera Remote • Compass (Compass, Elevation) • Contacts • Controls (Battery, Cellular) • Cycle Tracking • ECG • Find Devices • Find Items • Find People • Heart Rate • Home • Mail • Maps (Maps, Nearby Transit) • Messages • Mindfulness • Music • News • Noise (Sound Levels) • Now Playing • Phone • Podcasts • Reminders • Remote • Shortcuts • Sleep • Stocks • Stopwatch • Time (Analog Seconds, Analog Time, Digital Seconds, Digital Time) • Timer • Tips • Voice Memos • Walkie-Talkie • Weather • Workout • World Clock (Sunrise/Sunset)

Kaleidoscope

Select a photo to create a watch face with evolving patterns of shapes and colors. Turn the Digital Crown to change the pattern.

- Customizable features: Image • Style
- Available complications (Facet, Radial, and Rosette styles): Activity • Alarms • Astronomy (Moon Phase) • Audiobooks • Blood Oxygen • Calculator • Calendar (Today's Date, Your Schedule) • Camera Remote • Compass (Compass, Compass/Elevation, Elevation) • Contacts • Controls (Battery, Cellular) • Cycle Tracking • ECG • Find Devices • Find Items • Find People • Heart Rate • Home • Mail • Maps (Maps, Nearby Transit) • Messages • Mindfulness • Music • News • Noise (Sound Levels) • Now Playing • Phone • Podcasts • Reminders • Remote • Shortcuts • Sleep • Stocks • Stopwatch • Time (Digital Time) • Timer • Tips • Voice Memos • Walkie-Talkie • Weather • Workout • World Clock (Sunrise/Sunset)

Liquid Metal

This watch face animates whenever you raise your wrist or tap the display.

- Customizable features: Color • Face shape
- Available complications (Circular style only): Activity • Alarms • Astronomy (Moon Phase) • Audiobooks • Blood Oxygen • Calculator • Calendar (Today's Date, Your Schedule) • Camera Remote • Compass (Compass, Compass/Elevation, Elevation) • Contacts • Controls (Battery, Cellular) • Cycle Tracking • ECG • Find Devices • Find Items • Find People • Heart Rate • Home • Mail • Maps (Maps, Nearby Transit) • Messages • Mindfulness • Music • News • Noise (Sound Levels) • Now Playing • Phone • Podcasts • Reminders • Remote • Shortcuts • Sleep • Stocks • Stopwatch • Timer • Tips • Voice Memos • Walkie-Talkie • Weather • Workout • World Clock (Sunrise/Sunset)

Memoji

This watch face features Memoji you've created and all the Memoji characters.

- Customizable features: Character
- Available complications: Activity • Alarms • Astronomy (Moon Phase) • Audiobooks • Calendar (Today's Date, Your Schedule) • Compass (Compass, Compass/Elevation, Elevation) • Controls (Battery) • Heart Rate • Messages • Music • News • Noise (Sound Levels) • Now Playing • Podcasts • Reminders • Shortcuts • Stocks • Stopwatch • Timer • Weather • Workout • World Clock (Sunrise/Sunset)

Meridian

This full-screen watch face features a classic look with four subdials.

- Customizable features: Color • Dial (Black or White)
- Available complications: Activity • Alarms • Astronomy (Earth, Moon, Solar, Solar System) • Audiobooks • Blood Oxygen • Calculator • Calendar (Today's Date) • Camera Remote • Compass (Compass, Elevation) • Contacts • Controls (Battery, Cellular) • Cycle Tracking • ECG • Find Devices • Find Items • Find People • Heart Rate • Home • Mail • Maps (Maps, Nearby Transit) • Messages • Mindfulness • Monogram • Music • News • Noise (Sound Levels) • Phone • Podcasts • Reminders • Remote • Shortcuts • Sleep • Stocks • Stopwatch • Time (Analog Seconds, Analog Time, Digital Seconds, Digital Time) • Timer • Tips • Voice Memos • Walkie-Talkie • Weather • Workout • World Clock (Sunrise/Sunset)

Mickey Mouse and Minnie Mouse

Let Mickey Mouse or Minnie Mouse give you a whimsical view of the time—their arms rotate to indicate the hours and minutes, while their feet tap out each second.

- Customizable features: Color • Character
- Available complications: Activity • Alarms • Astronomy (Moon Phase) • Audiobooks • Blood Oxygen • Calculator • Calendar (Today's Date, Your Schedule) • Camera Remote • Compass (Compass, Compass/Elevation, Elevation) • Contacts • Controls (Battery, Cellular) • ECG • Find Devices • Find Items • Find People • Heart Rate • Home • Mail • Maps (Maps, Nearby Transit) • Messages • Mindfulness • Music • News • Noise (Sound Levels) • Now Playing • Phone • Podcasts • Reminders • Shortcuts • Sleep • Stocks • Stopwatch • Timer • Tips • Voice Memos • Walkie-Talkie • Weather • Workout • World Clock (Sunrise/Sunset)

To hear Mickey Mouse or Minnie Mouse tell you the time, open the Settings app on your Apple Watch, tap Clock, then turn on Speak Time. Raise your wrist, then place two fingers on the watch face to hear the time.

Modular

This watch face has a digital time display and a grid layout that lets you add many features to give you a thorough view of your day.

- Customizable features: Color
- Available complications: Activity • Alarms • Astronomy (Moon Phase) • Audiobooks • Blood Oxygen • Calculator • Calendar (Today's Date, Your Schedule) • Camera Remote • Compass (Compass, Elevation) • Contacts • Controls (Battery, Cellular) • Cycle Tracking • ECG • Find Devices • Find Items • Find People • Heart Rate • Home • Mail • Maps (Maps, Nearby Transit) • Messages • Mindfulness • Music • News • Noise (Sound Levels) • Now Playing • Phone • Podcasts • Reminders • Remote • Shortcuts • Sleep • Stocks • Stopwatch • Timer • Tips • Voice Memos • Walkie-Talkie • Weather • Workout • World Clock (Sunrise/Sunset)

Modular Compact

With this watch face, you can choose up to three complications as well as a digital or analog dial.

- Customizable features: Color • Dial (Analog or Digital)
- Available complications: Activity • Alarms • Astronomy (Earth, Moon, Solar, Solar System) • Audiobooks • Blood Oxygen • Calculator • Calendar (Today's Date, Your Schedule) • Camera Remote • Compass (Compass, Elevation) • Contacts • Controls (Battery, Cellular) • Cycle Tracking • ECG • Find Devices • Find Items • Find People • Heart Rate • Home • Mail • Maps (Maps, Nearby Transit) • Messages • Mindfulness • Music • News • Noise (Sound Levels) • Now Playing • Phone • Podcasts • Reminders • Remote • Shortcuts • Sleep • Stocks • Stopwatch • Time (Analog Seconds, Analog Time, Digital Seconds, Digital Time) • Timer • Tips • Voice Memos • Walkie-Talkie • Weather • Workout • World Clock (Sunrise/Sunset)

Modular Duo

This watch faces features digital time and up to three complications. Two of them are large, rectangular options that let you see more details in the complications you care about most.

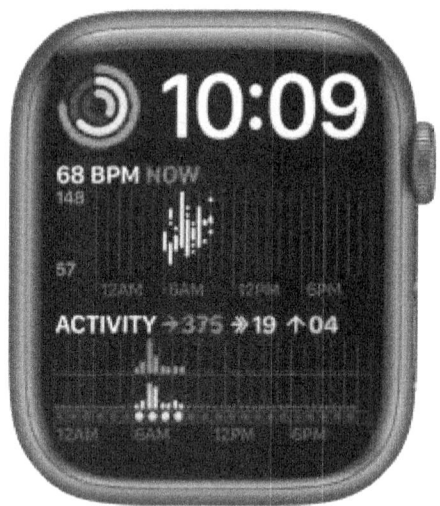

- Customizable features: Color
- Available complications: Activity • Alarms • Astronomy (Earth, Moon, Solar, Solar System) • Audiobooks • Blood Oxygen • Calculator • Calendar (Today's Date, Your Schedule) • Camera Remote • Compass (Compass, Elevation) • Contacts • Controls (Battery, Cellular) • Cycle Tracking • ECG • Find Devices • Find Items • Find People • Heart Rate • Home • Mail • Maps (Maps, Nearby Transit) • Messages • Mindfulness • Music • News • Noise (Sound Levels) • Now Playing • Phone • Podcasts • Reminders • Remote • Shortcuts • Sleep • Stocks • Stopwatch • Time (Analog Seconds, Analog Time, Digital Seconds, Digital Time) • Timer • Tips • Voice Memos • Walkie-Talkie • Weather • Workout • World Clock (Sunrise/Sunset)

Motion

This watch face displays a beautiful animated theme.

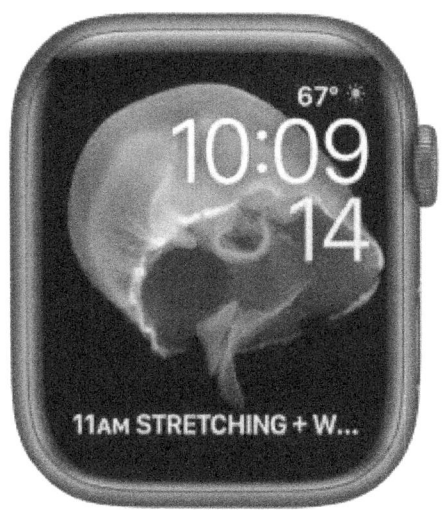

- Customizable features: Choose animated butterflies, flowers, or jellyfish
- Available complications: Activity • Alarms • Astronomy (Moon Phase) • Audiobooks • Calendar (Today's Date, Your Schedule) • Compass (Compass, Compass/Elevation, Elevation) • Controls (Battery) • Heart Rate • Messages • Music • News • Noise (Sound Levels) • Now Playing • Podcasts • Reminders • Shortcuts • Stocks • Stopwatch • Timer • Weather • Workout • World Clock (Sunrise/Sunset)

Numerals

This watch face displays the time with analog hands over a large hour marker. You can choose from seven different typefaces and countless colors for the perfect combination.

- Customizable features: Color • Symbols
- Available complications: Activity • Alarms • Astronomy (Moon Phase) • Audiobooks • Blood Oxygen • Calculator • Calendar (Today's Date, Your Schedule) • Compass (Compass, Compass/Elevation, Elevation) • Controls (Battery) • Heart Rate • Messages • Music • News • Noise (Sound Levels) • Now Playing • Podcasts • Reminders • Shortcuts • Stocks • Stopwatch • Timer • Tips • Weather • Workout • World Clock (Sunrise/Sunset)

Numerals Duo

This watch face displays large numbers in an Apple-designed font made specifically for Apple Watch.

- Customizable features: Colors • Symbols (Arabic, Arabic Indic, Devanagari) • Style (Filled, Hybrid, Outline)

Numerals Mono

This watch face displays large numbers in an Apple-designed font made specifically for Apple Watch.

- Customizable features: Color • Symbols (Arabic, Arabic Indic, Devanagari, Roman) • Style (Filled or Outline)

Photos

This watch face displays a new photo every time you raise your wrist or tap the display. Choose an album, Memory, or up to 24 custom photos.

- Customizable features: Color filters • Content (Synced Album, Favorites, Photos, Dynamic) • Time Position
- Available complications: Activity • Alarms • Astronomy (Moon Phase) • Audiobooks • Calendar (Today's Date, Your Schedule) • Compass (Compass, Compass/Elevation, Elevation) • Controls (Battery) • Heart Rate • Messages • Music • News • Noise (Sound Levels) • Now Playing • Podcasts • Reminders • Shortcuts • Stocks • Stopwatch • Timer • Weather • Workout • World Clock (Sunrise/Sunset)

Create a Photos face on your Apple Watch: With the current watch face showing, touch and hold the display, swipe all the way to the right, tap the New button (+), then tap Photos. Or, while browsing in the Photos app on your Apple Watch, tap ⬆, scroll to the bottom of the screen, then tap Create Face.

Create a Photos face on your iPhone: Open the Photos app on your iPhone, tap a photo, tap ⬆, swipe up, then tap Create Watch

Face. Choose to create a Portraits watch face, Photos watch face, or a Kaleidoscope watch face.

Add a color filter: On Apple Watch, touch and hold a Photos watch face, tap Edit, then turn the Digital Crown to choose a color filter. To choose from a wider selection of colors, scroll to the bottom of the list, tap "Tap to add more colors," choose a color, then tap Done. On iPhone, open the Apple Watch app, go to Face Gallery > Photos, then choose a color filter. Tap ⊕ to choose from a wider selection of colors.

If you're not seeing photos, make sure the photos are in your synced album.

Portraits

The Portraits watch face uses Portrait mode photos from your iPhone to create a multilayered watch face with depth. You can choose from three different type styles and select up to 24 photos. A new photo appears each time you raise your wrist or tap the display. The Portraits watch face requires Portrait mode photos taken on an iPhone with iOS 10.1 or later.

- Customizable features: Style (Classic, Modern, Rounded)
- Available complications: Activity • Alarms • Astronomy (Moon Phase) • Audiobooks • Calendar (Today's Date, Your

Schedule) • Compass (Compass, Compass/Elevation, Elevation) • Controls (Battery) • Heart Rate • Messages • Music • News • Noise (Sound Levels) • Now Playing • Podcasts • Reminders • Shortcuts • Stocks • Stopwatch • Timer • Weather • Workout • World Clock (Sunrise/Sunset)

Tip: Turn the Digital Crown to zoom in on the face.

Pride Analog

This face is inspired by the rainbow flag. The threads of color move when you tap the face or turn the Digital Crown.

- Customizable features: Style (Apple Watch includes a full-screen facet)
- Available complications (complications available only with Circular style): Activity • Alarms • Astronomy (Moon Phase) • Audiobooks • Blood Oxygen • Calculator • Calendar (Today's Date, Your Schedule) • Camera Remote • Compass (Compass, Elevation) • Contacts • Controls (Battery, Cellular) • Cycle Tracking • ECG • Find Devices • Find Items • Find People • Heart Rate • Home • Mail • Maps (Maps, Nearby Transit) • Messages • Mindfulness • Music • News • Noise (Sound Levels) • Phone • Podcasts • Reminders • Remote • Shortcuts • Sleep • Stocks • Stopwatch • Timer •

Tips • Voice Memos • Walkie-Talkie • Weather • Workout • World Clock (Sunrise/Sunset)

Pride Digital

This face is inspired by the rainbow flag. The threads of color move when you tap the face or turn the Digital Crown.

- Customizable features: Style (I, II, III)
- Available complications: Activity • Alarms • Astronomy (Moon Phase) • Audiobooks • Calendar (Today's Date, Your Schedule) • Compass (Compass, Compass/Elevation, Elevation) • Controls (Battery) • Heart Rate • Messages • Music • News • Noise (Sound Levels) • Now Playing • Podcasts • Reminders • Shortcuts • Stocks • Stopwatch • Timer • Weather • Workout • World Clock (Sunrise/Sunset)

Pride Woven

This face is inspired by the rainbow flag. The threads of color move when you turn the Digital Crown.

- Customizable features: Style (Rectangle, Circle)
- Available complications (complications available only with Circular style): Activity • Alarms • Astronomy (Moon) • Audiobooks • Blood Oxygen • Calculator • Calendar (Today's Date, Your Schedule) • Camera Remote • Compass (Compass, Elevation) • Contacts • Controls (Battery, Cellular) • Cycle Tracking • ECG • Find Devices • Find Items • Find People • Heart Rate • Home • Mail • Maps (Maps, Nearby Transit) • Messages • Mindfulness • Music • News • Noise (Sound Levels) • Phone • Podcasts • Reminders • Remote • Shortcuts • Sleep • Stocks • Stopwatch • Timer • Tips • Voice Memos • Walkie-Talkie • Weather • Workout • World Clock (Sunrise/Sunset)

Simple

This minimalistic and elegant watch face lets you add detail to the dial and features to the corners.

- Customizable features: Color • Style (I, II, III, IV)
- Available complications: Activity • Alarms • Astronomy (Moon) • Audiobooks • Blood Oxygen • Calculator • Calendar (Today's Date, Your Schedule) • Camera Remote • Compass (Compass, Elevation) • Contacts • Controls (Battery, Cellular) • Cycle Tracking • ECG • Find Devices • Find Items • Find People • Heart Rate • Home • Mail • Maps (Maps, Nearby Transit) • Messages • Mindfulness • Music • News • Noise (Sound Levels) • Phone • Podcasts • Reminders • Remote • Shortcuts • Sleep • Stocks • Stopwatch • Timer • Tips • Voice Memos • Walkie-Talkie • Weather • Workout • World Clock (Sunrise/Sunset)

Siri

This face displays information that's timely and helpful. It might be your next appointment, the traffic on your way home, or the time the sun sets, and you can tap to get more information. You can also turn the Digital Crown to scroll through your day.

- Customizable features: Color
- Available complications: Activity • Alarms • Astronomy (Moon Phase) • Audiobooks • Blood Oxygen • Calculator • Calendar (Today's Date, Your Schedule) • Camera Remote • Compass (Compass, Elevation) • Contacts • Controls (Battery, Cellular) • Cycle Tracking • ECG • Find Devices • Find Items • Find People • Heart Rate • Home • Mail • Maps (Maps, Nearby Transit) • Messages • Mindfulness • Music • News • Noise (Sound Levels) • Phone • Podcasts • Reminders • Remote • Shortcuts • Siri • Sleep • Stocks • Stopwatch • Timer • Tips • Voice Memos • Walkie-Talkie • Weather • Workout • World Clock (Sunrise/Sunset)

Solar Dial

This watch face features a 24-hour, circular dial that tracks the sun as well as an analog or digital dial that moves opposite to the sun's path.
Tip: Tap the watch face to see the day's length.

- Customizable features: Dial (Analog or Digital)
- Available complications: Activity • Alarms • Astronomy (Moon) • Audiobooks • Blood Oxygen • Calculator • Calendar (Today's Date, Your Schedule) • Camera Remote • Compass (Compass, Elevation) • Contacts • Controls (Battery, Cellular) • Cycle Tracking • ECG • Find Devices • Find Items • Find People • Heart Rate • Home • Mail • Maps (Maps, Nearby Transit) • Messages • Mindfulness • Music • News • Noise (Sound Levels) • Phone • Podcasts • Reminders • Remote • Shortcuts • Sleep • Stocks • Stopwatch • Timer • Tips • Voice Memos • Walkie-Talkie • Weather • Workout • World Clock (Sunrise/Sunset)

Solar Graph

Based on your current location and time of day, the Solar Graph watch face displays the sun's position in the sky, as well as the day, date, and current time.

Turn the Digital Crown to move through the day's solar events.

- Available complications: Activity • Alarms • Astronomy (Moon Phase) • Audiobooks • Calendar (Today's Date, Your Schedule) • Camera Remote • Compass (Compass, Compass/Elevation, Elevation) • Controls (Battery) • Heart Rate • Messages • Music • News • Noise (Sound Levels) • Now Playing • Podcasts • Reminders • Shortcuts • Stocks • Stopwatch • Timer • Weather • Workout • World Clock (Sunrise/Sunset)

Stripes

On this watch face you can select the number of stripes you want, choose colors, and rotate the angle.

- Customizable features: Style • Number of stripes • Color of stripes
- Available complications (complications available only with Circular style): Activity • Alarms • Astronomy (Moon) • Audiobooks • Blood Oxygen • Calculator • Calendar (Today's Date, Your Schedule) • Camera Remote • Compass (Compass, Elevation) • Contacts • Controls (Battery, Cellular) • Cycle Tracking • ECG • Find Devices • Find Items • Find People • Heart Rate • Home • Mail • Maps (Maps, Nearby Transit) • Messages • Mindfulness • Music • News • Noise (Sound Levels) • Phone • Podcasts • Reminders • Remote • Shortcuts • Sleep • Stocks • Stopwatch • Timer • Tips • Voice Memos • Walkie-Talkie • Weather • Workout • World Clock (Sunrise/Sunset)

Timelapse

This watch face shows a timelapse video of a natural setting or cityscape of your choice.

- Customizable features: Choose video of Mack Lake, New York, Hong Kong, London, Paris, or Shanghai
- Available complications: Activity • Alarms • Astronomy (Moon Phase) • Audiobooks • Calendar (Today's Date, Your Schedule) • Compass (Compass, Compass/Elevation, Elevation) • Controls (Battery) • Heart Rate • Messages • Music • News • Noise (Sound Levels) • Now Playing • Podcasts • Reminders • Shortcuts • Stocks • Stopwatch • Timer • Weather • Workout • World Clock (Sunrise/Sunset)

Toy Story

Your favorite Toy Story characters come to life with a raise of the wrist.

- Customizable features: Characters (choose Toy Box, Buzz, Jessie, or Woody)
- Available complications: Activity • Alarms • Astronomy (Moon Phase) • Audiobooks • Calendar (Today's Date, Your Schedule) • Compass (Compass, Compass/Elevation, Elevation) • Controls (Battery) • Heart Rate • Messages • Music • News • Noise (Sound Levels) • Now Playing • Podcasts • Reminders • Shortcuts • Stocks • Stopwatch • Timer • Weather • Workout • World Clock (Sunrise/Sunset)

Typograph

This watch face features three custom fonts.

- Customizable features: Color • Dial • Style • Symbols
- Available complications (complications available only with Dial II): Date • Monogram • Stopwatch • Digital Time • Timer

Unity

This watch face is inspired by the colors of the Pan-African Flag. The shapes change as you move, creating a face that's unique to you.

- Customizable features: Color

- Available complications: Activity • Alarms • Astronomy (Moon Phase) • Audiobooks • Calendar (Today's Date, Your Schedule) • Compass (Compass, Compass/Elevation, Elevation) • Controls (Battery) • Heart Rate • Messages • Music • News • Noise (Sound Levels) • Now Playing • Podcasts • Reminders • Shortcuts • Stocks • Stopwatch • Timer • Weather • Workout • World Clock (Sunrise/Sunset)

Utility

This watch face is practical and functional; add up to three complications to display what you want to see at a glance.

- Customizable features: Color • Style • Typeface
- Available complications: Activity • Alarms • Astronomy (Moon Phase) • Audiobooks • Blood Oxygen • Calculator • Calendar (Today's Date, Your Schedule) • Camera Remote • Compass (Compass, Elevation) • Contacts • Controls (Battery, Cellular) • Cycle Tracking • ECG • Find Devices • Find Items • Find People • Heart Rate • Home • Mail • Maps (Maps, Nearby Transit) • Messages • Mindfulness • Music • News • Noise (Sound Levels) • Phone • Podcasts • Reminders • Remote • Shortcuts • Sleep • Stocks • Stopwatch • Timer • Tips • Voice Memos • Walkie-Talkie • Weather • Workout • World Clock (Sunrise/Sunset)

Vapor

This watch face animates whenever you raise your wrist or tap the display.

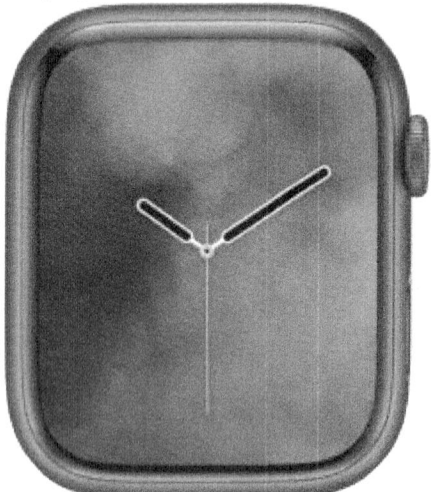

- Customizable features: Color • Style
- Available complications (Circular style only): Activity • Alarms • Astronomy (Moon Phase) • Audiobooks • Blood Oxygen • Calculator • Calendar (Today's Date, Your Schedule) • Camera Remote • Compass (Compass, Compass/Elevation, Elevation) • Contacts • Controls (Battery, Cellular) • Cycle Tracking • ECG • Find Devices • Find Items • Find People • Heart Rate • Home • Mail • Maps (Maps, Nearby Transit) • Messages • Mindfulness • Music • News • Noise (Sound Levels) • Now Playing • Phone • Podcasts • Reminders • Remote • Shortcuts • Sleep • Stocks • Stopwatch • Timer • Tips • Voice Memos • Walkie-Talkie • Weather • Workout • World Clock (Sunrise/Sunset)

World Time

This watch face lets you track the time in 24 time zones at once. The locations around the outer dial represent the different time zones, while the inner dial shows the current time in each location.

Tapping the globe centers it to the time zone you're in, which is also noted by the arrow at 6 o'clock.

The sun and moon icons represent sunrise and sunset where you are, and the light and dark zones on the globe reflect night and day moving across the earth.

- Customizable features: Analog or digital time
- Available complications: Activity • Alarms • Astronomy (Moon Phase) • Audiobooks • Blood Oxygen • Calculator • Calendar (Today's Date, Your Schedule) • Camera Remote • Compass (Compass, Elevation) • Contacts • Controls (Battery, Cellular) • Cycle Tracking • ECG • Find Devices • Find Items • Find People • Heart Rate • Home • Mail • Maps (Maps, Nearby Transit) • Messages • Mindfulness • Music • News • Noise (Sound Levels) • Phone • Podcasts • Reminders • Remote • Shortcuts • Sleep • Stocks • Stopwatch • Timer • Tips • Voice Memos • Walkie-Talkie • Weather • Workout • World Clock (Sunrise/Sunset)

X-Large

For when you need the largest available display. When you add a complication, it fills the screen.

- Customizable features: Color
- Available complications: Activity • Alarms • Astronomy (Earth, Moon, Solar, Solar System) • Audiobooks • Blood Oxygen • Calculator • Calendar (Today's Date, Your Schedule) • Camera Remote • Compass (Compass, Elevation) • Contacts • Controls (Battery, Cellular) • Cycle Tracking • ECG • Find My (Find People) • Heart Rate • Home • Mail • Maps (Maps, Nearby Transit) • Messages • Mindfulness • Music • News • Noise (Sound Levels) • Phone • Podcasts • Reminders • Remote • Shortcuts • Sleep • Stocks • Stopwatch • Timer • Tips • Voice Memos • Walkie-Talkie • Weather • Workout • World Clock (Sunrise/Sunset

Apple Fitness+

Subscribe to Apple Fitness+

You can choose to bundle your Apple Fitness+ subscription with other Apple services by subscribing to Apple One Premier.
Note: Apple Fitness+ and Apple One Premier aren't available in all countries or regions.

Get the Fitness app

To use Apple Fitness+, you need the Fitness app on your iPhone, iPad, or Apple TV. If you don't have the Fitness app on your device, you can download it from the App Store.

Subscribe to Apple Fitness+

1. Open the Fitness app on iPhone, iPad, or Apple TV. Then, if you're on your iPhone, tap Fitness+.
2. Select the free trial button, then follow the onscreen instructions to sign in with your Apple ID and confirm your subscription.

Cancel your Apple Fitness+ subscription

1. Do one of the following:
    - On iPhone or iPad: Open the Fitness app, then, if you're on your iPhone, tap Fitness+. Tap   , tap [account name], then tap Apple Fitness+.
    - On Apple TV: Open the Settings app, go to Users and Accounts > [account name] > Subscriptions, then select Apple Fitness+.
2. Follow the onscreen instructions to change or cancel your subscription.

Share your Apple Fitness+ subscription with Family Sharing

When you subscribe to Apple Fitness+ or Apple One Premier, you can use Family Sharing to share your subscription with up to five other family members. Your family group members don't need to do anything—Apple Fitness+ is available to them the first time they open the Fitness app after your subscription begins, as long as they have an Apple Watch Series 3 or later. If a family member has an Apple Watch, but no iPhone (because their Apple Watch was set up

by a family member), they can still use Apple Fitness+ with Apple TV or with an iPad.
Note: To stop sharing your Apple Fitness+ subscription with a family group, you can cancel the subscription, leave the family group, or (if you're the family group organizer) stop using Family Sharing.

All about Apple Fitness+

When you subscribe to Apple Fitness+, you get access to a catalog of workouts, including Cycling, Strength, Treadmill (running and walking), Yoga, and more. Your metrics, like heart rate and calories burned, are shared from your Apple Watch to your iPhone, iPad, or Apple TV while you work out, and sync with your daily activity data when you finish a workout.
You can also participate in guided Meditations—five, ten, or twenty minute long Meditations designed to help you develop a regular Meditation routine and improve your overall sense of well-being.
Apple Fitness+ requires Apple Watch Series 3 or later with watchOS 7.2 or later and one of the following Apple devices: iPhone 6s or later with iOS 14.3 or later, iPad with iPadOS 14.3 or later, or Apple TV 4K or Apple TV HD with tvOS 14.3 or later.
Use the latest version of iOS, iPadOS, watchOS, or tvOS to get the newest features.
Note: Apple Fitness+ isn't available in all countries or regions.

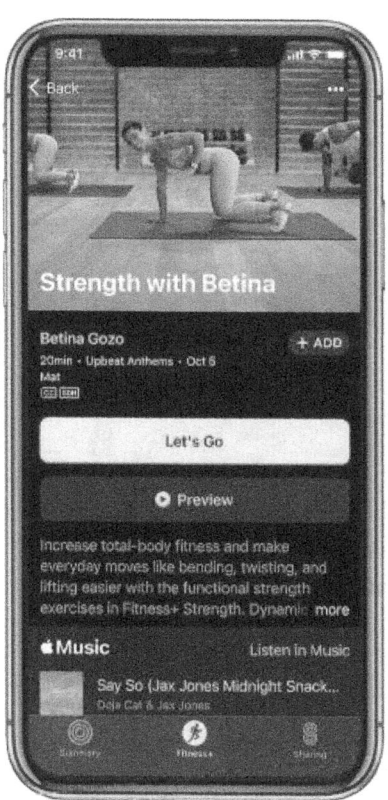

Choose a workout

When it's time to work out, you have lots of options. To help you pick, you can see details for every workout like its playlist and music genre, whether the workout has closed captions, as well as any equipment you need, such as dumbbells or a mat. You can also preview the workout before you get started.

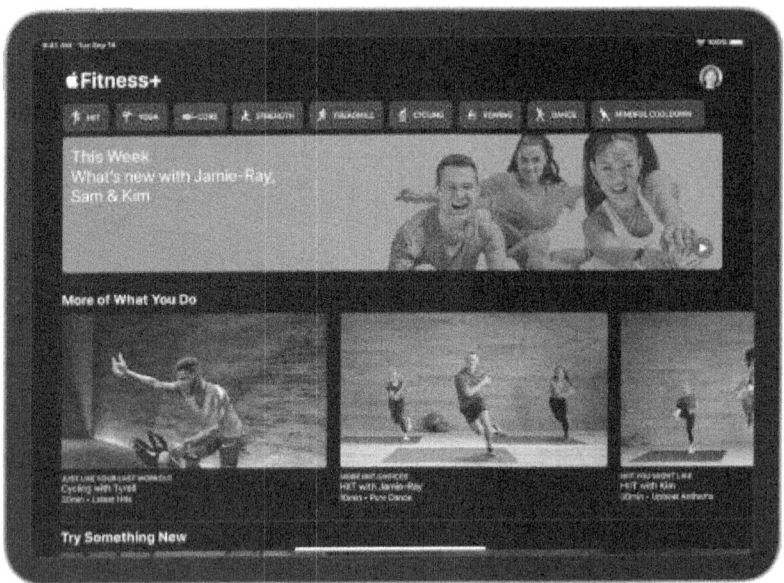

Find a trainer

Each of the Apple Fitness+ trainers bring their unique personality, taste in music, and training style to their workouts. You can read a bio for each trainer and see a list of every trainer's workouts in the Fitness app.

See your stats

During your workout, track your progress for each of your rings, as well as your heart rate and calories burned, right on your iPhone, iPad, or Apple TV.

Cycling, HIIT, Rowing, and Treadmill workouts also display the Burn Bar, which shows how your metrics compare to others who have done the workout before. The more calories you burn, the higher you land on the Burn Bar. Your position on the Burn Bar is saved in your workout summary along with your other metrics.

Set up Apple Fitness+ on Apple TV

Your Apple Watch syncs with the Fitness app on Apple TV 4K or Apple TV HD with tvOS 14.3 or later, so you can work out with Apple Fitness+ at home, in the office, or while you're traveling.

Connect your Apple Watch to Apple TV

To use Apple Fitness+ with Apple TV, you need to connect your Apple Watch.
1. Open the Fitness app on Apple TV.
2. Select your name, or select Other if you don't see your name.
   If no one is signed in on your Apple TV, you may need to choose Sign In in the Fitness app first.
3. On your Apple Watch, tap Connect.
   Note: You may need to open the Workout app on your Apple Watch before you can tap Connect.
4. If prompted, tap Continue, then enter the code from Apple TV on your Apple Watch.

Note: To start a workout on Apple TV, your Apple Watch must be updated to watchOS 7.2 or later, be unlocked, and have Bluetooth turned on.

Choose who is working out

If you use Family Sharing, you can easily switch between family members in the Fitness app on Apple TV. Friends or family outside of your Family Sharing group who are Apple Fitness+ subscribers can also work out using your Apple TV.

1. Open the Fitness app on your Apple TV.
2. Select your name, or select Other if you don't see your name.
   If no one is signed in on your Apple TV, you may need to select Sign In in the Fitness app first.
3. To switch to another family member or guest, select the account icon in the top left corner of the Fitness app, select Sign out, then select another user.

Browse Apple Fitness+ workouts and Meditations

Apple Fitness+ can help you find a workout, Meditation, or routine that works for you. You can browse for individual workouts or Meditations, start a program with multiple episodes, sort and filter workouts of a specific type, or choose a recommended workout based on your activity. Mindful Cooldown workouts begin at five minutes and all other workout types start at ten minutes, with new workouts added every week. Meditations can be five, ten, or twenty minutes.

Browse workouts and get recommendations

Apple Fitness+ recommends workouts based on the things you typically do with the Workout app on Apple Watch, as well as your favorite apps that work with the Health app. Apple Fitness+ will even suggest new trainers and workouts to help you round out your routine.

1. Open the Fitness app on iPhone, iPad, or Apple TV. Then, if you're on your iPhone, tap Fitness+.
2. Explore workouts and trainers:
    - Browse by workout type: Navigate left or right to browse the workout types at the top of the screen.
    - Time to Walk (iPhone only): Choose audio workouts to play on your Apple Watch.
    Tap the Add button to add a Time to Walk episode to Apple Watch. When you're ready to listen to an episode, open the Workout app 🏃 on Apple Watch, then tap Time to Walk. Tap 📋, then turn

186

the Digital Crown to scroll through other episodes on your Apple Watch.
- Browse featured workouts: Navigate down to a category such as New This Week, For Beginners, Popular, or Simple and Quick.
- Browse by trainer: Navigate down to the row of trainers, then navigate left or right and select a trainer to see their workouts and filter workouts by type, length, and music genre.
  On iPhone or iPad, tap Show All to see a list of all trainers.
- More of What You Do: Browse workouts with trainers you often work out with, and workout types you typically do with your Apple Watch or in other fitness apps that work with the Health app.
- Try Something New: Explore workouts similar to what you already do, but with different trainers and suggested workout types to balance your routine.
- My Library (iPhone and iPad only): Workouts added to My Library from the workout detail or workout summary screen. My Library can be used to keep a list of your favorite workouts, build a workout routine, or save workouts for playing offline.

Browse and start Meditations

1. Open the Fitness app on iPhone, iPad, or Apple TV. Then, if you're on your iPhone, tap Fitness+.
2. Tap Meditation at the top of the screen.
3. Do one of the following:
   - Tap a Meditation session, then tap Let's Begin to start the session.
   - Tap Filter; choose a specific trainer, time, or theme; tap Done; tap a session; then tap Let's Begin.

During the Meditation, your Apple Watch shows the elapsed time of the Meditation as well as your current heart rate. Swipe right to find

controls to pause, resume, and end the Meditation. Tap the Workout button to start a workout while the Meditation continues to play.
Tip: If you subscribe to Apple Fitness+ you can listen to guided Meditations in the Mindfulness app on your Apple Watch.

Try a workout program with multiple episodes

1. Open the Fitness app on iPhone, iPad, or Apple TV. Then, if you're on your iPhone, tap Fitness+.
2. Choose a program.
   Each program tile shows the workout types and number of episodes.
3. Do any of the following:
   - Preview the program: Select View Film to watch a video about the goals of the program and the kind of workouts you'll do. You can also read about the program to learn more.
   - Add episodes to My Workouts: Select   next to the episode you want to add, or select **+ ADD ALL** to add all episodes to My Workouts.
   - Start an episode from the program: Select an episode from the list, then select the button that begins the workout.

To help you keep your place after completing an episode, the next episode is automatically displayed under Next Workout, but you can choose any episode at any time.

Sort and filter workouts

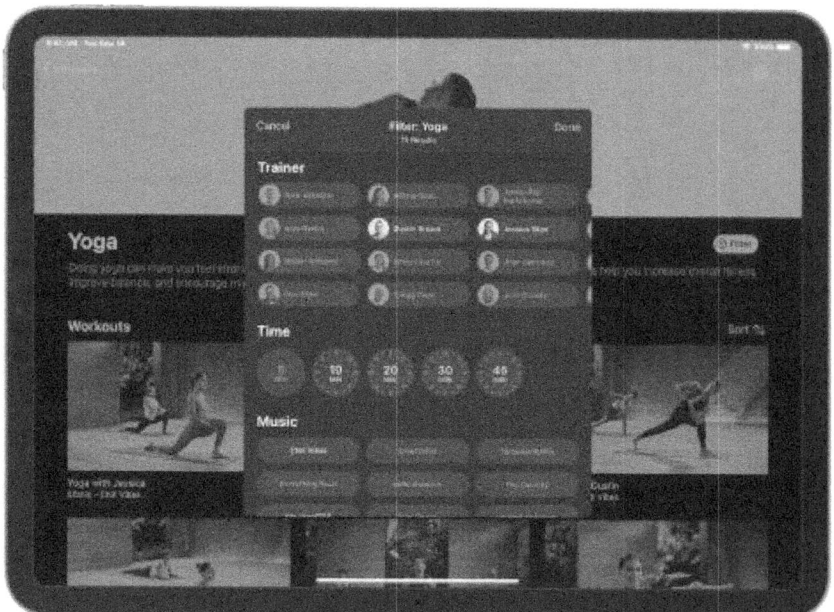

To make it easier to find the workout you're looking for, you can sort and filter specific types of workouts (like Rowing or Dance) by trainer, length of the workout, music genre, and more.

1. Open the Fitness app on iPhone, iPad, or Apple TV. Then, if you're on your iPhone, tap Fitness+.
2. Select a workout type, then do any of the following:
    - Sort workouts: Choose Sort, then select an option like Trainer or Time.
    - Filter workout: Choose Filter, then select the filter(s) you want to apply.
    If you can't select a filter, there are no workouts that apply to that filter.

Start an Apple Fitness+ workout

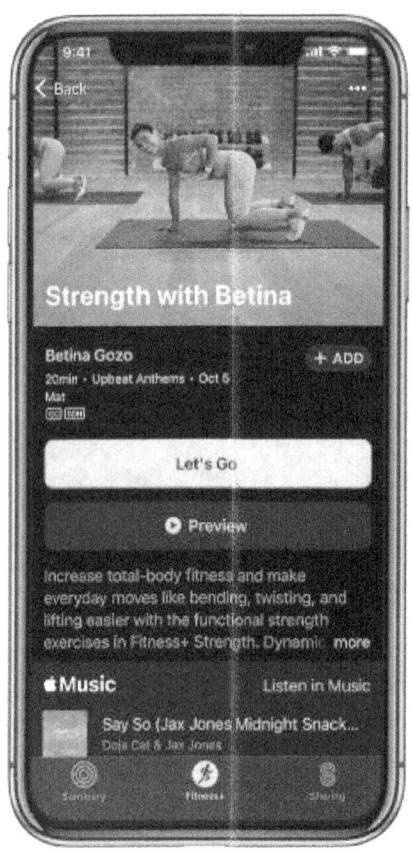

You can start an Apple Fitness+ workout from your iPhone, iPad, or Apple TV. Apple Fitness+ workouts are for all levels, so you can challenge yourself whether you're just starting out or repeating your favorite workouts. In all workouts, additional trainers demonstrate modifications of the exercises to help you make the workout easier or more advanced. Trainers may also offer directions on how to modify an exercise, such as doing the movement with bodyweight instead of a dumbbell.

Start a workout on iPhone or iPad

1. Open the Fitness app. Then, if you're on your iPhone, tap Fitness+.

If you don't have the Fitness app on your device, you can download it from the App Store.
2. Select a workout type at the top of the screen, then select a workout, or select a workout from one of the categories (like Try Something New).
3. Do any of the following:
    ○ Add the workout to My Workouts: Tap .
    ○ Preview the workout: Tap Preview.
      You can also see the playlist for the workout. If you subscribe to Apple Music, tap Listen in Music to open the playlist in Apple Music.
    ○ Start the workout: Tap the button that begins the workout, then tap ⏵ on iPhone, iPad, or Apple Watch. If you're starting a Treadmill workout, choose Run or Walk to get the most accurate metrics.
      If you're not wearing your Apple Watch, you can still start the workout, but your metrics (like calories burned) aren't collected. Tap Work Out Without Watch to start the workout.
      To stream your workout to an AirPlay 2.0 compatible device such as a TV or HomePod, tap the screen during a workout, tap 📡, then choose a destination.

You can also start a workout on Apple TV. See the task below to learn more.

Start a workout on Apple TV

1. Open the Fitness app, then choose who is working out.
2. Select a workout type, then choose a workout, or choose a workout from one of the categories (like Try Something New).

3. Do any of the following:
    - Preview the workout: Select Preview.
    - Start the workout: Select the free trial button if you haven't subscribed, or click the button to begin the workout if you're a subscriber.
    If you're starting a Treadmill workout, choose Run or Walk to get the most accurate metrics.
    - Play featured songs from the workout in Music: Navigate down to the list of songs, then select a song to open the workout playlist in the Music app (Apple Music subscription required).
    - Browse related workouts: Navigate down to the Related Workouts row, then navigate left or right to browse another workout.

Pause and resume an Apple Fitness+ workout

You can pause a workout from the device playing the workout, or your Apple Watch.

- On Apple Watch, do any of the following:
    - Pause a workout: Press the side button and the Digital Crown at the same time. You can also swipe right, then tap Pause.
    - Resume a workout: Press the side button and the Digital Crown at the same time, or swipe right and tap Resume.
- On iPhone or iPad, do any of the following:
    - Pause a workout: Tap the screen, then tap the Pause button ▮▮.
    - Resume a workout: Tap the Play button ▶.
- On Apple TV:
    - Pause or resume a workout: Press the clickpad center (second-generation Siri Remote) or the touch

surface (first-generation Siri Remote). On the Siri Remote, press the Play/Pause button ▶︎❚❚.

End and review an Apple Fitness+ workout

You can end a workout from the device playing the workout, or your Apple Watch.
When your workout ends, you can share your workout, cooldown, and more.

- On Apple Watch: Swipe right, then tap End.
  Your workout summary is displayed. Tap Done to return to the Workout app.
- On iPhone or iPad: Tap ⊗, then tap End Workout.
  Your workout summary is displayed. Tap  to add the workout to My Workouts, tap   to share your workout, tap Mindful Cooldown to choose a cooldown workout, or tap Done to return to Apple Fitness+.
- On Apple TV: Press the MENU button on the Siri Remote/Apple TV Remote, then select End Workout.
  Your workout summary is displayed. Select Mindful Cooldown to choose a cooldown workout, or select Done to return to Apple Fitness+.

You can view your workout summary again later in the Fitness app on iPhone.
Once you've taken a class, it appears in the list of workouts with on the thumbnail.

Work out together using SharePlay

Group Workouts, powered by SharePlay, let you and up to 32 of your favorite people work out together. You can start a FaceTime call on your iPhone or iPad, then start a Group Workout in the Fitness app on iPhone, iPad, or Apple TV.

The workout plays in sync with everyone on the call, and everyone can control playback from their devices—so you and your friends can cheer each other on, see when someone closes an Activity ring, and get notifications when someone moves ahead of the pack on the Burn Bar during HIIT, Treadmill, Cycling, and Rowing workouts. Group Workouts with Apple Fitness+ requires Apple Watch Series 3 or later with watchOS 8.1 or later and one of the following Apple devices: iPhone 6s or later with iOS 15.1 or later, iPad with iPadOS 15.1 or later. Playback on Apple TV requires tvOS 15.1 or later. FaceTime, some FaceTime features, and other Apple services may not be available in all countries or regions, and features may vary by area.

Start a Group Workout on iPhone or iPad

1. Start a FaceTime call.
2. Open the Fitness app on iPhone or iPad. Then, if you're on your iPhone, tap Fitness+.
   If you don't have the Fitness app on your device, you can download it from the App Store.
3. Select a workout, start the workout, then tap SharePlay to begin the workout with everyone on the call. (To participate in the Group Workout, others on the call may have to tap Open when prompted to use SharePlay.)
   For everyone on the call who has access, the workout starts playing at the same time. Those who don't have access are asked to get access (through a subscription or a free trial, if available).
   Everyone can use playback controls on their respective devices (including Apple Watch) to play or pause the workout.

To end a workout before it completes, tap X in the top-left corner of the iPhone or iPad screen. On Apple Watch, swipe right, then tap End.

Join a Group Workout on Apple TV

You can join a Group Workout using SharePlay on Apple TV.
Note: SharePlay controls appear only when a user is signed in with the same Apple ID on both Apple TV and FaceTime on an iPhone or iPad. To switch users on Apple TV, press and hold the TV button on the Siri Remote to open Control Center, then select or add a new user.

1. Start a FaceTime call on an iPhone or iPad.
   Apple TV detects when a FaceTime call is in progress, and a SharePlay indicator appears in the upper-right corner of the Home Screen on Apple TV.
2. Open the Fitness app on Apple TV, then do either of the following:
   - Start a workout, then select SharePlay when prompted and confirm on your iPhone or iPad.
   - Press and hold the TV button on the Siri Remote to open Control Center, select the SharePlay button, select Join, then confirm on your iPhone or iPad.
3. If you haven't already, browse to a workout in Fitness, then start it.
   The workout plays in sync on Apple TV and on all the devices on the FaceTime call. Everyone can use playback controls on their respective devices to play or pause in real time.

Change what's on the screen during an Apple Fitness+ workout

Change onscreen metrics

During your workout, you can track your progress onscreen for each of your rings, as well as your heart rate and calories burned, all shown in real time on your device.

Some workouts also display the Burn Bar, which shows how your metrics compare to others who have done the workout before. The more calories you burn, the higher you land on the Burn Bar. Your position on the Burn Bar is saved in your workout summary along with your other metrics.

You can change the metrics from Apple Watch that you see on the screen during a workout. Metrics settings sync in the Fitness app on all your devices where you're signed in with your Apple ID.

1. During a workout, tap [icon].
   If you're working out with Apple TV, use these gestures:
   - Siri Remote (2nd generation): Press down on the clickpad ring or swipe down on the clickpad to show the Info pane, then navigate to the Metrics pane.
   - Siri Remote (1st generation): Swipe down on the touch surface to show the Info pane, then navigate to the Metrics pane.
2. Do one of the following:
   - Turn off all metrics: Turn off Show Metrics.
     Your metrics are still collected, but they aren't displayed on the screen.
   - Change how time is displayed: Select Off, Show Time Elapsed, or Show Time Remaining.

Turning off Time still shows the timer for intervals in your workout.
- Turn off the Burn Bar: Turn off Burn Bar.
  If you turn off the Burn Bar, your workouts don't contribute to the community burn bar and you won't see your position at the end of your workout.

Turn on captions and subtitles

All Fitness+ workouts support standard captions, as well as subtitles for the deaf and hard of hearing (SDH). After you choose a workout, you can see if it includes closed captions and SDH below the length, music genre, and date added.

- On iPhone or iPad: During a workout, tap ⌐⌐, then choose a language.
- On Apple TV: During a workout, do one of the following, depending on the remote you have:
  - Siri Remote (2nd generation): Press down on the clickpad ring or swipe down on the clickpad to show the Info pane, then navigate to the Subtitles pane and choose a language.
  - Siri Remote (1st generation): Swipe down on the touch surface to show the Info pane, then navigate to the Subtitles pane and choose a language.

Download an Apple Fitness+ workout on iPhone or iPad

You can download workouts to your iPhone or iPad so you can work out even when you're offline.
1. Open the Fitness app. Then, if you're on your iPhone, tap Fitness+.
2. Do any of the following:

- Download a workout to your device: Choose a workout, tap **+ ADD** to add the workout to My Workouts, then tap .
- View all downloaded workouts: Scroll to the bottom of the Fitness+ tab, then tap Downloaded Workouts. To start a downloaded workout, tap the one you want, then tap the button to begin the workout.
- Remove a downloaded workout from your device: Tap , then tap Remove Download.

APPS

Activity

Track daily activity with Apple Watch

The Activity app ⊙ on your Apple Watch keeps track of your movement throughout the day and encourages you to meet your fitness goals. The app tracks how often you stand, how much you move, and how many minutes of exercise you do. Three rings in different colors summarize your progress. The goal is to sit less, move more, and get some exercise by completing each ring every day.

The Fitness app on your iPhone keeps a record of your activity. If you've tracked at least six months of activity, it displays daily trend data for active calories, exercise minutes, stand hours, stand minutes, walk distance, flights climbed, and more. In the Fitness app on iPhone, tap Summary, then scroll to Trends to see how you're doing compared to your average activity.

Note: Your Apple Watch is not a medical device.

Get started

When you set up your Apple Watch, you're asked if you'd like to configure the Activity app. If you choose not to, you can do so later when you open the Activity app for the first time.

1. Open the Activity app ⊚ on your Apple Watch.
2. Swipe left to read the Move, Exercise, and Stand descriptions, then tap Get Started.
3. Use the Digital Crown to set your sex, age, height, weight, and whether you use a wheelchair.
4. Choose an activity level and start moving.

Check your progress

Open the Activity app ⊚ on your Apple Watch at any time to see how you're doing. The Activity app displays three rings.

- The red Move ring shows how many active calories you've burned.
- The green Exercise ring shows how many minutes of brisk activity you've done.
- The blue Stand ring shows how many times in the day you've stood and moved for at least one minute per hour.

If you specified that you use a wheelchair, the blue Stand ring becomes the Roll ring and shows how many times in the day you've rolled for at least one minute per hour.

Turn the Digital Crown to see your current totals—keep scrolling to see your progress as a graph, your total steps, total distance, workouts, and flights climbed.

An overlapping ring means you exceeded your goal. Turn the Digital Crown, then tap Weekly Summary to see how you're doing for the week.

See your weekly summary

1. Open the Activity app on your Apple Watch.
2. Turn the Digital Crown to scroll to the bottom of the screen, then tap Weekly Summary.

The summary includes a week's totals for calories, average calories, steps, distance, flights climbed, and active time.

Change your goals

If you find your activity goals either too challenging or not challenging enough, you can change them.

1. Open the Activity app on your Apple Watch.
2. Turn the Digital Crown to scroll to the bottom of the screen, then tap Change Goals.
3. Tap − or + to adjust a goal, then tap Next.

Every Monday, you're notified about the previous week's achievements, and you can adjust your goals for the next week. Your Apple Watch suggests goals based on your previous performance.

Check your activity history

1. Open the Fitness app on your iPhone, then tap Summary.

2. Tap the Activity area, tap   , then tap a date.

Check your trends

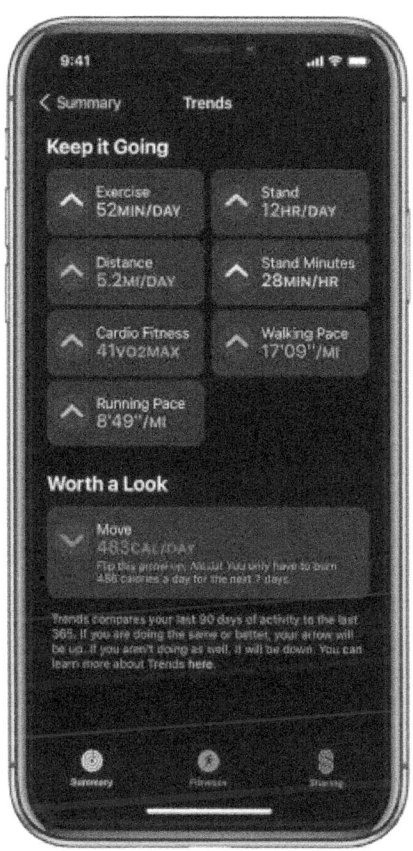

In the Fitness app on iPhone, the Trends area shows you daily trend data for active calories, exercise minutes, stand hours, stand minutes, walk distance, and cardio fitness. Trends compares your last 90 days of activity to the last 365.
To see how you're trending, follow these steps:
1. Open the Fitness app on your iPhone, then tap Summary.
2. Swipe up to see trends.
3. To learn how to turn a trend around, tap See More.
4. To see the history of a specific trend, tap it.

If the Trend arrow for a particular metric points up, then you're maintaining or improving your fitness levels. If an arrow points down, your 90 day average for that metric has started to decline. To help motivate you to turn the trend around, you'll receive coaching—"Walk an extra quarter of a mile a day," for example.

See your awards

You can earn awards for personal records, streaks, and major milestones using your Apple Watch. To see all your awards, including Activity Competition awards and awards you're making progress towards, follow these steps:

1. Open the Activity app ⊙ on your Apple Watch.
2. Swipe left two times to view the Awards screen.
3. Scroll up to see your awards. Tap an award to learn more about it.

You can also open the Fitness app on your iPhone, tap the Summary tab, then swipe up to see Awards at the bottom of the screen.

Control activity reminders

Reminders can help when it comes to meeting goals. Your Apple Watch lets you know if you're on track or falling behind your activity goals. To choose which reminders and alerts you'd like to see, follow these steps:

1. Open the Settings app ⚙ on your Apple Watch.
2. Tap Activity, then configure the notifications.

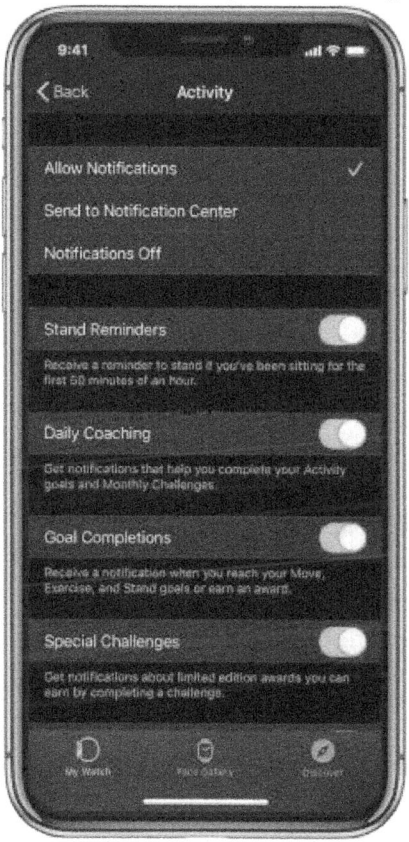

Suspend daily coaching

To turn off activity reminders, follow these steps:
1. Open the Apple Watch app on your iPhone, then tap My Watch.
2. Tap Activity, then turn off Daily Coaching.

203

Share your activity from Apple Watch

Keep your fitness routine on track by sharing your activity with your family and friends—you can even share with a trainer or coach. You can get notifications when your friends meet their goals, finish workouts, and earn achievements.

Add or remove a friend

If you've never shared activity before, open the Fitness app on your iPhone, then tap Sharing. Tap Get Started, then follow these steps:

1. Open the Activity app ⊙ on your Apple Watch.
2. Swipe left, then turn the Digital Crown to scroll to the bottom of the screen.
3. To add a friend, tap Invite a Friend, then tap a friend.
   To remove a friend, tap a friend you're sharing with, then tap Remove.

After a friend accepts your invitation, you can see their activity and they can see yours. If a friend hasn't accepted an invitation, tap their name in the Invited area of the Sharing screen, then tap Invite Again.

To add a friend, you can also open the Fitness app on your iPhone, tap Sharing, tap   , then tap ＋ to send an email invitation, or tap   to send an invitation with Messages.

Note: If you're using a managed Apple Watch, just open the Activity app, swipe left, tap Add Friends, then tap a name.

Check your friends' progress

1. Open the Activity app ⊙ on your Apple Watch.
2. Swipe left, then turn the Digital Crown to scroll your friends list.
3. Tap friends to see their stats for the day.

Compete with your friends

Stay motivated with a little healthy competition. You can challenge a friend to a competition in which you earn points based on the percentage of your Activity Rings that you close. You get a point for every percent you add to your rings each day. The competition lasts 7 days and you can earn up to 600 points a day for a maximum of 4,200 points for the week. The person with the most points at the end of the competition wins. During a competition, alerts tell you if you're ahead of or falling behind your competitor—along with the score.

1. Open the Activity app ⊚ on your Apple Watch.
2. Swipe left, tap a friend, then tap Compete.
3. Tap Invite, then wait for your friend to accept.

Or, when you receive an Activity sharing notification—your friend just closed their rings or doubled their move goal, for example—you can scroll down and tap Compete.

You can also open the Fitness app on your iPhone, tap Sharing, tap a friend, then tap Compete with [your friend's name].

Change your friend settings

You can easily adjust friend settings. Just open the Activity app ⊚ on your Apple Watch, swipe left, tap a friend, scroll down, then do any of the following:

- Mute notifications for the friend: Tap Mute Notifications.
- Hide your activity from the friend: Tap Hide my Activity.
- Remove the friend: Tap Remove Friend.

Add an alarm on Apple Watch

Use the Alarms app to play a sound or vibrate your Apple Watch at a set time.

Ask Siri. Say something like: "Set repeating alarm for 6 a.m."

Set an alarm on Apple Watch

1. Open the Alarms app on your Apple Watch.
2. Tap Add Alarm.
3. Tap AM or PM, then tap the hours or minutes.
   This step is unnecessary when using 24-hour time.
4. Turn the Digital Crown to adjust, then tap .
    5. To turn the alarm on or off, tap its switch. Or tap the alarm time to set repeat, label, and snooze options.

Don't let yourself snooze

When an alarm sounds, you can tap Snooze to wait several minutes before the alarm sounds again. If you don't want to allow snooze, follow these steps:

1. Open the Alarms app on your Apple Watch.

2. Tap the alarm in the list of alarms, then turn off Snooze.

Delete an alarm

1. Open the Alarms app on your Apple Watch.
2. Tap the alarm in the list.
   3. Scroll to the bottom, then tap Delete.

Skip a wake-up alarm

If you have a wake-up alarm that's part of your sleep schedule, you can skip it for just that evening.

1. Open the Alarms app on your Apple Watch.
2. Tap the alarm that appears under Sleep | Wake Up, then tap Skip for Tonight.

See the same alarms on both iPhone and Apple Watch

1. Set the alarm on your iPhone.
2. Open the Apple Watch app on your iPhone.
3. Tap My Watch, tap Clock, then turn on Push Alerts from iPhone.

Your Apple Watch alerts you when an alarm goes off so you can snooze or dismiss the alarm. (You aren't alerted on your iPhone when your Apple Watch alarms go off.)

Set up Apple Watch as a nightstand clock with alarm

1. Open the Settings app on your Apple Watch.
2. Go to General > Nightstand Mode, then turn on Nightstand Mode.

When you connect your Apple Watch to its charger with nightstand mode turned on, it displays charging status, the current time and date, and the time of any alarm you've set. To see the time, tap the display or lightly nudge your Apple Watch. Even nudging or tapping the table might work.

If you set an alarm using the Alarms app, your Apple Watch in nightstand mode will gently wake you with a unique alarm sound. When the alarm sounds, press the side button to turn it off, or press the Digital Crown to snooze for another 9 minutes.

Press to snooze.

Press to turn off alarm.

Audiobooks

Add audiobooks to Apple Watch

Apple Watch can sync audiobooks from the Apple Books.
Note: Audiobooks from other sources aren't synced to Apple Watch.
1. Open the Apple Watch app on your iPhone.
2. Tap My Watch, then tap Audiobooks.
3. Tap Add Audiobook, then select audiobooks to add them to your Apple Watch.

If there's available storage space, the entire contents of the audiobook you're currently listening to—as well as the one listed below Want to Read—are automatically synced to your Apple Watch. Five hours from each audiobook you add is also downloaded to your Apple Watch when there's available space. Audiobooks sync to Apple Watch when it's connected to power.

Play audiobooks on Apple Watch

You can use the Audiobooks app to play audiobooks from the Book Store on your Apple Watch.

Play audiobooks stored on Apple Watch

1. After you connect Apple Watch to Bluetooth headphones or speakers, open the Audiobooks app on your Apple Watch.
2. Turn the Digital Crown to scroll through the artwork.
3. Tap an audiobook to play it.

Play audiobooks on iPhone

1. Open the Audiobooks app on your Apple Watch.
2. Tap On iPhone.
3. Tap an audiobook to play it on your iPhone.

Play audiobooks from your library

If your Apple Watch is near your iPhone or connected to a Wi-Fi network (or a cellular network, for Apple Watch models with cellular), you can stream audiobooks from your audiobooks library to your Apple Watch.

1. Open the Audiobooks app on your Apple Watch.
2. Tap Library, then tap an audiobook to play it.

You can also play audiobooks purchased from the Book Store by members of your Family Sharing group. Just tap My Family on the Audiobooks screen, then tap an audiobook.

Use Siri to play audiobooks

Use Siri to play an audiobook in your library.
"Play the audiobook 'In the Time of the Butterflies.'"

Control playback

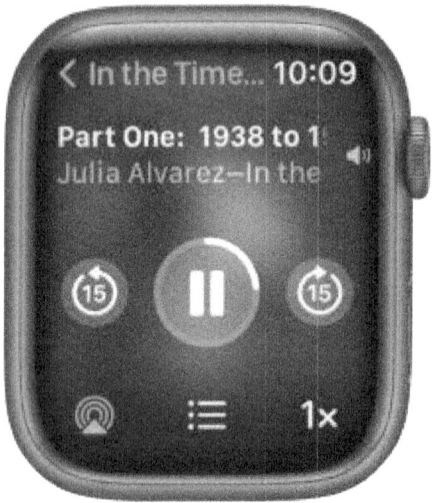

Turn the Digital Crown to adjust volume. Use these controls to play audiobooks:

≡	Choose a track or chapter.
1x	Playback speed. Options include 1x, 1 1/4x, 1 1/2x, 1 3/4x, 2x, and 3/4x.
⟲15	Skip back 15 seconds.
⟳15	Skip ahead 15 seconds.

❙❙	Pause playback.
▶	Play the audiobook.

Measure blood oxygen levels on Apple Watch

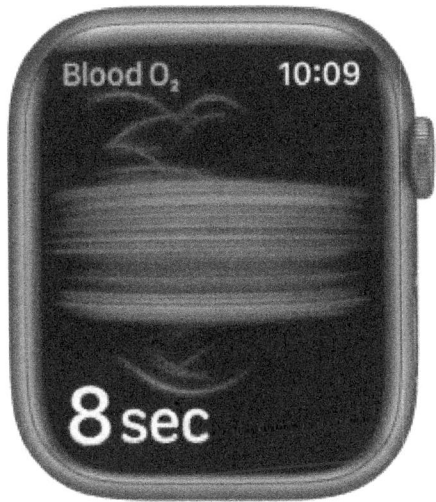

Use the Blood Oxygen app to measure the percentage of oxygen your red blood cells carry from your lungs to the rest of the body. Knowing how well oxygenated your blood is can help you understand your overall health and wellness.
Note: The Blood Oxygen app is not available in all regions. Blood Oxygen app measurements are not intended for medical use.

Set up Blood Oxygen

1. Open the Settings app on your Apple Watch.
2. Tap Blood Oxygen, then turn on Blood Oxygen Measurements.

Turn off background measurements in sleep mode and theater mode

Blood oxygen measurements use a bright red light that shines against your wrist, which may be more visible in dark places. You can turn off measurements if you find the light distracting.

1. Open the Settings app on your Apple Watch.
2. Tap Blood Oxygen, then turn off In Sleep Mode and In Theater Mode.

Measure your blood oxygen level

The Blood Oxygen app periodically measures your blood oxygen level throughout the day if background measurements are turned on, but you can also take an on-demand measurement at any time.

1. Open the Blood Oxygen app on your Apple Watch.
2. Rest your arm on a table or in your lap, and make sure your wrist is flat, with the Apple Watch display facing up.
3. Tap Start, then hold your arm very still during the 15-second countdown.
4. At the end of the measurement, you receive the results. Tap Done.

Note: For best results, the back of your Apple Watch needs skin contact. Wearing your Apple Watch not too tight or too loose, with room for your skin to breath, helps ensure successful Blood Oxygen measurements.

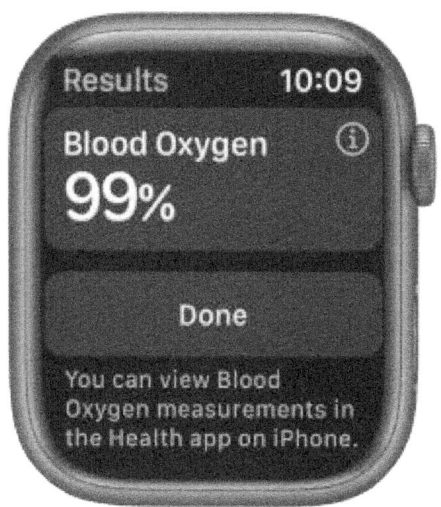

View your Blood Oxygen measurements history

1. Open the Health app on your iPhone.
2. Tap Browse, tap Respiratory, then tap Blood Oxygen.

Use Calculator on Apple Watch

In the Calculator app , you can perform basic arithmetic calculations. You can also quickly calculate a tip and split the check. Ask Siri. Say something like: "What's 73 times 9?" or "What's 18 percent of 225?"

Perform a quick calculation

1. Open the Calculator app on your Apple Watch.
2. Tap numbers and operators to get a result.

Split the check and calculate a tip

1. Open the Calculator app on your Apple Watch.
2. Enter the total amount of the bill, then tap Tip.
3. Turn the Digital Crown to choose a tip percentage.
4. Tap People, then turn the Digital Crown to enter the number of people sharing the bill.
   You see the tip amount, the total amount, and how much each person owes if the bill is split evenly.
   Note: The Tip feature is not available in all regions.

Check and update your calendar on Apple Watch

The Calendar app 14 on your Apple Watch shows events you've scheduled or been invited to today and for the next week. Your Apple Watch shows events for all calendars on your iPhone or just those calendars you choose.

Ask Siri. Say something like: "What's my next event?"

See calendar events on Apple Watch

1. Open the Calendar app 14 on your Apple Watch, or tap the date or a calendar event on the watch face.
2. Turn the Digital Crown to scroll through upcoming events.

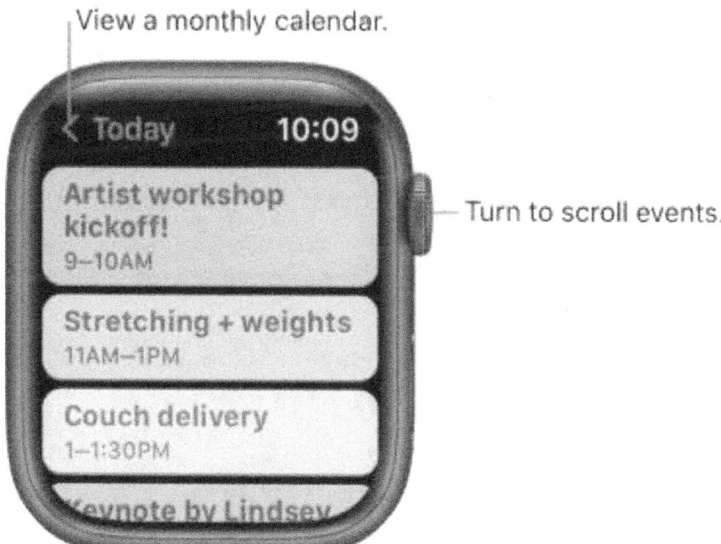

3. Tap an event to see details about it, including time, location, invitee status, and notes.
   Tip: To return to the next event, tap < in the top-left corner.
You can also see your events by week or month.

Change how you view your calendar

To switch views, open the Settings app on your Apple Watch, tap Calendar, then tap an option:
- Up Next: Shows your upcoming events for the week.
- List: Shows all your events from yesterday through six days from today.
- Day: Shows just the events for this day.

To see the whole month, tap < in the top-left corner of any calendar in List or Day view. Tap the monthly calendar to return to Today view.

To see another day, swipe left or right if you're in Day view; if you're in List view or Up Next view, turn the Digital Crown.

To jump back to the current day and time, tap the current time in the top-right corner of the display.

Add, delete, or change an event

- Add an event: Say something like "Create a calendar event titled FaceTime with Mom for May 20 at 4 p.m."
- Delete an event you created: Tap an event, tap Delete, then tap Delete Event.

If this is a recurring event, you can delete this event only, or all future events.
- Change an event: Use the Calendar app on your iPhone.

Respond to a Calendar invitation

You can respond on your Apple Watch to event invitations when you receive them, or later.
- If you see the invitation when it arrives: Scroll to the bottom of the notification, then tap Accept, Decline, or Maybe.
- If you discover the notification later: Tap it in your list of notifications, then scroll and respond.
- If you're already in the Calendar app: Tap the event to respond.

To contact an event organizer, tap the organizer's name in the event details, then tap the phone, message, email, or Walkie-Talkie button. You can also email the organizer by tapping an event, scrolling to the bottom, then tapping Email Sender.

Get directions to an event

If an event includes a location, your Apple Watch can provide directions to it.

1. Open the Calendar app 14 on your Apple Watch.
2. Tap an event, then tap the address.

Change "leave now" alerts

If an event includes a location, you automatically get a "leave now" alert on your Apple Watch based on estimated travel time and traffic conditions. To choose a specific time interval such as two hours before the event, do the following:
1. Open the Calendar app on your iPhone.
2. Tap the event.
3. Tap Alert, then choose a different interval.

Adjust calendar settings

To change the kind of calendar notifications you receive and choose specific calendars to appear on Apple Watch, follow these steps:
1. Open the Apple Watch app on your iPhone.
2. Tap My Watch, then tap Calendar.
3. Tap Custom under Notifications or Calendars.

Use Camera Remote and timer on Apple Watch

If you want to position your iPhone for a photo and then take the photo from a distance, you can use your Apple Watch to view the iPhone camera image and take the photo. You can also use your Apple Watch to set a shutter timer—this gives you time to lower your wrist and raise your eyes when you're in the shot.

To function as a camera remote, your Apple Watch needs to be within normal Bluetooth range of your iPhone (about 33 feet or 10 meters).

Ask Siri. Say something like: "Take a picture."

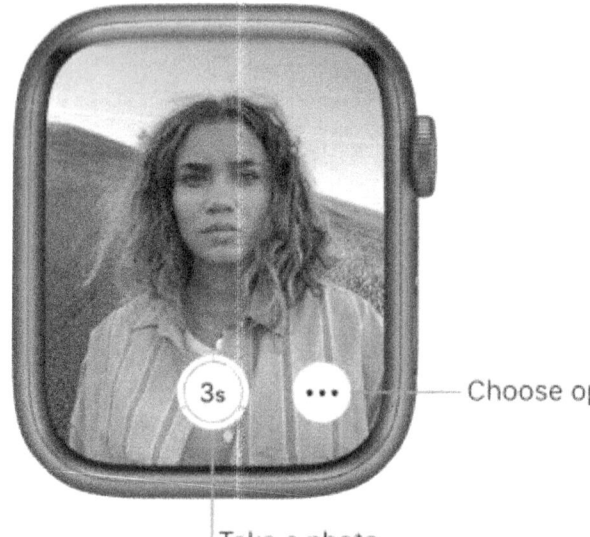

Choose options.

Take a photo.

Take a photo

1. Open the Camera Remote app 📷 on your Apple Watch.
2. Position your iPhone to frame the shot using your Apple Watch as a viewfinder.
3. To zoom, turn the Digital Crown.
4. To adjust exposure, tap the key area of the shot in the preview on your Apple Watch.
5. To take the shot, tap the Shutter button.

The photo is captured in Photos on your iPhone, but you can review it on your Apple Watch.

Review your shots

Use the following actions to review your shots on your Apple Watch.
- View a photo: Tap the thumbnail in the bottom left.
- See other photos: Swipe left or right.
- Zoom: Turn the Digital Crown.
- Pan: Drag on a zoomed photo.
- Fill the screen: Double-tap the photo.
- Show or hide the Close button and the shot count: Tap the screen.

When you're finished, tap Close.

Choose a different camera and adjust settings

1. Open the Camera Remote app 📷 on your Apple Watch.
2. Tap •••, then choose from among these options:
    - Timer (3-second timer on or off)
    - Camera (front or rear)
    - Flash (auto, on, or off)
    - Live Photo (auto, on, or off)
    - HDR (on or off)

Use Compass on Apple Watch

The Compass app shows the direction your Apple Watch SE or Apple Watch Series 5 or later is facing, as well as your current location and elevation.
Note: If you remove the Compass app from your iPhone, it's also removed from Apple Watch.

See your bearings, elevation, incline, and coordinates

Your bearing is shown at the top left. Turn the Digital Crown to scroll up and see your incline, elevation, and coordinates.

1. Open the Compass app on your Apple Watch.
2. For accurate bearings, hold Apple Watch flat to align the crosshairs at the center of the compass.
3. To add a bearing, turn the Digital Crown to scroll up, tap Add Bearing, turn Apple Watch to the bearing, then tap Done.
To edit the bearing, turn the Digital Crown to scroll up, tap Edit Bearing, turn Apple Watch to the new bearing, then tap Done.
4. To clear the bearing, turn the Digital Crown to scroll up, then tap Clear Bearing.

Add the elevation complication to the watch face

The always-on altimeter lets you track your current elevation in real time. Add the elevation complication to the watch face to see your elevation with a glance.

1. With the watch face showing, touch and hold the display, then tap Edit.
2. Swipe left all the way to the end.
   If a face offers complications, they're shown on the last screen.
3. Tap a complication to select it, turn the Digital Crown to Compass, then choose Elevation.
4. Press the Digital Crown to save your changes, then tap the face to switch to it.

Note: Compass won't display elevation or coordinates if Location Services is turned off. To turn Location Services on or off, open the Settings app on your Apple Watch, tap Privacy, then tap Location Services.

To use true north rather than magnetic north, open the Settings app on your Apple Watch, tap Compass, then turn on Use True North.

Note: Compass can be affected by magnetic materials in some watch bands.

Use Cycle Tracking on Apple Watch

Use the Cycle Tracking app to log details about your menstrual cycle. You can add flow information and record symptoms such as headaches or cramps. Using information you've logged, the Cycle Tracking app can alert you when it predicts that your next period or fertile window is about to start. The app can also use heart rate data from Apple Watch to improve predictions.

Set up Cycle Tracking

1. Open the Health app on your iPhone.
2. Tap Browse at the lower right to display the Health Categories screen.
3. Tap Cycle Tracking.
4. Tap Get Started, then follow the onscreen instructions to set notifications and other options.
5. Tap Options, then turn on the options you want—Period Predictions, Fertility Predictions, and Heart Rate Data.

Log your cycle on Apple Watch

1. Open the Cycle Tracking app on your Apple Watch.
2. Tap the buttons and choose options that describe your period—your flow level and symptoms, for example.

The observations you provide appear in the Cycle log on iPhone. If you've turned on Period Prediction and Fertility Prediction in the Health app on iPhone, you will receive notifications on Apple Watch about upcoming periods and fertility windows.

On iPhone, you can also log factors in the Health app that could impact your cycle, such as pregnancy, lactation, and contraceptive use. Depending on the factors you select, your period or fertile window predictions on iPhone and Apple Watch may be turned off.

Important: Fertile window predictions should not be used as a form of birth control.

Contacts

In the Contacts app, you can view, edit, and share contacts from other devices that use the same Apple ID. You can also create contacts and set up a contact card with your own information.

See contacts on your Apple Watch

1. Open the Contacts app on your Apple Watch.
2. Turn the Digital Crown to scroll through your contacts.
3. Tap a contact to view address information and notes.

If you have an image associated with the contact, tap it to enlarge the image.

Communicate with contacts

You can call, text, email, or begin a Walkie-Talkie conversation directly from the Contacts app.

1. Open the Contacts app on your Apple Watch.
2. Turn the Digital Crown to scroll through your contacts.
3. Tap a contact, then do any of the following:

    - Tap to see the contact's phone numbers. Tap a phone number to call.
    - Tap to open an existing message thread or begin a new one.
    - Tap to create an email message.
    - Tap to invite the person to Walkie-Talkie or—if they've already accepted your invitation and they have Walkie-Talkie turned on—begin a Walkie-Talkie conversation.

Create a contact

1. Open the Contacts app on your Apple Watch.
2. At the top of the screen, tap New Contact.
3. Enter the contact's name and, optionally, company.
4. Add a phone number, email, and address, then tap Done.

Share, edit, or delete a contact

1. Open the Contacts app on your Apple Watch.
2. Turn the Digital Crown to scroll through your contacts.
3. Tap a contact, scroll down, then tap Share Contact, Edit, or Delete Contact.

Record an electrocardiogram with the ECG app on Apple Watch

Apple Watch Series 4 and later have an electrical heart rate sensor that, along with the ECG app, allows you to take an electrocardiogram (or ECG). To use the ECG app, update your iPhone 6s or later to the latest version of iOS and Apple Watch to the latest version of watchOS. The ECG app is not available in all regions.

1. Open the Health app on your iPhone, then follow the onscreen steps to set up ECG.
   If you don't see a prompt to set up, tap Browse at the bottom right, tap Heart, then tap Electrocardiogram (ECG).
2. Open the ECG app on your Apple Watch.
3. Rest your arm on a table or in your lap.
4. With the hand opposite your watch, hold your finger on the Digital Crown, then wait while Apple Watch records the ECG.
   You don't need to press the Digital Crown during the session.

At the end of the recording, you receive a classification. You can then tap Add Symptoms and choose your symptoms. Tap Save to note any symptoms, then tap Done. To view your results on iPhone, open the Health app on iPhone, tap Browse at the bottom right, then tap Heart > Electrocardiograms (ECG).

Find People, Devices, and Items

Find People

View a friend's location with Apple Watch

The Find People app is a great way to find people who are important to you and share your location with them. Friends and family members who use iPhone, iPad, iPod touch, Apple Watch SE, or Apple Watch Series 3 or later and share their locations with you appear on a map, so you can quickly see where they are. You can set notifications to alert you when friends or family members leave from or arrive at various locations.

Add a friend

1. Open the Find People app on your Apple Watch.
2. Tap Share My Location.
3. Tap the Dictation, Contacts, or Keypad button to choose a friend.
4. Select an email address or phone number.
5. Choose how long to share your location—for one hour, until the end of the day, or indefinitely.

Your friend receives a notification that you've shared your location. They can choose to also share their location with you. After your friend agrees to share their location, you can see where they are in a list or on a map in the Find My app on iPhone, iPad, iPod touch, and Mac, or the Find People app on Apple Watch.

To stop sharing your location with a friend, tap your friend's name on the Find People screen, then tap Stop Sharing.

To stop sharing your location with everyone, open the Settings app on your Apple Watch, go to Privacy > Location Services, then turn off Share My Location.

Find out where your friends are

1. Open the Find People app on your Apple Watch to see a list of your friends, with each friend's approximate location and distance from you. Turn the Digital Crown to see more friends.
2. Tap a friend to see their location on a map.

3. Tap < in the top-left corner to return to your friends list.

Or use Siri. Say something like, "Where is Julie?"
Note: If your friend is wearing an Apple Watch with cellular and is sharing their location, but they don't have their iPhone with them, their location will be tracked using their Apple Watch.

Notify a friend of your departure or arrival

1. Open the Find People app on your Apple Watch.
2. Tap a friend, scroll down, then tap Notify [name of friend].
3. Turn on Notify [name of friend] on the next screen, then choose to notify your friend when you leave your location or arrive at their location.

Get a notification about your friend's location

1. Open the Find People app on your Apple Watch.
2. Tap your friend, scroll down, then tap Notify Me.
3. Turn on Notify Me, then choose to be notified when your friend leaves their location or arrives at your location.

Use Apple Watch to get directions or contact a friend

Use Find People to quickly get directions to a friend.

Get directions to a friend

1. Open the Find People app on your Apple Watch.
2. Tap your friend, scroll down, then tap Directions to open the Maps app .
3. Tap the route to get step-by-step directions from your current location to your friend's location.

Contact a friend

1. Open the Find People app on your Apple Watch.
2. Tap your friend, scroll down, then tap Contact to call, email, use Walkie-Talkie, or send a message to your friend.

Find misplaced devices with Apple Watch

The Find Devices app on Apple Watch can help you locate Apple devices you've lost or misplaced. To find your Apple devices you must connect them to your Apple ID.

See the location of a device

If your device is online, you can see its location in the Find Devices app. For supported devices, Find Devices can locate the device even if it's powered off, in low power mode, or if airplane mode is turned on.

Open the Find Devices app on your Apple Watch, then tap a device.
- If the device can be located: It appears on the map so you can see where it is. The device's approximate distance, time it last connected to Wi-Fi or cellular, and charge level appears above the map. An approximate location appears below the map.
- If the device can't be located: You see "No location" under the device's name. Under Notifications, turn on Notify When Found. You receive a notification once it's located.

Play a sound on your iPhone, iPad, iPod touch, Mac, or Apple Watch

1. Open the Find Devices app on your Apple Watch, then tap a device.
2. Tap Play Sound.
    - If the device is online: A sound starts after a short delay and gradually increases in volume, then plays for about two minutes. The device vibrates (if applicable). A Find My [device] alert appears on the device's screen.
    A confirmation email is also sent to your Apple ID email address.
    - If the device is offline: You see Sound Pending. The sound plays the next time the device connects to a Wi-Fi or cellular network.

Play a sound on your AirPods or Beats headphones

If your AirPods or Beats headphones are paired with your Apple Watch, you can play a sound on them using Find Devices.
For supported AirPods models, you can even play a sound on your AirPods if they are in their case.

1. Open the Find Devices app on your Apple Watch, then tap a device.
2. Tap Play Sound. If your AirPods or AirPods Pro are separated, you can mute one by tapping Left or Right to find them one at a time.
    - If the device is online: It plays a sound immediately for two minutes.
    A confirmation email is also sent to your Apple ID email address.
    - If the device is offline: You receive a notification the next time your device is in range of your Apple Watch.

Get directions to a device

You can get directions to a device's current location in the Maps app 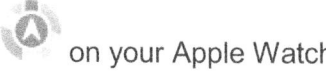 on your Apple Watch.

1. Open the Find Devices app on your Apple Watch, then tap a device you want directions to.
2. Tap Directions to open Maps.
3. Tap the route to get directions from your current location to the device's location.

Receive a notification when you've left a device behind

To help keep you from misplacing your device, you can receive a notification when you've left your device behind. You can also set Trusted Locations—locations where you can leave your device without receiving a notification.

1. Open the Find My app on your iPhone, then tap Devices.
2. Tap the device you want to set up a notification for.
3. Below Notifications, tap Notify When Left Behind.
4. Turn on Notify When Left Behind, then follow the onscreen instructions.
5. If you want to add a Trusted Location, you can choose a suggested location, or tap New Location, select a location on the map, then tap Done.

You can also open the Find Devices app on your Apple Watch, tap a device, scroll up, tap Notify When Left Behind, then turn on Notify When Left Behind.

Mark a device as lost

If your device is lost or stolen, you can turn on Lost Mode for your iPhone, iPad, iPod touch, or Apple Watch, or lock your Mac.

1. Open the Find Devices app on your Apple Watch, then tap a device.

2. Tap Lost Mode, then turn on Lost Mode.

When you mark a device as lost, the following occurs:

- A confirmation email is sent to your Apple ID email address.
- A message indicating the device is lost and how to contact you appears on the device's Lock Screen.
- Your device doesn't display alerts or make noise when you receive messages or notifications, or if any alarms go off. Your device can still receive phone calls and FaceTime calls.
- Apple Pay is disabled for your device. Any credit or debit cards set up for Apple Pay, student ID cards, and Express Transit cards are removed from your device. Credit, debit, and student ID cards are removed even if your device is offline. Express Transit cards are removed the next time your device goes online.
- For an iPhone, iPad, iPod touch, or Apple Watch, you see your device's current location on the map as well as any changes in its location.

Find Items

Locate an AirTag or other item in Find Items

You can use the Find Items app on your Apple Watch to locate a missing AirTag or third-party item that you've registered to your Apple ID.

See the location of an item

Open the Find Items app on your Apple Watch, then tap an item you want to find.

- If the item can be located: It appears on the map so you can see where it is. The device's approximate distance, time it last connected to Wi-Fi or cellular, and charge level appears above the map. An approximate location appears below the map.
- If the item can't be located: You see where and when it was last located. Under Notifications, tap Notify When Found, then turn on Notify When Found. You receive a notification once it's located again.

Play a sound

If the item is nearby, you can play a sound on it to help you find it. Note: If you can't play a sound on an item, you won't see the Play Sound button.

1. Open the Find Items app on your Apple Watch, then tap the item you want to play a sound on.

2. Tap Play Sound.

   To stop playing the sound before it ends automatically, tap Stop Sound.

Get directions to an item

You can get directions to an item's current or last known location in the Maps app on your Apple Watch.

1. Open the Find Items app on your Apple Watch, then tap the item you want to get directions to.
2. Tap Directions to open Maps.
3. Tap the route to get directions from your current location to the item's location.

Receive a notification when you've left an item behind

To help keep you from misplacing your items, you can receive a notification when you've left them behind. You can also set Trusted Locations—locations where you can leave your item without receiving a notification.

1. Open the Find My app on your iPhone, then tap Items.
2. Tap the item you want to set up a notification for.
3. Below Notifications, tap Notify When Left Behind.
4. Turn on Notify When Left Behind, then follow the onscreen instructions.
5. If you want to add a Trusted Location, you can choose a suggested location, or tap New Location, select a location on the map, then tap Done.

You can also open the Find Items app on your Apple Watch, tap an item, scroll up, tap Notify When Left Behind, then turn on Notify When Left Behind.

Change distance units

1. Open the Find Items app on your Apple Watch, then turn the Digital Crown to scroll to the bottom of the screen.
2. Tap Directions In, then choose miles or kilometers.

Mark an AirTag or other item as lost in Find Items on Apple Watch

Mark a device as lost

If you lose an AirTag or third-party item registered to your Apple ID, you can use the Find Items app to mark it as lost.

1. Open the Find Items app on your Apple Watch, then tap an item.
2. Tap Lost Mode, then turn on Lost Mode.

If someone finds your item, they can learn more about it by connecting to it.

Turn off Lost Mode for an item

When you find your lost item, turn off Lost Mode.

1. Open the Find Items app on your Apple Watch, then tap the item.
2. Tap Lost Mode, then turn off Lost Mode.

Check your heart rate on Apple Watch

Your heart rate is an important way to monitor how your body is doing. You can check your heart rate during a workout; see your resting, walking, breathe, workout, and recovery rates throughout the day; or take a new reading at any time.

See your heart rate

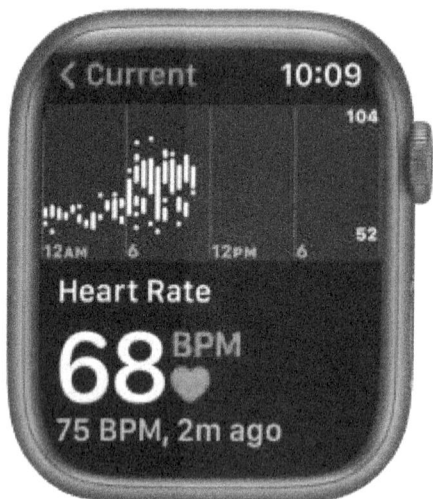

Open the Heart Rate app on your Apple Watch to view your current heart rate, resting rate, and walking average rate.
Your Apple Watch continues measuring your heart rate as long as you're wearing it.

Check your heart rate during a workout

By default, your current heart rate shows on the Multiple Metric workout view. To customize which metrics appear during a workout, follow these steps:
1. Open the Apple Watch app on your iPhone.
2. Tap My Watch, go to Workout > Workout View, then tap a workout.

See a graph of your heart rate data

1. Open the Health app on your iPhone.
2. Tap Browse at the bottom right, tap Heart, then tap Heart Rate.
3. To add Heart Rate to your Summary, swipe up, then tap Add to Favorites.

You can see your heart rate over the last hour, day, week, month, or year. Tap Show More Heart Rate Data and you can also see the range of your heart rate during the selected time period; your resting, walking average, workout, sleep, and Breathe rates; and any high or low heart rate notifications.

Turn on heart rate data

By default, your Apple Watch monitors your heart rate for the Heart Rate app, workouts, and Breath and Reflect sessions. If you've turned off heart rate data, your can turn it back on.

1. Open the Settings app on your Apple Watch.
2. Go to Privacy > Health.
3. Tap Heart Rate, then turn on Heart Rate.

You can also open the Apple Watch app on your iPhone, tap My Watch, tap Privacy, then turn on Heart Rate.

Receive high or low heart rate notifications

Your Apple Watch can notify you if your heart rate remains above a chosen threshold or below a chosen threshold after you've been inactive for at least 10 minutes. You can turn on heart rate notifications when you first open the Heart Rate app, or at any time later.

1. Open the Settings app on your Apple Watch, then tap Heart.
2. Tap High Heart Rate Notifications or Low Rate Notifications, then set a heart rate threshold.

You can also open the Apple Watch app on your iPhone, tap My Watch, then tap Heart. Tap High Heart Rate or Low Heart Rate, then set a threshold.

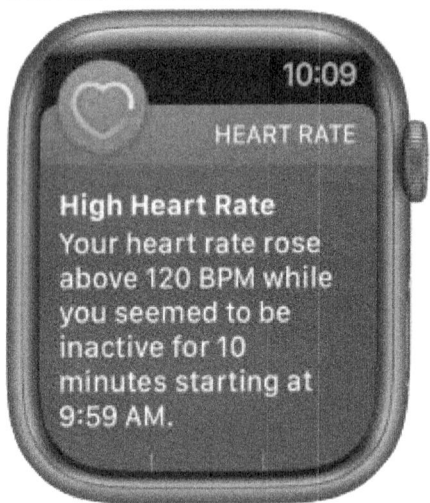

Receive irregular heart rhythm notifications (not available in all regions)

You can receive a notification if Apple Watch has identified an irregular heart rhythm that appears to be atrial fibrillation (AFib).

1. Open the Settings app  on your Apple Watch.
2. Tap Heart, then turn on Irregular Rhythm Notifications.

You can also open the Apple Watch app on your iPhone, tap My Watch, tap Heart, then turn on Irregular Rhythm.

Receive low cardio fitness notifications

Apple Watch can provide you with cardio fitness estimates by measuring how hard your heart is working during an outdoor walk, run, or hike, and send you a notification when it's low. Depending on your age and sex, your cardio fitness will fall into one of four ranges: Low, Below Average, Above Average, or High. If your cardio fitness level falls in the "Low" range, you'll receive a notification on your Apple Watch. If it stays low, you'll receive a notification every four months.

Note: This feature may not be available in all regions.

1. In the Health app on your iPhone, tap Browse, tap Respiratory, then tap Cardio Fitness.
2. Follow the onscreen prompts to turn on Cardio Fitness notifications.

You can also look in the Cardio Fitness section of the Health app to see your cardio fitness measurements and the range they fall into. Tap Show All Cardio Fitness Levels.

Note: For best results, the back of your Apple Watch needs skin contact for features like wrist detection, haptic notifications, blood oxygen level measurements, and the heart rate sensor. Wearing your Apple Watch with the right fit—not too tight, not too loose, and with room for your skin to breathe—keeps you comfortable and lets the sensors do their job.

Home

Control your home with Apple Watch

The Home app provides a secure way to control HomeKit-enabled accessories, such as lights, locks, smart TVs, thermostats, window shades, and smart plugs. You can also send and receive Intercom messages on supported devices and view the video streams of HomeKit Secure Video cameras. With your Apple Watch, all your controls are right on your wrist.
The first time you open the Home app on your iPhone, the setup assistant helps you create a home. Then you can define rooms, add HomeKit-enabled accessories, and create scenes. Accessories, scenes, and rooms that you add on your iPhone are available on your Apple Watch.
Ask Siri. Say something like: "Turn off the lights in the office."

View your home status

The Home app shows you the status of accessories you're currently using—for example, the temperature registered by your thermostat or an unlocked front door. Just tap a button to control the accessory or learn more.

1. Open the Home app on your Apple Watch.
2. Tap any of the round buttons that appear just below your home's name.

When multiple accessories appear in a status, tapping the status lets you control each device or set of grouped devices. For example, if all the lights are on in the living room and bedroom, you can tap the status, then turn off just the lights in the living room.

Control smart home accessories and scenes

In the Home app on your Apple Watch, the relevant scenes and accessories for that moment appear near the top of the screen. For example, a coffee maker may appear in the morning and be replaced by your bedside lamp at night.

You can see the rest of your accessories by scrolling up, then tapping Cameras, Favorites, or a room.

To control an accessory, do any of the following:
- Turn an accessory on or off: Tap the accessory—a light, for example—or, if you want to unlock a compatible lock, a home key.

- Adjust an accessory's settings: Tap   for an accessory. Tap Done to return to the list of accessories.
  The available controls depend on the type of accessory. For example, with some lightbulbs, there are controls for both brightness and changing colors. Swipe left to see additional controls.
- Control favorite accessories or accessories in a room: Tap Favorites or a room, then tap an accessory or tap   to adjust the accessory's settings.
- View a camera's video stream: Tap Cameras, then tap a camera.

To run a scene, open the Home app   on your Apple Watch, then tap the scene.

View a different home

If you have more than one home set up, you can choose which one to view on your Apple Watch.

Open the Home app   on your Apple Watch, then do one of the following:
- If the Home Screen is showing, tap a home.
- If a specific home is showing, tap <, then tap a different home.

Send and receive Intercom messages from Apple Watch

Using the Home app   on Apple Watch, you can send an Intercom message to all members of your home. You can also send Intercom messages to specific rooms or zones.

1. Open the Home app 🏠 on your Apple Watch, then tap the Intercom button.
2. Say something like "Who ate the last piece of pizza?"
3. Tap Done.

A recording of your voice is sent to all the HomePod speakers in your home, and to the iOS, iPadOS, and watchOS devices of all members of your home who can send and receive Intercom messages.

To send a message to a HomePod in a specific room or zone, raise your Apple Watch and say something like "Hey Siri, tell the office 'The movie is starting'" or "Hey Siri, announce upstairs 'I'm going to the store.'"

Remotely access your smart home accessories from Apple Watch

If you have an Apple TV (3rd generation or later), HomePod, or an iPad (iPadOS 13 or iOS 10 or later) that you leave at home, you can remotely access HomeKit-enabled accessories from your iPhone and your paired Apple Watch. The Apple TV, HomePod, or iPad acts as a home hub that lets you communicate with your accessories when you're away from home.

Allow remote access

On your iPhone, go to Settings > [your name] > iCloud, then turn on Home. Make sure you're signed in using the same Apple ID on all the devices.

If you have an Apple TV and you're signed in using the same Apple ID as your iPhone, it will be paired automatically.

Mail

Read mail on Apple Watch

Read mail on your Apple Watch, then reply using the QWERTY keyboard, dictation, Scribble, emoji, or a prepared response, or switch to your iPhone to type a response.

Read mail in a notification

1. To read a new message, just raise your wrist when the notification arrives.
2. To dismiss the notification, swipe down from the top or tap Dismiss at the end of the message.

If you miss the notification, swipe down on the watch face later to see unread notifications, then tap it there.

To control email notifications on your Apple Watch, open the Apple Watch app on your iPhone, tap My Watch, then go to Mail > Custom.

Read mail in the Mail app

1. Open the Mail app on your Apple Watch.
2. Turn the Digital Crown to scroll the message list.
3. Tap a message to read it.
4. To jump to the top of a long message, turn the Digital Crown, or tap the top of the screen.

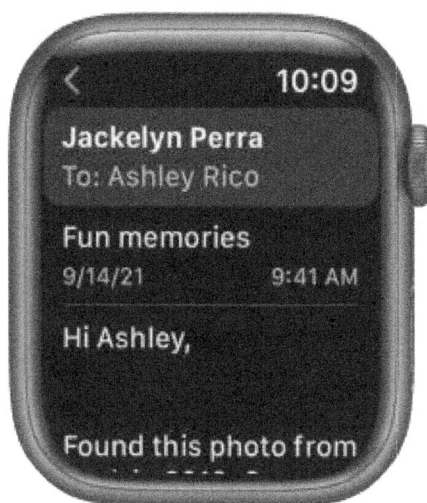

Messages are formatted to be viewed on your Apple Watch. Most text styles are preserved, and you can tap website links in Mail and view web-formatted content optimized for Apple Watch. Double-tap to zoom in on the content.

Website links may not be available in all regions.

Tip: You can make a call, open a map, or view web-formatted content from a mail message—just tap a phone number, address, or link.

Switch to iPhone

When you receive a message you want to read on your iPhone, follow these steps:
1. Wake your iPhone.
2. On an iPhone with Face ID, swipe up from the bottom edge and pause to show the App Switcher. (On an iPhone with a Home button, double-click the Home button to show the App Switcher.)
3. Tap the button at the bottom of the screen to open Mail.

Write and reply to mail on Apple Watch

Create a message

1. Open the Mail app on your Apple Watch.
2. Use the Digital Crown to scroll to the top of the screen, then tap New Message.
3. Tap Add Contact to add a recipient, tap Add Subject to create a subject line, then tap Create Message.

If you've set up your Apple Watch to use more than one language, tap Language, choose a language, then tap the Create Message field.

Compose a message

You can compose a message in a variety of ways—most of them on a single screen. Tap the Create Message field, then do one or a combination of the following:

- Use the QWERTY and QuickPath keyboard: (Apple Watch Series 7 only) Tap characters to enter them or use the QuickPath keyboard to slide from one letter to the next without lifting your finger (not available for all languages). To end a word, lift your finger.

If you don't see the keyboard, swipe up from the bottom, then tap the Keyboard button.

- Use Scribble: Use your finger to write your message. To edit your message, turn the Digital Crown to move the cursor into position, then make your edit.
  To use predictive text, tap a finished or unfinished word to highlight it, then turn the Digital Crown to see suggested words. Stop turning the Digital Crown to enter the highlighted suggestion.
  Tip: If you've set up your Apple Watch to use more than one language, you can choose a different language when using Scribble. Just swipe up from the bottom of the screen, then choose a language.
  Scribble is not available in all languages.

- Dictate text: Tap , say what you want to say, then tap Done. You can speak punctuation, too—for example, "did it arrive question mark."
  To return to using Scribble, turn the Digital Crown or tap.

- Include emoji: Tap , tap a frequently used emoji or a category, then scroll to browse available images. When you find the right symbol, tap it to add it to your message.

- Enter text with your iPhone: When you start composing a message and your paired iPhone is nearby, a notification appears on the iPhone, offering to let you enter text using the iOS keyboard. Tap the notification, then type the text on your iPhone.

Reply to a message on Apple Watch

Scroll to the bottom of a message you've received in the Mail app , then tap Reply. If there are multiple recipients, tap Reply All. Tap Add Message, then do either of the following:

251

- Send a smart reply: Scroll to see a list of handy phrases that you can use—just tap one to send it.
To add your own phrase, open the Apple Watch app on your iPhone, tap My Watch, go to Messages > Default Replies, then tap Add Reply. To customize the default replies, tap Edit, then drag to reorder them or tap ⊖ to delete one.
If the smart replies aren't in the language you want to use, scroll down, tap Languages, then tap a language. The available languages are those you enabled on your iPhone in Settings > General > Keyboard > Keyboards.
- Compose a reply: Tap the Add Message field, then compose a reply.

Open the email on iPhone

1. If you prefer to reply on your iPhone, wake your iPhone, then open the App Switcher. (On an iPhone with Face ID, swipe up from the bottom edge and pause; on an iPhone with a Home button, double-click the Home button.)
2. Tap the button that appears at the bottom of the screen to open the email in Mail.

Manage mail on Apple Watch

Choose which mailboxes appear on Apple Watch

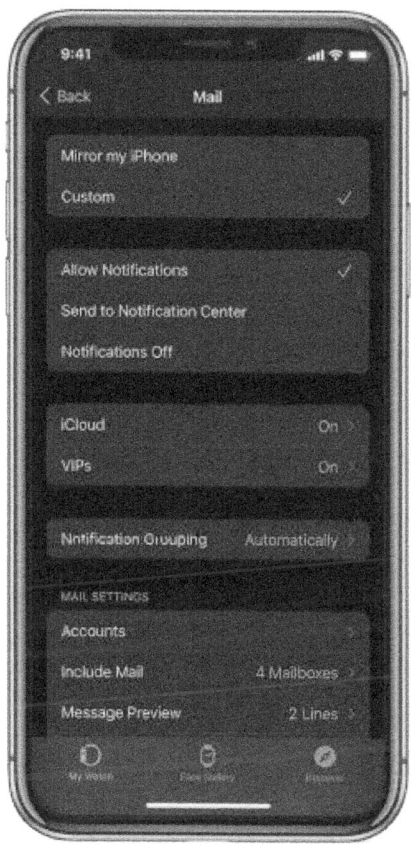

1. Open the Apple Watch app on your iPhone.
2. Tap My Watch, then go to Mail > Include Mail.
3. Tap the accounts you want to see on your Apple Watch under Accounts. You can specify multiple accounts—for example, iCloud and the account you use at work.
4. If you want, tap an account, then tap specific mailboxes to see their contents on your Apple Watch.

By default you see messages from all inboxes. You can also choose to view messages from VIPs, flagged messages, unread messages, and more.

You can also choose the accounts and mailboxes you see, right on Apple Watch. Open the Mail app , scroll down, tap Edit, then tap an account or mailbox.

View specific accounts on Apple Watch

1. Open the Mail app on your Apple Watch.
2. Tap < in the top-left corner to see a list of accounts and special mailboxes, such as Flagged and Unread.
3. Tap an account or mailbox to view its contents.

To see your email from all accounts, tap All Inboxes.

Delete, mark as unread or read, or flag a message

Open the Mail app on your Apple Watch, open a mail message, then scroll to the bottom to:

- Mark a message unread or read: Tap "Mark as Unread" or "Mark as Read."
  If you're looking at the message list, swipe right on the message, then tap the Read or Unread button .
- Delete a message: Tap Trash Message.
  If you're looking at the message list, swipe left on the message, then tap .
- Flag a message: Tap Flag. (You can also unflag a message that's already been flagged.)
  If you're looking at the message list, swipe left on the message, then tap .

If you swipe on a message thread, the action you choose (Trash, Flag, Read, or Unread) applies to the entire thread.

Customize alerts

1. Open the Apple Watch app on your iPhone.
2. Tap My Watch, go to Mail > Custom, tap an account, then turn on Show Alerts from [name of account].
3. Turn Sound and Haptic on or off.

Shorten your message list

To make your mail list more compact, reduce the number of preview text lines shown for each email in the list.

1. Open the Apple Watch app on your iPhone.
2. Tap My Watch, tap Mail, then tap Message Preview.
3. Choose to show only 1 or 2 lines, or none.

Load remote images

Some emails can contain links that point to online images. If you allow remote images to load, those images appear in the email. To allow these images, follow these steps:

1. Open the Apple Watch app on your iPhone.
2. Tap My Watch, tap Mail, tap Custom, then turn on Load Remote Images.

Note: Loading remote images can cause email to download more slowly to your Apple Watch.

Organize by thread

To see all responses to an email combined in one thread, follow these steps:

1. Open the Apple Watch app on your iPhone.
2. Tap My Watch, tap Mail, tap Custom, then turn on Organize By Thread.

Maps

Find places and explore with Apple Watch

Your Apple Watch has a Maps app for exploring your surroundings and getting directions.
Ask Siri. Say something like:
- "Where am I?"
- "Find coffee near me."

Search the map

1. Open the Maps app on your Apple Watch.
2. Tap Search, then tap to dictate or to scribble.
Note: Scribble is not available in all languages.

Find a nearby service

1. Open the Maps app on your Apple Watch.
2. Tap Search, then, under Nearby, tap a category such as Food Delivery or Charging Stations.
3. Tap a result, then turn the Digital Crown to scroll the information.
4. Tap < in the top-left corner to return to the list of results.

Note: Nearby suggestions aren't available in all areas.

View a guide to nearby attractions and services

1. Open the Maps app on your iPhone, tap the search field, swipe up, then do any of the following:
    - Tap a cover that appears below Editors' Picks.
    - Tap Explore Guides, browse the guides, then tap a cover.
    - Swipe up, choose a publisher, then tap a cover.
2. Tap Save.
3. Open the Maps app on your Apple Watch.
4. Scroll down, then tap a guide under Recents.

To add a location mentioned in a guide, open the guide on your iPhone, tap next to the location's name—the name of a park or restaurant, for example—then tap My Places or a guide you've created. The location will appear on your Apple Watch in the guide you chose.

Note: Guides are not available in all regions.

See and search your current location and surroundings

1. Open the Maps app ![icon] on your Apple Watch.
2. Tap Location.

    3. To search around your location, tap ●●● , then tap Search Here.
    Tap Transit Map to see nearby transit options.

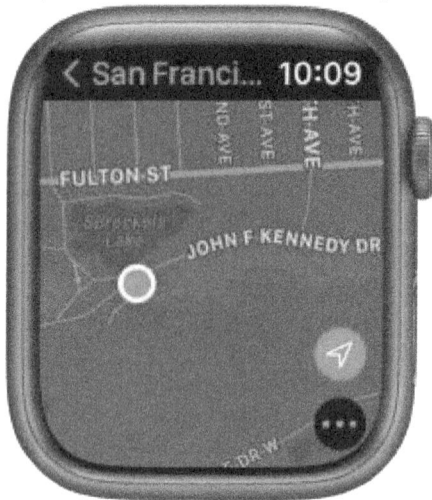

A blue cone on the map shows the direction your watch is facing.

Pan and zoom

- Pan the map: Drag with one finger.
- Zoom the map in or out: Turn the Digital Crown.
  You can also double-tap the map to zoom in on the spot you tap.

- Go back to your current location: Tap ◢ at the bottom left.

Get info about a landmark or marked location

1. Tap the location marker on the map.
2. Turn the Digital Crown to scroll the information.
3. Tap < in the top-left corner to return to the map.

Tip: To call a location, tap the phone number in the location info. To switch to your iPhone, open the App Switcher. (On an iPhone with Face ID, swipe up from the bottom edge and pause; on an iPhone with a Home button, double-click the Home button.) Tap the button at the bottom of the screen to open Phone.

Drop, move, and remove map pins

- Drop a pin: Touch and hold the map where you want the pin to go, wait for the pin to drop, then let go.
- Move a pin: Drop a new pin in the new location.
  - Remove a pin: Tap it to see address information, turn the Digital Crown to scroll, then tap Remove Marker.

Tip: To find the approximate address of any spot on the map, drop a pin on the location, then tap the pin to see address info.

See a contact's address on the map

1. Open the Maps app on your Apple Watch.
2. Tap Search, then tap .
3. Turn the Digital Crown to scroll, then tap the address.
4. Scroll down, then tap the map.

Get directions on Apple Watch

Ask Siri. Say something like:
- "Directions to the nearest gas station?"
- "Get directions home"
- "How far to the airport?"

Get directions

1. Open the Maps app on your Apple Watch.
2. Turn the Digital Crown to scroll to Favorites, Guides, and Recents.
3. Tap an entry to get driving, walking, transit, and cycling directions.
   Note: Not all transportation modes are available in all locations.
   4. Tap a mode to see suggested routes, then tap a route to begin your trip and to see an overview of it—with turns, distance between turns, and street names.
   Look in the top-left corner to see your estimated arrival time.

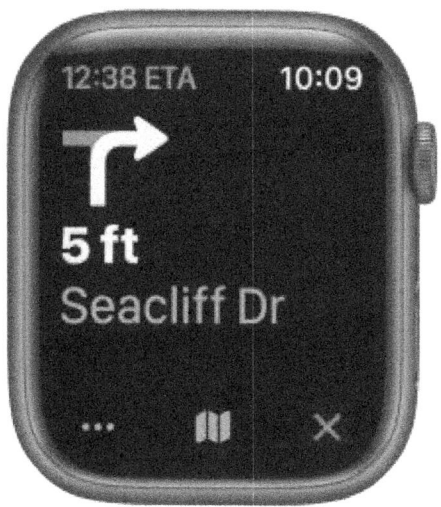

Tip: When you choose Cycling, you see an overview of elevation changes along the route. Tap ••• to learn about the kind of roads you'll ride—whether they have a bike path, are a side or main road, or require you to dismount your bike and walk.

See transportation options

With suggested routes showing in the Maps app , you can select various options before you begin.
- Choose an alternate route: If alternate routes appear, tap one to take it.
- Switch to a driving, walking, transit, or cycling route: Tap Walking, Driving, Transit, or Cycling.
- Avoid tolls or highways: With a driving route showing, tap > next to the destination's address, then turn on an option.
- Avoid hills, or busy roads: With a cycling route showing, tap > next to the destination's address, then turn on an option.
- Choose preferred public transit: With a transit route showing, tap >, then choose the kinds of public transit you prefer—bus, subway & light rail, commuter rail, and ferry, for example.

Get directions to a landmark or map pin

1. Open the Maps app on your Apple Watch.
2. Tap Location, then tap the destination landmark or map pin.
3. Scroll the location information until you see Directions, then choose walking, driving, transit, or cycling directions.
4. When you're ready to go, tap a route, then follow the directions.

Ask Siri. Say something like, "How long will it take me to get home?"

Use Maps while en route

Your Apple Watch has many ways to help keep you on the right path. Choose these options as you travel:

- See turn-by-turn directions: When you start your journey, Apple Watch displays a list of each turn you'll take, complete with street and highway names. Turn the Digital Crown to see upcoming turns, then tap the top of the display to return to the next turn you'll take.
  Note: Location services must be turned on to use turn-by-turn directions. On Apple Watch, go to Settings > Privacy > Location Services to turn location services on or off.

- Open a map: When viewing a list of turn-by-turn directions, tap to open a map that shows the turn's location. Turn the Digital Crown to zoom in and out on the map. Tap to return to the turn-by-turn list.

    - Listen for directions: After you head off on your first leg, your Apple Watch uses sounds and taps to let you know when to turn. A low tone followed by a high tone (tock tick, tock tick) means turn right at the intersection you're approaching; a high tone followed by a low tone (tick tock, tick tock) means turn left. Not sure what your destination looks like? You'll feel a vibration when you're on the last leg, and again when you arrive.

You can choose the transportation modes that provide alerts. Open the Apple Watch app on your iPhone, tap My Watch, tap Maps, then turn on the alerts you want to receive—Driving, Driving with CarPlay, Walking, and Cycling.

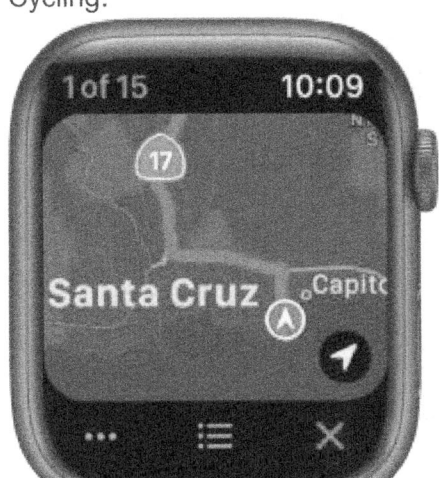

To end directions before you get there, tap ✕ in the bottom right of the display. Or tap •••, scroll up, then tap End.

Quickly return to Maps from the watch face

You can switch to the watch face while you're getting directions. To quickly return to Maps, tap ⓐ at the top of the screen.

Use Memoji on Apple Watch

With the Memoji app 👦, you can design your own personalized Memoji—choose skin color and freckles, hairstyle and color, facial features, headwear, glasses, and more. You can create multiple Memoji for different moods.

Create Memoji

1. Open the Memoji app on your Apple Watch.
2. If you're using the Memoji app for the first time, tap Get Started.

   If you've already made a Memoji, scroll up, then tap ⊕ to add a new one.
3. Tap each feature and scroll the Digital Crown to choose the options you want for your Memoji. As you add features such as hairstyle and eyewear, your character comes to life.
4. Tap Done to add the Memoji to your collection.
   Memoji you create can be used as Memoji stickers in Messages.

To create another Memoji, tap ⊕, then add features.

Edit Memoji and more

Open the Memoji app on your Apple Watch, tap a Memoji, then choose an option:

- Edit a Memoji: Tap features such as eyes and headwear, then turn the Digital Crown to choose a variation.
- Create a Memoji watch face: Scroll down, then tap Create Watch Face.
  Return to the watch face and swipe left to see your new Memoji watch face. The watch face is also added to the watch face collection in the Apple Watch app on iPhone.
- Duplicate a Memoji: Scroll down, then tap Duplicate.
- Delete a Memoji: Scroll down, then tap Delete.

Messages

Read messages on Apple Watch

Read incoming text messages right on your Apple Watch, then reply using the QWERTY keyboard, dictation, Scribble, or a prepared response, or switch to your iPhone to type a response.

Read a message on Apple Watch

1. When you feel a tap or hear an alert sound telling you that a message has arrived, raise your Apple Watch to read it.
2. Turn the Digital Crown to scroll to the bottom of the message.
3. To jump to the top of the message, tap the top of the screen. Tip: You can tap a website link within a message to view web-formatted content optimized for Apple Watch. Double-tap to zoom in on the content.

If the message arrived a while ago, touch and hold the top of the screen, swipe down on the display to see the message notification, then tap it. To mark the message as read, scroll down, then tap Dismiss. To dismiss the notification without marking the message as read, press the Digital Crown.

See when messages were sent

Tap a conversation in the Messages conversation list, then swipe left on a message in the conversation.

Mute or delete a conversation

- Mute a conversation: Swipe left on the conversation in the Messages conversation list, then tap 🌙.
- Delete a conversation: Swipe left on the conversation in the Messages conversation list, then tap 🗑.

Access photos, audio, and video in a message

Messages can contain photos, audio, and videos. To access them from your Apple Watch, follow these steps:

- Photo: Tap the photo to view it, double-tap it to fill the screen, and drag it to pan. When you're finished, tap < in the top-left corner to return to the conversation.

  If you want to share the photo, tap it, tap ⬆, then tap a sharing option—choose people you often exchanges messages with, or tap Messages or Mail. To save the image, scroll past the sharing options, then tap Save Image. The image is saved to the Photos app on your iPhone.
- Audio clip: Tap the clip to listen.
  The clip is deleted after two minutes to save space—if you want to keep it, tap Keep below the clip. The audio remains for 30 days, and you can set it to remain longer on your iPhone: Go to Settings, tap Messages, scroll to Audio Messages, tap Expire, then tap Never.
- Video: Tap a video in a message to start playing the video full-screen. Tap once to display the playback controls. Double-tap to zoom out and turn the Digital Crown to adjust the volume. Swipe or tap the Back button to return to the conversation.
  To save the video, open the message in the Messages app on your iPhone, and save it there.

Decide how to be notified

1. Open the Apple Watch app on your iPhone.
2. Tap My Watch, then tap Messages.
3. Tap Custom to set options for how you want to be notified when you receive a message.

You won't receive a notification if you're using a Focus that doesn't allow Messages notifications.

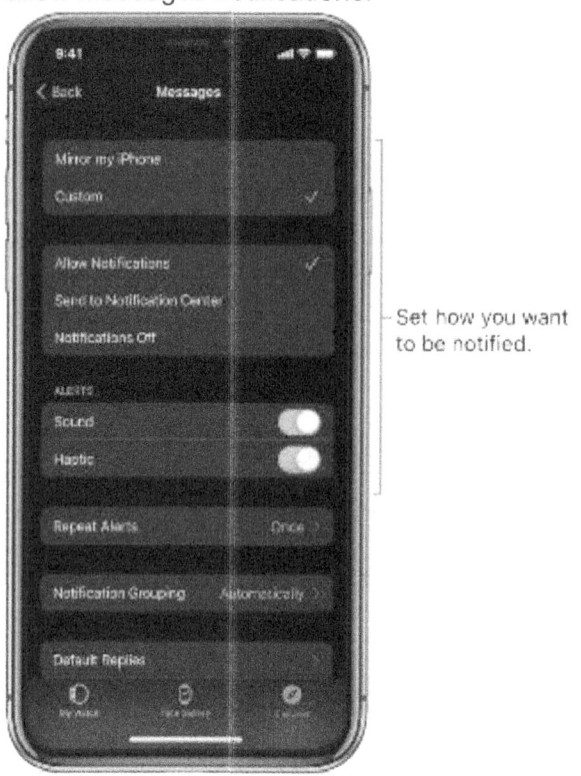

Set how you want to be notified.

Send messages from Apple Watch

In the Messages app on your Apple Watch, you can compose and send messages that contain not only text, but also images, emoji, Memoji stickers, and audio clips. You can also send money through Apple Pay and let people know where you are by including your location in a message.

Create a message on Apple Watch

1. Open the Messages app on your Apple Watch.
2. Scroll to the top of the screen, then tap New Message.
3. Tap Add Contact, tap a contact in the list of recent conversations that appears, or choose an option:

    - Tap to search for someone in your contacts or to dictate a phone number.

    - Tap to choose from your full list of contacts.

    - Tap to enter a phone number.
4. Tap Create Message.
5. If you've set up your Apple Watch to use more than one language, tap Language, then choose a language.

Compose a text message

You can compose a message in a variety of ways—most of them on a single screen. After creating a message, tap the Create Message field, then do one or a combination of the following:

- Use the QWERTY and QuickPath keyboard: (Apple Watch Series 7 only) Tap characters to enter them or use the QuickPath keyboard to slide from one letter to the next without lifting your finger (not available for all languages). To end a word, lift your finger.
  If you don't see the keyboard, swipe up from the bottom, then tap the Keyboard button.
- Use Scribble: Use your finger to write your message. To edit your message, turn the Digital Crown to move the cursor into position, then make your edit.
  To use predictive text, tap a finished or unfinished word to highlight it, then turn the Digital Crown to see suggested words. Stop turning the Digital Crown to enter the highlighted suggestion.
  Tip: If you've set up your Apple Watch to use more than one

language, you can choose a different language when using Scribble. Just swipe up from the bottom of the screen, then choose a language.
Scribble is not available in all languages.

- Dictate text: Tap 🎤 , say what you want to say, then tap Done. You can speak punctuation, too—for example, "did it arrive question mark."
To return to using Scribble, turn the Digital Crown or tap .

- Include emoji: Tap 😀, tap a frequently used emoji or tap a category, then scroll to browse available images. When you find the right symbol, tap it to add it to your message.
- Enter text with your iPhone: When you start composing a message and your paired iPhone is nearby, a notification appears on the iPhone, offering to let you enter text using the iOS keyboard. Tap the notification, then type the text using the iPhone keyboard.

Send a smart reply, Memoji sticker, sticker, GIF, or audio clip

You can also compose messages without entering a single character. Try one of these options after creating a message:

- Send a smart reply: Scroll to see a list of handy phrases that you can use—tap one, then tap Send.
To add your own phrase, open the Apple Watch app on your iPhone, tap My Watch, go to Messages > Default Replies, then tap Add Reply. To customize the default replies, tap Edit, then drag to reorder them or tap ⊖ to delete one.
If the smart replies aren't in the language you want to use, scroll down, tap Languages, then tap a language. The available languages are those you enabled on your iPhone in Settings > General > Keyboard > Keyboards.

- Send a Memoji sticker: Tap 🅰, tap 😀, tap an image in the Memoji Stickers collection, tap a variation, then tap Send.

- Send a sticker: Tap 🅰, tap 😀, scroll to the bottom, then tap More Stickers. Tap one, then tap Send. To create new stickers or see all your stickers, use Messages on your iPhone.

- Send a GIF: Tap 🅰, tap 🔍, tap a GIF, then tap Send. To search for an appropriate GIF, tap the Search field, enter a search term, tap a resulting GIF, then tap Send.

- Send an audio clip: Tap 🅰, tap 🎤, record what you want to say, tap Done, then tap Send.

Use Apple Pay to send and receive money

1. In a conversation, tap 🅰 next to the iMessage field.
2. Tap ⓔPay.
3. Select an amount to send using the Digital Crown, then tap Pay.
4. Double-click the side button to send.

Note: Apple Cash is not available in all regions.

Send a sketch from Apple Watch

You can use Digital Touch to send sketches to friends who have an Apple Watch or iPhone with iOS 10 or later.
To see a sketch someone has sent you, tap the notification.

1. Create a message, then tap 🅰.
2. Tap ❤ to open the drawing canvas.
3. Use your finger to draw on the screen.

4. Tap the dot in the top-right corner to choose a different color.
5. Tap Done when you're finished sketching, then tap Send.

Express your feelings with a Digital Touch

You can use Digital Touch to send taps, a kiss, or your heartbeat to friends who have an Apple Watch or iPhone with iOS 10 or later. To see (or feel) a tap or heartbeat someone has sent you, tap the notification.

1. Create a message, then tap .
2. Tap to open the drawing canvas, then use gestures to send any of the following:
    - Tap: Tap the screen to send a single tap or tap repeatedly to send a tap pattern.
    - Kiss: Tap two fingers on the display one or more times. Stop tapping to send.
    - Heartbeat: Place two fingers on the display until you feel your heartbeat and see it animated on the screen.
    - Heartbreak: Place two fingers on the display until you feel your heartbeat, then drag them down to send.

- Fireball: Touch and hold one finger on the display until you see a flame. Lift to send.

Share your location

To send someone a map showing your current location, scroll down, then tap Send Location.

On your paired iPhone, make sure Share My Location is turned on in Settings > [your name] > Find My > Share My Location. Or, on your Apple Watch with cellular, open the Settings app , go to Privacy > Location Services, then turn on Share My Location.

Share your location in a message.

Contact the person you're messaging

1. While viewing a conversation, scroll down.
2. Tap Details, then tap , , , or .

Scroll down and tap Share Contact to share the contact with others.

Reply to messages on Apple Watch

Reply to a message

Turn the Digital Crown to scroll to the bottom of the message, then choose how to reply.
To quickly respond with a Tapback, touch and hold a specific message in a conversation, then choose a Tapback—like thumbs-up or a heart.

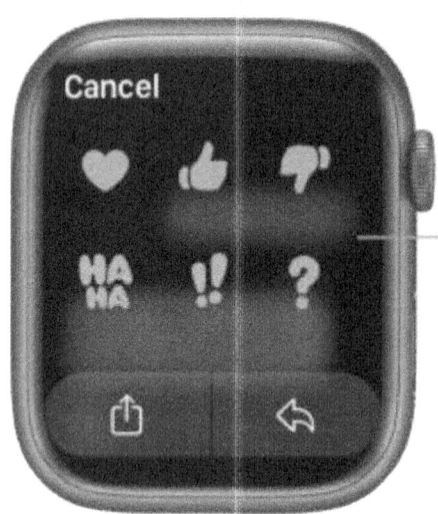

Double-tap a message, then tap to choose a Tapback.

Reply directly to one message in a conversation

In a group conversation, you can respond to a specific message inline to help keep conversations organized.

1. In a Messages conversation, touch and hold a specific message to reply to, then tap ↩.
2. Create your response, then tap Send.
   Only the person you reply to sees the message.

Share a message

Friends often include information and sentiments in their messages that you want to share with others. To share a message, follow these steps:
1. In a Messages conversation, touch and hold a specific message, then tap ⬆️.
2. Choose people you often exchange messages with, or tap Messages or Mail.
3. If you've chosen Messages or Mail, add contacts and, if you're sending an email, a subject.
4. Tap Send.

Mindfulness

Use Apple Watch to practice mindfulness

The Mindfulness app on your Apple Watch encourages you to set aside a few minutes a day to focus, center, and connect as you breathe. With an Apple Fitness+ subscription, you can listen to guided Meditations on Apple Watch.

Start a Reflect or Breathe session

Open the Mindfulness app ✿ on your Apple Watch, then do one of the following:
- Reflect: Tap Reflect, read the theme, focus your attention, then tap Begin.
- Breathe: Tap Breathe, inhale slowly as the animation grows, then exhale as it shrinks.

To end a session before it completes, swipe right, then tap End.

Set the duration of a session

1. Open the Mindfulness app ✿ on your Apple Watch.
2. Tap •••, tap Duration, then choose a duration.
   You can choose a time between one and five minutes.

Adjust mindfulness settings

You can change how frequently you get mindfulness reminders, mute mindfulness reminders for the day, change your breath rate, and choose haptics settings.

Open the Settings app on your Apple Watch, tap Mindfulness, then do any of the following:

- Set mindfulness reminders: Under Reminders, turn Start of Day and End of Day on or off; tap Add Reminder to create additional reminders.
- Get or stop a weekly summary: Turn Weekly Summary on or off.
- Mute mindfulness reminders: Turn on "Mute for today."
- Change your breathing rate: Tap Breath Rate to change the number of breaths per minute.
- Choose haptics settings: Tap Haptics, then choose None, Minimal, or Prominent.
- Get new meditations: Turn on Add New Meditations to Watch to download new meditations when your Apple Watch is connected to power. Meditations you've completed are deleted automatically.

You can also open the Apple Watch app on your iPhone, tap My Watch, tap Mindfulness, then adjust a setting.

See your heart rate during mindfulness sessions

Complete a Reflect or Breathe session. Your heart rate appears in the Summary screen.

You can also review your heart rate later. Open the Health app on your iPhone, tap Browse, tap Heart, then tap Heart Rate. Tap Show More Heart Rate Data, swipe up, then tap Breathe.

Use the Breathe watch face

Add the Breathe watch face to get quick access to mindfulness sessions.
1. With the current watch face showing, touch and hold the display.
2. Swipe left all the way to the end, then tap the New button (+).
3. Turn the Digital Crown to select Breathe, then tap Add.
4. Tap the watch face to open the Mindfulness app.

Listen to guided Meditations on Apple Watch (Apple Fitness+ subscription required)

If you subscribe to Apple Fitness+, you can listen to guided Meditations with your Apple Watch when it's paired with AirPods or other Bluetooth headphones or speakers.

Note: Apple Fitness+ isn't available in all countries or regions.

Start a guided Meditation

1. Open the Mindfulness app on your Apple Watch.
2. Tap Fitness+ Audio Meditations.
3. Scroll to browse through the Meditations.
   The theme, trainer, and duration of the Meditation appear near the bottom of each episode.
4. Tap to learn more about the Meditation, add it to your library, or play its playlist in the Music app .
5. Tap a Meditation to begin.

As the Meditation plays, its elapsed time and your current heart rate appear on Apple Watch.

To pause or end a guided Meditation, swipe right as the Meditation plays, then tap Pause or End. To begin a workout while the Meditation continues to play, tap Workout, then choose a workout.

Browse your completed Meditations

When you complete most or all of a Meditation, it appears in My Library, which you can find on your Apple Watch and in the Fitness app on your iPhone.

1. Open the Mindfulness app on your Apple Watch.
2. Tap Fitness+ Audio Meditations.
3. Scroll to the bottom of the screen, then tap My Library to show any Meditations you've played.

4. Tap ⓘ to learn more about the Meditation, add it to your library, or play its playlist in the Music app 🎵.
5. Tap a Meditation to play it again.

You can also browse My Library on your iPhone, iPad, or Apple TV. Open the Fitness app on your device (tap Fitness+ on iPhone), then go to My Library.

Music

Add music to Apple Watch

When you add music to your Apple Watch, you can listen to it wherever you go, even when you don't have your iPhone with you. You can add specific playlists and albums to your Apple Watch using the Apple Watch app on your iPhone. If you're an Apple Music subscriber, you can also add music with the Music app 🎵 directly on your Apple Watch.

Note: You don't have to choose specific music to add to your Apple Watch if you're an Apple Music subscriber. Music you've recently listened to is added automatically. (If you haven't listened to anything, music recommended by Apple Music is added.)

Add music using your iPhone

1. Open the Apple Watch app on your iPhone.
2. Tap My Watch, then tap Music.
3. Below Playlists & Albums, tap Add Music.
4. Select albums and playlists to sync to your Apple Watch.

Music is added when Apple Watch is connected to power and placed near your iPhone.

Tip: Use the Music app on your iPhone to create playlists specifically for music you want to listen to on your Apple Watch—music that motivates you during a workout, for example.

Add music using your Apple Watch

If you're an Apple Music subscriber, you can add music using your Apple Watch.

1. Open the Music app on your Apple Watch.
2. Tap Library, Listen Now, or Search, then navigate to music you want to add.
3. Tap a playlist or album, tap ⋯ , then tap Add to Library. A message confirms that the item was added.
   Note: You can stream music you add to Apple Watch when you have an internet connection. To play music when you're not connected to the internet, you must first download it.
4. To download the music to Apple Watch, tap ⋯ again, then tap Download.
   Music is added when Apple Watch is connected to power and Wi-Fi.

Add a workout playlist to Apple Watch

You can add a playlist from your music library that plays automatically when you start a workout in the Workout app on Apple Watch.

1. Open the Apple Watch app on your iPhone.
2. Tap My Watch, then tap Workout.
3. Tap Workout Playlist, then choose a playlist.

The playlist is added to My Watch > Music in the Apple Watch app on your iPhone.

Note: A workout playlist won't play if you're currently listening to other music or audio.

Remove music from Apple Watch

If you're running out of room to store music on your Apple Watch, you may want to remove the music that was automatically added to your watch or music that you no longer listen to.

Note: To see how much music is stored on your Apple Watch, open the Settings app on your Apple Watch, then go to General > Storage. You can also open the Apple Watch app on your iPhone, tap My Watch, then go to General > Storage.

Remove music using your iPhone

1. Open the Apple Watch app on your iPhone.
2. Tap My Watch, tap Music, then do any of the following:

    - For music you've added: Tap Edit, then tap next to the items you want to remove.
    - For music that was automatically added: Turn off Recent Music or other music automatically added to your Apple Watch.
    Note: Music you've recently played won't be automatically added to Apple Watch until you turn on Recent Music again.

Music you remove from your Apple Watch remains on your iPhone.

Remove music using your Apple Watch

If you're an Apple Music subscriber, you can remove music directly on Apple Watch, whether it was added automatically or you chose to add it.

1. Open the Music app on your Apple Watch.
2. Tap Library, scroll down, tap Downloaded, then tap Playlists or Albums.
3. Swipe left on a playlist or album, tap , then tap Remove.

4. Tap Remove Download or Delete from Library.
   If you tap Remove Download, the item is removed from your Apple Watch but remains in your music library, allowing you to easily find it later. If you tap Delete from Library, it's removed from your Apple Watch and from all other devices that use the same Apple ID.

Note: You can also remove individual songs. If you swipe left on a song, tap Remove, then tap Delete, the song is removed from your Apple Watch and from all other devices that use the same Apple ID.

Play music on Apple Watch

Use the Music app to choose and play music on Apple Watch. You can play music stored on Apple Watch, control music on your iPhone, and stream music from Apple Music if you're a subscriber.
Ask Siri. Say something like:
- "Play 'enough for you' by Olivia Rodrigo"
- "Play more songs from this album"
- "Play my workout playlist"

Play music

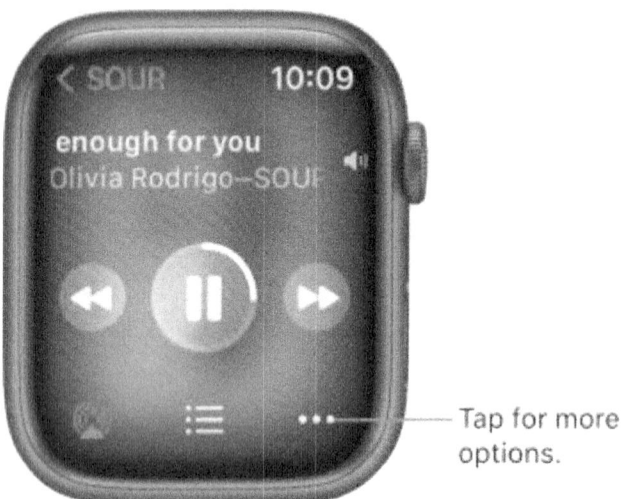

Tap for more options.

After you connect Apple Watch to Bluetooth headphones or speakers, open the Music app on your Apple Watch, then do any of the following:

- Play music on your Apple Watch: Turn the Digital Crown to scroll through album artwork, then tap a playlist or album to play it.
  Use the Apple Watch app on your iPhone to choose which songs to add to Apple Watch.
- Play music from iPhone (Bluetooth pairing not required): Scroll to the top of the screen, tap On iPhone, then tap a playlist, artist, album, or song to play it.
- Play music from your music library: Tap Library, then tap a playlist, artist, album, or song. To play music downloaded to your Apple Watch, tap Downloaded, then choose music.
- Request music from Apple Music (Apple Music subscription required): Raise your wrist, then request an artist, album, song, genre, or portion of a song lyric.

Play music for you

If you're an Apple Music subscriber, you can play music chosen just for you.

1. Open the Music app on your Apple Watch.
2. Scroll to the top of the screen, then tap Listen Now to view a curated feed of playlists and albums based on your likes and dislikes.
3. Tap a category, tap an album or playlist, then tap .

Open the queue

When playing music, you can see a list of upcoming songs in the queue.

1. Open the Music app on your Apple Watch.
2. Play an album or playlist, then tap .
3. To play a track in the queue, tap it.

By default, Auto Play adds music to the end of the queue that's similar to what you're playing. To turn off Auto Play, tap .

Note: When you turn off Auto Play on a device that uses your Apple ID—your Apple Watch, for example—it's turned off only for that device. Other devices will continue to use Auto Play until you turn it off on each one.

To add music you choose to the queue, swipe left on a song, playlist, or album; tap ; then tap Play Next or Play Later. Music you choose to play later is added to the end of the queue.

Control playback

Turn the Digital Crown to adjust volume. Use these controls to play music on your Apple Watch and iPhone:

285

▶	Play the current song.
❙❙	Pause playback.
▶▶	Skip to the next song.
◀◀	Skip to the beginning of the song; double-tap to skip to the previous song.

Shuffle or repeat music

- Shuffle albums, songs, artists, from the Music screen: Tap an album, artist, or playlist, then tap ⤭.
- Shuffle or repeat music from the playback screen: While viewing the playback screen, tap ☰, then tap ⤭ or ↻.

Tap Repeat twice to repeat a song.

Listen to radio on Apple Watch

In the Music app 🎵 on Apple Watch, Radio is the home of Apple Music 1, Apple Music Hits, and Apple Music Country—three Apple Music stations that feature the latest music from a variety of genres as well as exclusive interviews. You can also listen to broadcast radio and featured stations crafted by music experts.
No subscription is required to listen to Apple Music 1, Apple Music Hits, or Apple Music Country.

Listen to Apple Music radio

To listen to Apple Music radio, make sure your Apple Watch is near your iPhone or connected to a Wi-Fi network—or a cellular network, if you have an Apple Watch with cellular.

1. Open the Music app 🎵 on your Apple Watch.
2. Tap Radio, then tap Apple Music 1, Apple Music Hits, or Apple Music Country.

Listen to a featured or genre station

1. Open the Music app ![icon] on your Apple Watch.
2. Tap Radio, then turn the Digital Crown to scroll through stations and genres created by music experts.
3. Tap a genre to see its stations, then tap a station to play it.

Listen to broadcast radio

You can listen to thousands of broadcast radio stations on your Apple Watch.
Ask Siri. Say something like "Play Wild 94.9" or "Tune in to ESPN Radio."
You can ask for stations by name, call sign, frequency, and nickname.
Note: You don't need a subscription to Apple Music to listen to broadcast radio. Broadcast radio isn't available in all countries or regions. Not all stations are available in all countries or regions.

Read news stories on Apple Watch

The News app ![icon] on your Apple Watch helps keep you up to date with current events, presenting stories selected with your interests in mind.
Note: The News app is not available in all countries or regions.

View stories in the News app

You can view news stories in several ways:

- Open the News app ![icon] on your Apple Watch.
- Tap the News complication on a watch face.
- Tap a news item on the Siri watch face.
- Tap a notification from News.

Read a news story

1. Open the News app on your Apple Watch.
2. Scroll through the story summary by turning the Digital Crown.
3. To read the story on your iPhone, iPad, or Mac, scroll to the bottom of the story, then tap Save for Later.
4. To open the story on your compatible device, do one of the following:
    - iPhone or iPod touch: Open the News app on an iPhone or iPod touch, tap Following, tap Saved Stories, then tap the story.
    - iPad: On an iPad, open the News app, tap Saved Stories in the sidebar, then tap the story.
    - Mac: On a Mac, open the News app, click Saved Stories in the sidebar, then click the story.

To read stories from just the channels you follow, open the Settings app on your iPhone, tap News, then turn on Restrict Stories in Today.

Note: Restricting stories significantly limits the variety of stories that appear in Today and all other feeds. For example, if you restrict stories and follow only one entertainment-related channel, your Entertainment topic feed will contain stories only from that channel. When you restrict stories, you won't see Top Stories and Trending Stories.

Go to the next or previous news story

1. Open the News app on your Apple Watch.
2. Swipe left to read the next story, if one is available.
3. Swipe right to see the previous story.

If you've scrolled to read the summary, tap Next Story at the bottom of the screen.

Open news stories on iPhone

1. Open the News app ![icon] on your Apple Watch.
2. Wake iPhone, then open the App Switcher. (On an iPhone with Face ID, swipe up from the bottom edge and pause; on an iPhone with a Home button, double-click the Home button.)
3. Tap the button that appears at the bottom of the screen to open News.

Noise

Measure noise levels with Apple Watch

The Noise app ![icon] measures the ambient sound levels in your environment using the microphone and duration of exposure. When Apple Watch detects that the decibel level has risen to a point where hearing could be affected, it can notify you with a tap on the wrist.
Note: The Noise app uses the microphone to sample and measure the sound levels in your environment. Your Apple Watch doesn't record or save any sounds to measure these levels.

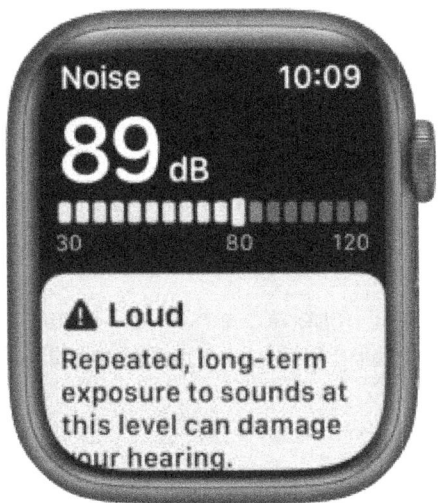

Set up the Noise app

1. Open the Noise app on your Apple Watch.
2. Tap Enable to turn on monitoring.
3. To measure the environmental noise around you in the future, open the Noise app or use the Noise complication.

Get noise notifications

1. Open the Settings app on your Apple Watch.
2. Go to Noise > Noise Notifications, then choose a setting.

You can also open the Apple Watch app on your iPhone, tap My Watch, then go to Noise > Noise Threshold.

Turn off noise measuring

1. Open the Settings app on your Apple Watch.
2. Go to Noise > Environmental Sound Measurements, then turn off Measure Sounds.

You can also open the Apple Watch app on your iPhone, tap My Watch, tap Noise, then turn off Environmental Sound Measurements.

Monitor your environmental noise exposure with Apple Watch

When you pair Apple Watch with your iPhone and set up the Noise app on Apple Watch, environmental sound levels are automatically sent from Apple Watch to the Health app on iPhone.

View the details about a noise notification

When noise in your environment reaches a level that might affect your hearing, you can get a notification from Apple Watch on your iPhone.
To view the details about a notification, do the following:
1. On your iPhone, open the Health app, then tap Summary at the bottom left.
2. Tap the notification at the top of the screen, then tap More Details.

See your exposure to environmental noise levels over time

1. On your iPhone, open the Health app, tap Browse at the bottom right, then tap Hearing.
2. Tap Environmental Sound Levels, then do any of the following:
    - View exposure levels over a time period: Tap the tabs at the top of the screen. (All levels are measured in decibels.)
    - Learn about the sound level classifications: Tap ⓘ .

- Change the time span displayed in the graph: Swipe the graph left or right.
- See details about a moment in time: Touch and hold the graph, then drag to move the selection.
- View details about average exposure: Tap Show More Data, then tap Daily Average.
- View a line representing average exposure: Tap Exposure below the graph.
- View the high and low range: Tap Show More Data, then tap Range.
- View highlights: Scroll down. To see more, tap Show All.

Use Now Playing on Apple Watch

Now Playing lets you control audio playback on Apple Watch, iPhone, and other devices.

Open Now Playing

You can open Now Playing in the following ways:

- Open the Now Playing app on your Apple Watch.
- While audio plays, tap the Now Playing icon at the top of the screen.
- Press the side button, then tap Now Playing in the Dock.
- Tap the Now Playing button if you've added it to the watch face.

Control music, podcasts, or audiobooks on iPhone

1. Open the Music, Podcasts, or Books app on your iPhone, then start playing a song, podcast, or audiobook.
2. Open Now Playing on your Apple Watch and use its controls to play, pause, and more.
3. Turn the Digital Crown to adjust volume.

Quickly open Music or Podcasts

When playing music on iPhone, tap the song title in Now Playing to open the Music app on Apple Watch. Tap the podcast episode title to open the Podcasts app.

Use Now Playing with a different device

If more than one device is available to play audio—an Apple Watch, iPhone, and HomePod for example—the name of the device you currently control appears in the top-left corner.
Tap < to see a list of devices, then tap one to control it.

Phone

Answer phone calls on Apple Watch

WARNING: For important information about avoiding distractions that could lead to dangerous situations.

Answer a call

When you hear or feel the call notification, raise your wrist to see who's calling.

- Send a call to voicemail: Tap the red Decline button in the incoming call notification.
- Answer on your Apple Watch: Tap the Answer button to talk using the built-in microphone and speaker or a Bluetooth device paired with your Apple Watch.
  - Answer using your iPhone or send a text message instead: Tap ●●●, then tap an option. If you tap Answer on iPhone, the call is placed on hold and the caller hears a repeated sound until you answer on your paired iPhone.
    If you can't find your iPhone, touch and hold the bottom of the screen, swipe up, then tap 📱 on your Apple

Watch.

While you're on a call

If you're on a call that doesn't use FaceTime audio, you can switch a call to your iPhone, adjust the call volume, enter numbers using the keypad, and switch the call to another audio device.

- Switch a call from your Apple Watch to your iPhone: While talking on your Apple Watch, unlock your iPhone, then tap the green button or bar at the top of the screen.
  You can quickly silence an incoming call by pressing the palm of your hand on the watch display for three seconds. Just make sure you have Cover to Mute turned on—open the Settings app on your Apple Watch, tap Sounds & Haptics, then turn on Cover to Mute.

- Adjust call volume: Turn the Digital Crown. Tap to mute your end of the call (if you're listening on a conference call, for example).

- Enter additional digits during a call: Tap , tap Keypad, then tap the digits.

296

- Switch the call to an audio device: Tap •••, then choose a device.

During a FaceTime Audio call, you can adjust the volume, mute the call by tapping 🎤, or tap ••• and choose an audio destination.

Listen to voicemail

If a caller leaves voicemail, you get a notification—tap the Play button in the notification to listen. To listen to voicemail later, open the Phone app 📞 on your Apple Watch, then tap Voicemail. On the voicemail screen you have these options:
- Adjust volume with the Digital Crown
- Start and stop playback
- Skip ahead or back five seconds
- Call back
- Delete the voicemail

Make phone calls on Apple Watch

Ask Siri. Say something like:
- "Call Max"

297

- "Dial 555 555 2949"
- "Call Pete FaceTime audio"

Make a call

1. Open the Phone app on your Apple Watch.
2. Tap Contacts, then turn the Digital Crown to scroll.
3. Tap the contact you want to call, then tap the phone button.
4. Tap FaceTime Audio to start a FaceTime audio call, or tap a phone number.
5. Turn the Digital Crown to adjust volume during the call.

Tip: To call someone you've recently spoken with, tap Recents, then tap a contact. To call a person you've designated as a favorite in the Phone app on your iPhone, tap Favorites, then tap a contact.

Enter a phone number on Apple Watch

1. Open the Phone app on your Apple Watch.

2. Tap Keypad, enter the number, then tap .

You can also use the keypad to enter additional digits during a call.

Just tap , then tap the Keypad button.

Make calls over Wi-Fi

If your cellular carrier offers Wi-Fi calling, you can use your Apple Watch to make and receive calls over Wi-Fi instead of the cellular network—even when your paired iPhone isn't with you or is turned off. Your Apple Watch just has to be within range of a Wi-Fi network that your iPhone has connected to in the past.

1. On your iPhone, go to Settings > Phone, tap Wi-Fi Calling, then turn on both Wi-Fi Calling on This iPhone and Add Wi-Fi Calling For Other Devices.

2. Open the Phone app on your Apple Watch.
3. Choose a contact, then tap .
4. Select the phone number or FaceTime address you want to call.

Note: You can make emergency calls over Wi-Fi, but when possible, use your iPhone over a cellular connection instead—your location information is more accurate. Make sure your emergency address is up to date—on your iPhone, go to Settings > Phone > Wi-Fi Calling, then tap Update Emergency Address. If emergency services can't locate you, they go to your emergency address.

See call info on Apple Watch

While you're talking on your iPhone, you can view call information on your Apple Watch in the Phone app . You can also end the call from your Apple Watch (for example, if you're using earphones or a headset).

Make an emergency phone call on Apple Watch

In case of emergency, use your Apple Watch to quickly call for help.

Make an emergency call

Do one of the following:

- Press and hold the side button until the sliders appear, then drag the Emergency SOS slider to the right.

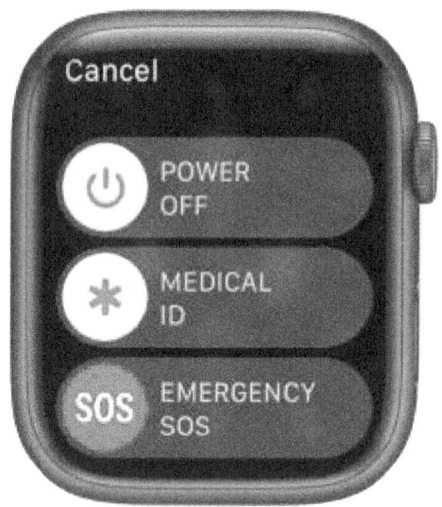

Your Apple Watch calls the emergency services in your region—for example, 911. (In some regions, you may be required to press a keypad number to complete the call.) After the call ends, your Apple Watch alerts your emergency contacts that you made a call and sends them your current location (if available).

- Press and keep holding the side button until your Apple Watch beeps and starts a countdown. When the countdown ends, your Apple Watch calls emergency services. The Apple Watch beeps even if it's in silent mode, so if you're in an emergency situation where you don't want to make noise, use the Emergency SOS slider to call emergency services without a countdown.

If you don't want your Apple Watch to automatically start the emergency countdown when you press and hold the side button, turn off Automatic Dialing. Open the Settings app on your Apple Watch, tap SOS, tap Hold Side Button, then turn off Hold Side Button. (Or open the Apple Watch app on your iPhone, tap My Watch, tap Emergency SOS, then turn off Hold Side Button.) You can still make an emergency call with the Emergency SOS slider.

If fall detection is enabled and you have been immobile for about a minute after Apple Watch detects a hard fall, it will attempt to make a call to emergency services automatically.

You can user Apple Watch Series 7 (GPS + Cellular) to make an emergency call in many locations, provided that cellular service is available. Some cellular networks may not accept an emergency call from your Apple Watch Series 7 (GPS + Cellular) if your Apple Watch isn't activated, if it isn't compatible with or configured to operate on a particular cellular network, or if isn't set up for cellular service.

When you start an Emergency SOS call while abroad, your watch connects to local emergency services, but it doesn't send your location or a text message to your emergency contacts. In some countries and regions, international emergency calling works even if you haven't set up cellular service on the watch.

Share your Medical ID with emergency services

1. Open the Apple Watch app on your iPhone.
2. Tap My Watch, then go to Health > Medical ID.
3. Tap Edit, then turn on Share During Emergency Call.

Cancel an emergency call

If you started an emergency call by accident, tap , then tap End Call to cancel.

Add an emergency contact

1. Open the Health app on your iPhone.
2. Tap your profile picture, tap Medical ID, then tap Edit.
3. Tap "add emergency contact," then tap Done to save your changes.

Use Dual SIM iPhone with Apple Watch cellular models

If you set up multiple cellular plans using an iPhone with Dual SIM, you can add multiple lines to your Apple Watch with cellular, then choose the one your watch uses when it connects to cellular networks.
Note: Each iPhone cellular plan must be provided by a supported carrier and must support Apple Watch cellular.

Set up multiple carrier plans

You can add one plan when you set up your watch for the first time. You can set up a second plan later in the Apple Watch app by following these steps:
1. Open the Apple Watch app on your iPhone.
2. Tap My Watch, then tap Cellular.
3. Tap Set Up Cellular or Add a New Plan, then follow the steps to choose the plan you want to add to your Apple Watch.

You can add multiple lines to your Apple Watch, but your Apple Watch can connect to only one line at a time.

Switch between plans

1. Open the Settings app on your Apple Watch.
2. Tap Cellular, then choose the plan you want your watch to use.

You can also open the Apple Watch app on your iPhone, tap My Watch, then tap Cellular. Your plan should automatically switch. If it doesn't switch, tap the plan you want to use.

How Apple Watch receives calls when using multiple cellular plans

- When Apple Watch is connected to your iPhone: You can receive calls from both lines. Your watch shows a badge that tells you which cellular line you received a notification from—H for Home, and W for Work, for example. If you respond to a call, your watch automatically responds from the line that received the call.
- When Apple Watch is connected to cellular and your iPhone isn't nearby: You receive calls from the line you've chosen in the Apple Watch app. If you respond to a call, your watch automatically calls back from the line you've chosen in the Apple Watch app.
Note: If the line you've chosen in the Apple Watch app isn't available when you try to return a call, your watch asks if you want to respond from another available line that you've added.

How Apple Watch receives messages when using multiple plans

- When Apple Watch is connected to your iPhone: You can get messages from both plans. If you respond to a message, your watch automatically responds from the line that received the message.
- When your Apple Watch is connected to cellular and away from your iPhone: You can get SMS messages from your active plan. If you respond to an SMS message, your Apple Watch automatically texts back from the line that received the message.
- When your Apple Watch is connected to cellular or Wi-Fi and your iPhone is turned off: You can send and receive iMessage texts as long as your Apple Watch has an active data connection to a Wi-Fi or cellular network.

Photos

Choose a photo album and manage storage on Apple Watch

With the Photos app on your Apple Watch, you can view photos from the iPhone album of your choice, featured photos, and photo Memories.

Choose the album to store on Apple Watch

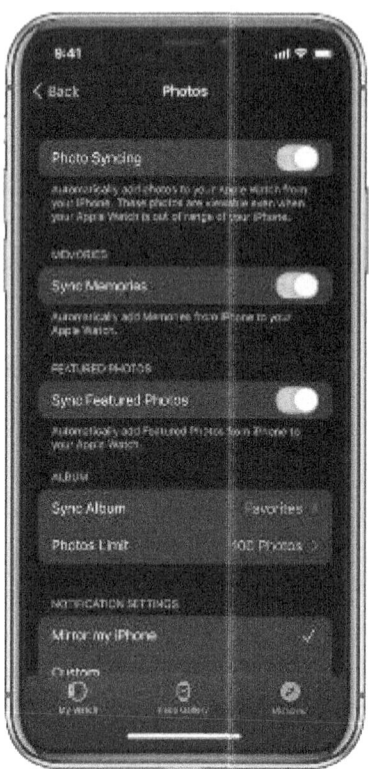

When you first get an Apple Watch, it's set to display photos from your Favorites album—photos you tagged as favorites—but you can change the album it uses.
1. Open the Apple Watch app on your iPhone.
2. Tap My Watch, go to Photos > Selected Photo Album, then choose the album.

To remove a photo from Apple Watch, open the Photos app on your iPhone, then remove the image from the album you've synced.

To create a new album for Apple Watch photos, use the Photos app on your iPhone.

Show featured photos and photo Memories on Apple Watch

Your Apple Watch can automatically sync featured photos and photo Memories from the photos library on your iPhone.
1. Open the Apple Watch app on your iPhone.
2. Tap My Watch, tap Photos, then turn on Sync Memories and Sync Featured Photos.

Stop photo syncing

If you don't want your iPhone to sync Memories, featured photos, or photos from an album you've chosen, follow these steps:
1. Open the Apple Watch app on your iPhone.
2. Tap My Watch, tap Photos, then turn off Photo Syncing.

Limit photo storage on Apple Watch

The number of photos stored on your Apple Watch depends on available space. To save space for songs or other content, you can limit the number of photos stored on it.
1. Open the Apple Watch app on your iPhone.
2. Tap My Watch, then go to Photos > Photos Limit.

To see how many photos are on your Apple Watch, do one of the following:

- Open the Settings app ⚙ on your Apple Watch, then go to General > About.
- Open the Apple Watch app on your iPhone, tap My Watch, then go to General > About.

To see how much space is used for your photos, open the Settings app ⚙ on your Apple Watch, then go to General > Storage. To do this on your iPhone, open the Apple Watch app, tap My Watch, then go to General > Storage.

Take a screenshot of Apple Watch

1. Open the Settings app ⚙ on your Apple Watch, go to General, then turn on Enable Screenshots.
2. Press the Digital Crown and the side button at the same time to take a picture of the screen.

Screenshots are saved in Photos on your iPhone.

View photos and Memories on Apple Watch

On Apple Watch, browse your photos in the Photos app 🌸 and show a photo on your watch face.

Tap to view a photo.

Browse photos in the Photos app on Apple Watch

Open the Photos app on your Apple Watch and use these actions to browse your photos.
1. Tap a Memory, Featured Photos, or an album you've synced to your Apple Watch.
2. Tap a photo to view it.
3. Swipe left or right to see other photos.
    - Turn the Digital Crown to zoom, or drag to pan a photo.
    - Zoom all the way out to see the entire photo album.

Swipe left or right to see the next photo.

Turn to zoom.

Drag to pan.

Double-tap to fill screen or see all.

View a photo memory on the watch face

In addition to viewing photo memories in the Photos app on your Apple Watch, you can view them on the Siri and Photos watch faces.

- See a recent memory from the Siri watch face: Choose the Siri watch face, then tap a memory.
- See photos from Memories on the Photos watch face: Open the Apple Watch app on your iPhone, tap Face Gallery, tap the Photos watch face, then tap Dynamic.
  The Dynamic watch face displays photos from your recent Memories, and it updates when you have new ones.

View a Live Photo on Apple Watch

Look for the Live Photo symbol 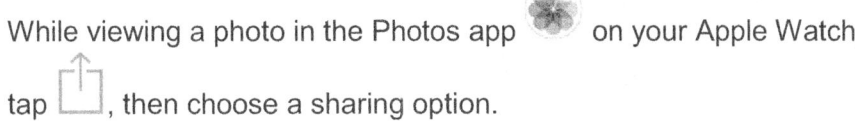 in the bottom-left corner of a photo, then touch and hold the photo.

Share a photo

While viewing a photo in the Photos app on your Apple Watch, tap , then choose a sharing option.

Create a photo watch face

While viewing a photo in the Photos app 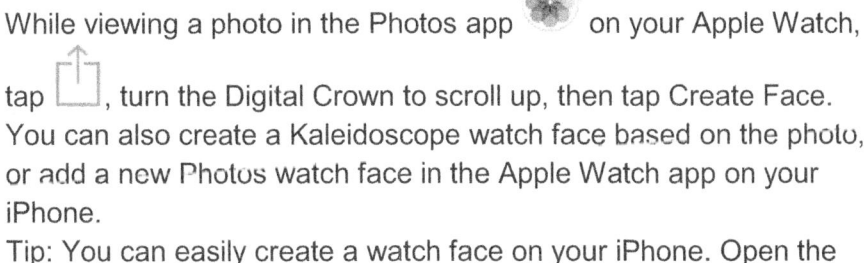 on your Apple Watch, tap , turn the Digital Crown to scroll up, then tap Create Face. You can also create a Kaleidoscope watch face based on the photo, or add a new Photos watch face in the Apple Watch app on your iPhone.
Tip: You can easily create a watch face on your iPhone. Open the Photos app on your iPhone, tap a photo, tap , swipe up, then tap Create Watch Face.

Podcasts

Add podcasts to Apple Watch

When you add podcasts to your Apple Watch, you can listen to them wherever you go, even when you don't have your iPhone with you. Just subscribe to shows in the Podcasts app on your iPhone and recent episodes of those shows are added to your Apple Watch when it's connected to power.

Download specific podcasts to Apple Watch

By default, Apple Watch downloads one episode from each of the top 10 shows in Listen Now on your iPhone. To sync specific podcasts, follow these steps:
1. Open the Apple Watch app on your iPhone.
2. Tap My Watch, then tap Podcasts.
3. Tap Custom, then turn on the stations and shows you want to download to your Apple Watch.
   Your Apple Watch will try to download three episodes from every show you select. If you select a custom station, your Apple Watch will try to add as many unplayed episodes as possible.

To once again download episodes from all the podcasts you subscribe to with your Apple Watch, tap Up Next.

See downloaded podcasts

1. Open the Podcasts app on your Apple Watch.
2. Tap Library, then tap Downloaded.

Play podcasts on Apple Watch

Play podcasts stored on Apple Watch

1. After you connect Apple Watch to Bluetooth headphones or speakers, open the Podcasts app on your Apple Watch.
2. Turn the Digital Crown to scroll through the artwork.
3. Tap a podcast to play it.

Play podcasts from iPhone

1. Open the Podcasts app on your Apple Watch.
2. Tap On iPhone.
3. Tap Up Next, Shows, Episodes, or Stations.
4. Navigate to an episode, then tap it.

Play podcasts from your library

If your Apple Watch is near your iPhone or connected to a Wi-Fi network (or a cellular network, for Apple Watch models with cellular), you can stream podcasts from your podcast library to your Apple Watch.

1. Open the Podcasts app on your Apple Watch.
2. Tap Library; tap Episodes, Stations, or a show; then tap an episode to play it.

Play podcasts with Siri

Say something like "Hey Siri, play the podcast Still Processing." Your Apple Watch plays the podcast's latest episode.

Control playback

View more episodes.
Change playback speed.
Choose playback destination.

Turn the Digital Crown to adjust volume. Use these controls to play podcasts on your Apple Watch:

▶	Play the current podcast.
❚❚	Pause playback.
⟳30	Skip ahead 30 seconds.
⟲15	Skip back 15 seconds.
1x	Playback speed. Options include 1x, 1 1/2x, 2x, and 1/2x.
☰	Choose an episode of the currently playing podcast.

312

Set and respond to reminders on Apple Watch

Your Apple Watch notifies you of reminders you create in the Reminders app on your Apple Watch or iPhone—and on any other iOS device, iPad, or Mac where you're signed in with your Apple ID.

See your reminders

1. Open the Reminders app on your Apple Watch.
2. Tap a list to open it.
3. Tap an item to mark it as completed.
4. Tap < in the top-left corner to return to your list view.
5. To see the completed reminders in a list, tap the list, tap View Options, then tap Show Completed.
   To see all completed reminders, tap the All list, tap View Options, then tap Show Completed.

You can share a list and collaborate with people who use iCloud. Shared lists show who a reminder has been assigned to. On Apple Watch you can join a shared list, but you can't share a list from Apple Watch.

Turn to see more lists.

Tap to view the items.

Respond to a reminder notification

- If you see the reminder notification when it arrives: Swipe (or turn the Digital Crown to scroll) the reminder, then tap Mark as Completed, or choose a time to be reminded.
- If you discover the notification later: Tap it in your list of notifications, then scroll and respond.

Create a reminder

- Use Siri: Say something like: "Remind me to pick up my dry cleaning at 5 PM."
  You can also use Siri to create a list on Apple Watch.
- Create a reminder in the Reminders app: Scroll to the bottom of the Lists screen or of any list, then tap Add Reminder.
  You can't assign a time or date to a reminder you create in this way.

Delete a reminder, choose a default list, reorder lists

For an Apple Watch that you set up for yourself, you manage some aspects of reminders on the paired iPhone.

- Delete a reminder: Open the Reminders app on your iPhone, tap a list that contains the reminder you want to delete, then swipe left on the reminder.
  To delete a list, swipe left on it.
- Choose a default list: If you create a new reminder outside of a specific list, it's added to the default list. Open the Settings app on your iPhone, then tap Reminders. Tap Default List, then tap a list.
- Change the order of your lists: Open the Reminders app on your iPhone. Tap Edit, then drag the list to a new location.

Remote

Use Apple Watch to control music on a Mac or PC

Use the Remote app ⏺ on your Apple Watch to play music on a computer that's on the same Wi-Fi network.

Add a music library

1. Open the Remote app ⏺ on your Apple Watch.
2. Tap Add Device.
    - If you're using the Music app on a Mac with macOS 10.15 or later: Open Apple Music and select your device from the list of devices shown with your library.
    - If you're using iTunes on your Mac or PC: Click the Remote button near the top left of the iTunes window.
3. Enter the 4-digit code displayed on your Apple Watch.

Control playback from Apple Watch

Do any of the following:

- Use the playback controls in the Remote app ⏺.
- Turn the Digital Crown to adjust volume.
- Tap 📶, then choose an audio destination.

Choose a media library to play from

- If you added more than one library: Tap the one you want when you open the Remote app ⏺ on your Apple Watch.

- If you're already playing music: Tap < at the top left of the playback controls, then tap the library.

Remove a media library

1. Open the Remote app ▶ on your Apple Watch.
2. Touch and hold a device.
3. When the device icon jiggles, tap X to remove it, then tap Remove.

Control Apple TV with Apple Watch

You can use Apple Watch as a remote control for an Apple TV when you're connected to the same Wi-Fi network.

Pair your Apple Watch with Apple TV

If your iPhone has never joined the Wi-Fi network that the Apple TV is on, join it now, then follow these steps:

1. Open the Remote app ▶ on your Apple Watch.
2. Tap your Apple TV. If you don't see it listed, tap Add Device.
3. On the Apple TV, go to Settings > Remotes and Devices > Remote App and Devices, then select Apple Watch.
4. Enter the passcode displayed on your Apple Watch.

When the pairing icon appears next to Apple Watch, it's ready to control the Apple TV.

Use your Apple Watch to control Apple TV

Make sure the Apple TV is awake, then follow these steps:

1. Open the Remote app ▶ on your Apple Watch.
2. Choose your Apple TV, then swipe up, down, left, or right to move through the Apple TV menu options.
3. Tap to choose the selected item.

4. Tap the Play/Pause button to pause or resume playback.
5. Tap the Menu button to go back, or touch and hold it to return to the main menu.

To start the screen saver, go to the top-left corner of the Home Screen on your Apple TV, then tap the Menu button.

Unpair and remove Apple TV

1. On the Apple TV, go to Settings > Remotes and Devices > Remote App and Devices.
2. Tap your Apple Watch under Remote App, then tap Unpair Device.
3. Open the Remote app on your Apple Watch and, when the "lost connection" message appears, tap Remove.

Track your sleep with Apple Watch

With the Sleep app on Apple Watch, you can create bedtime schedules to help you meet your sleep goals. Wear your watch to bed, and Apple Watch can track your sleep. When you wake up, open the Sleep app to learn how much sleep you got and see your sleep trends over the past 14 days.

If your Apple Watch is charged less than 30 percent before you go to bed, you're prompted to charge it. In the morning, just glance at the greeting to see how much charge remains.

You can create multiple schedules—for example, one for weekdays and another for weekends. For each schedule, you can set up the following:
- A sleep goal (how many hours of sleep you want to get)
- What time you want to go to bed and wake up
- An alarm sound to wake you up
- When to turn on sleep mode, which limits distractions before you go to bed and protects your sleep after you're in bed
- Sleep tracking, which uses your motion to detect sleep when Apple Watch is in sleep mode and worn to bed

Tip: To exit sleep mode, first turn the Digital Crown to unlock. Then swipe up to open Control Center and tap .

Set up Sleep on Apple Watch

1. Open the Sleep app on your Apple Watch.

2. Follow the onscreen instructions.

You can also open the Health app on iPhone, tap Browse, tap Sleep, then tap Get Started (under Set Up Sleep).

Change or turn off your next wake-up alarm

1. Open the Sleep app on your Apple Watch.
2. Tap your current bedtime.
3. To set a new wake-up time, tap the wake-up time, turn the Digital Crown to set a new time, then tap .
   If you don't want your Apple Watch to wake you in the morning, turn off Alarm.

The changes apply only to your next wake-up alarm, after which your normal schedule resumes.

Note: You can also turn off the next wake-up alarm in the Alarms app . Just tap the alarm that appears under Sleep | Wake up, then tap Skip for Tonight.

Change or add a sleep schedule

1. Open the Sleep app on your Apple Watch.
2. Tap Full Schedule, then do one of the following:
    - Change a sleep schedule: Tap the current schedule.
    - Add a sleep schedule: Tap Add Schedule.
    - Change your sleep goal: Tap Sleep Goal, then set the amount of time you want to sleep.
    - Change Wind Down time: Tap Wind Down, then set the amount of time you want sleep mode to be active before bedtime.
    To reduce distractions before your scheduled bedtime, sleep mode turns on during Wind Down. Sleep mode turns off the watch display and turns on Do Not Disturb.
3. Do any of the following:
    - Set the days for your schedule: Tap your schedule, then tap the area below Active On. Choose days, then tap Done.
    - Adjust your wake time and bedtime: Tap Wake Up or Bedtime, turn the Digital Crown to set a new time, then tap Set.
    - Set the alarm options: Turn Alarm off or on and tap Sound to choose an alarm sound.
    - Remove or cancel a sleep schedule: Tap Delete Schedule (at the bottom of the screen) to remove an existing schedule, or tap Cancel (at the top of the screen) to cancel creating a new one.

Change sleep options

1. Open the Settings app on your Apple Watch.
2. Tap Sleep, then tap Sleep Focus to adjust these settings:
    - Turn On at Wind Down: By default, Sleep Focus begins at the wind down time you set in the Sleep

app. If you'd prefer to control Sleep Focus manually in Control Center, turn this option off.
    - Sleep Screen: Your Apple Watch display and iPhone Lock Screen are simplified to reduce distractions.
    - Show time: Show the date and time on your iPhone and Apple Watch during sleep mode.
3. Turn Sleep Tracking and Charging Reminders on or off. When Sleep Tracking is on, your Apple Watch tracks your sleep and adds sleep data to the Health app on your iPhone. Turn on Charging Reminders to have your Apple Watch remind you to charge your watch before your wind down time and notify you when your watch is fully charged.

You can also change these and other sleep options on your iPhone. Open the Health app on iPhone, tap Browse, then go to Sleep > Options.

View your recent sleep history

1. Open the Sleep app on your Apple Watch.
2. Scroll down to see the amount of sleep you got the night before and your sleep average over the last 14 days.

To see your sleep history on iPhone, open the Health app on iPhone, tap Browse, then tap Sleep.

Review your sleeping respiratory rate

In watchOS 8, your Apple Watch can track your breathing rate as you sleep, which can give you greater insight into your overall health. After wearing your watch to bed, follow these steps:

1. Open the Health app on your iPhone, tap Browse, then tap Respiratory.
2. Tap Respiratory Rate, then tap Show More Respiratory Rate Data.
   The Sleep entry shows the range of your respiratory rate as you've slept.

Note: Respiratory Rate measurements are not intended for medical use.

Track stocks on Apple Watch

Use the Stocks app ![icon] on Apple Watch to see info on the stocks you follow on your iPhone.

Ask Siri. Say something like: "What was today's closing price for Apple stock?"

Add and remove stocks

Your Apple Watch displays the stocks found in the Stocks app on your iPhone, but you can add and remove stocks right on your Apple Watch. Just open the Stocks app ![icon] on your Apple Watch to:

- Add a stock: Scroll to the bottom of the screen, then tap Add Stock. Type the stock name, or use Scribble or dictation to enter the stock name. Tap the name of the stock in the list. To use Scribble on Apple Watch Series 7, swipe up from the bottom of the screen, then tap Scribble.
  Note: Scribble is not available in all languages.
- Remove a stock: Swipe left on the stock you want to remove, then tap X.

To reorder stocks on your Apple Watch, open the Stocks app on your iPhone, tap Edit, then drag them into your preferred position. The order changes on your Apple Watch to match.

See stock data on Apple Watch

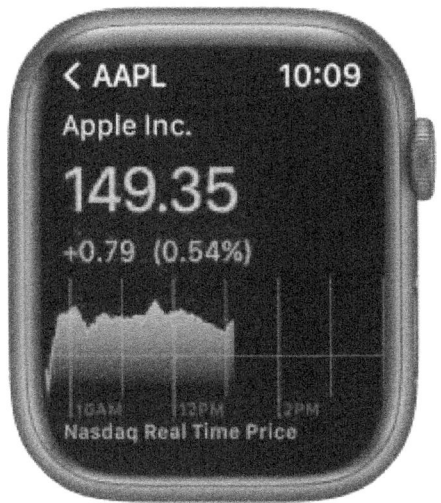

1. Open the Stocks app on your Apple Watch.
2. Tap a stock in the list.
3. Tap < in the top-left corner to return to the stocks list, or turn the Digital Crown to scroll to the next stock in the list.

Choose the stock shown on the Siri watch face

1. Open the Settings app on your Apple Watch.
2. Go to Stocks > Selected Stock, then choose a stock.

Choose the data you see

1. Open the Settings app on your Apple Watch.
2. Go to Stocks > Data Metric, then tap Current Price, Points Change, Percentage Change, or Market Cap.
   The selected data metric appears on the Siri watch face and any Stocks complications.

Tip: You can also open the Stocks app on your iPhone, then tap the price change for any stock to see percentage change or market cap.

Switch to Stocks on iPhone

1. Open the Stocks app ![icon] on your Apple Watch.
2. On iPhone, open the App Switcher. (On an iPhone with Face ID, swipe up from the bottom edge and pause; on an iPhone with a Home button, double-click the Home button.)
3. Tap the button that appears at the bottom of the screen to open Stocks.

Time events with a stopwatch on Apple Watch

Time events with accuracy and ease. Apple Watch can time full events (up to 11 hours, 55 minutes) and keep track of lap or split times, then show the results as a list, a graph, or live on your watch face. The Chronograph and Chronograph Pro watch faces have the stopwatch built in.

Open a stopwatch

Open the Stopwatch app ![icon] on your Apple Watch, or tap the stopwatch on your watch face (if you've added it or you're using the Chronograph or Chronograph Pro watch face).

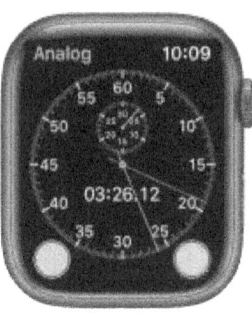

Start, stop, and reset the stopwatch

Open the Stopwatch app on your Apple Watch, then do any of the following:
- Start: Tap the Start button (the green button on the analog stopwatch).
- Record a lap: Tap the Lap button (the white button on the analog stopwatch).
- Record the final time: Tap the Stop button (the red button on the analog stopwatch).
- Reset the stopwatch: With the stopwatch stopped, tap the Reset button (the white button on the analog stopwatch).

The timing continues even if you switch back to the watch face or open other apps.

Review results on the display you used for timing, or change displays to analyze your lap times and fastest/slowest laps (marked with green and red) in the format you prefer. If the display includes a list of lap times, turn the Digital Crown to scroll.

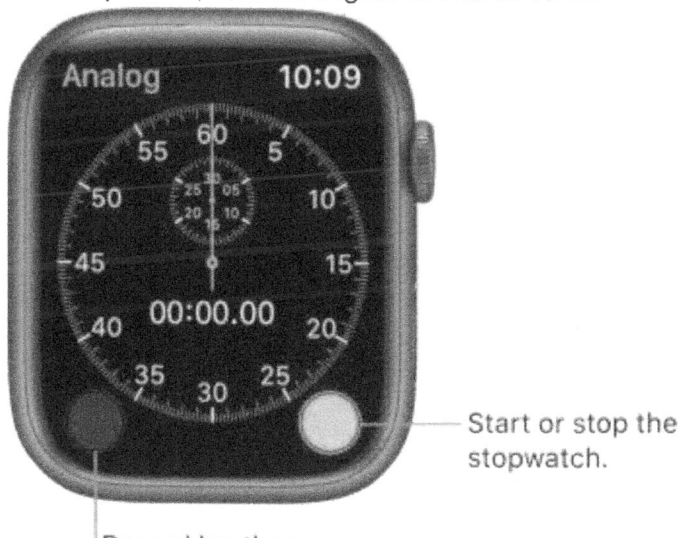

Start or stop the stopwatch.

Record lap times.

325

Change the stopwatch format

1. Open the Stopwatch app on your Apple Watch.
2. Tap the display to cycle through Digital, Analog, Graph, and Hybrid formats.

Set timers on Apple Watch

The Timers app on Apple Watch can help you keep track of time. With watchOS 8, you can set multiple timers that track time for up to 24 hours.
Ask Siri. Say something like: "Set a timer for 20 minutes."

Quickly set a timer

1. Open the Timers app on your Apple Watch.
2. Tap a timer duration to start the timer.
3. Scroll down to choose a recent or custom time.

When a timer goes off, you can tap Repeat to start a timer of the same duration.

Pause or end a timer

1. With a timer running, open the Timers app ⓢ on your Apple Watch.
2. Tap ❚❚ to pause, tap ▶ to resume, or tap ✕ to end.

Create a custom timer

1. Open the Timers app ⓢ on your Apple Watch.
2. Scroll down, then tap Custom.
3. Tap hours, minutes, or seconds; turn the Digital Crown to adjust.
4. Tap Start.

Tap hours, minutes, or seconds, then turn the Digital Crown.

Your Apple Watch displays the last several custom timers under Recents.

Create multiple timers

1. Open the Timers app on your Apple Watch.
2. Create and start a timer.
   Tip: To assign a label such as "Pizza" to a timer, use Siri to create the timer. Raise your Apple Watch, then say something like "Set a 12 minute pizza timer."
3. Tap < to return to the Timers screen, then create and start another timer.

All your running timers appear on the Timers screen. Tap ‖ to pause a timer, and tap ▶ to resume.
To delete a running or paused timer that appears on the Timers screen, swipe left, then tap X.

Tips

In the Tips app , see collections of tips that help you get the most from your Apple Watch.

Get Tips

Use the Tips app 💡 on your Apple Watch to discover new features in watchOS, learn how to customize your watch, and much more.

View tips on Apple Watch

1. Open the Tips app 💡 on your Apple Watch.
2. Tap a tips collection, then scroll up to read the tip.
3. If a tip includes a Try It button, tap the button to see how the tip works on your Apple Watch.
4. Swipe left to see the next tip.

Record and play voice memos on Apple Watch

Use the Voice Memos app on Apple Watch to record personal notes.

Record a voice memo

1. Open the Voice Memos app on your Apple Watch.
2. Tap .
3. Tap to end the recording.

Play a voice memo

1. Open the Voice Memos app on your Apple Watch.
2. Tap a recording on the Voice Memos screen, then tap to play it.
3. To delete the recording, tap , then tap Delete.

Voice memos you record on your Apple Watch automatically sync to your Mac, iPad, and any iOS devices where you're signed in with the same Apple ID.

Use Walkie-Talkie on Apple Watch

Walkie-Talkie is a fun, simple way to connect with another user with a compatible Apple Watch. Like using a real walkie-talkie, press a button to talk, and release to listen when you're ready for them to reply. Walkie-Talkie requires that both participants have connectivity—through a Bluetooth connection to the iPhone, Wi-Fi, or cellular.
Note: Walkie-Talkie is not available in all regions.

Invite a friend to use Walkie-Talkie

1. Open the Walkie-Talkie app on your Apple Watch for the first time.
2. Scroll down the list of contacts, then tap a name to send an invitation.

When your contact accepts the invitation, you can start a Walkie-Talkie conversation when both of you are available.
To add another contact, tap Add Friends on the Walkie-Talkie screen, then choose a contact.

Have a Walkie-Talkie conversation

1. Open the Walkie-Talkie app on your Apple Watch.
2. Tap your friend's name.
3. Touch and hold the Talk button, then speak.
   If your friend has made themselves available, Walkie-Talkie opens on their Apple Watch and they'll hear what you said.

To adjust the volume while you're talking, turn the Digital Crown.

Talk with a single tap

If you have difficulty keeping your finger pressed on the Talk button, you can use a single tap to talk.

1. Open the Settings app  on your Apple Watch.
2. Tap Accessibility, then, below Walkie-Talkie, turn on Tap to Talk.

When this is on, tap once to talk, then tap again when you're finished talking.
You can also open the Apple Watch app on your iPhone, tap My Watch, tap Accessibility, then, below Walkie-Talkie, turn on Tap to Talk.

Remove contacts

In the Walkie-Talkie app on your Apple Watch, swipe left on a contact, then tap X.

Make yourself unavailable

1. Touch and hold the bottom of the screen, then swipe up to open Control Center.

2. Scroll up, then tap .

Or, in the Walkie-Talkie app on your Apple Watch, scroll to the top of the screen, then turn off Walkie-Talkie.
Turning on theater mode also makes you unavailable for Walkie-Talkie.

Wallet and Apple Pay

About Wallet on Apple Watch

The Wallet app on your Apple Watch lets you easily access the cards, passes, and keys you added to the Wallet app on your iPhone. Supported cards and passes include the following:
- Cards for Apple Pay (not available in all regions): Apple Cash, credit, debit, store, transit, and prepaid cards
- Passes: Boarding passes, movie tickets, coupons, rewards cards, and more

- Keys: Car keys, home keys

Apple Pay on Apple Watch

Apple Pay offers an easy, secure, and private way to pay on your Apple Watch. With your cards stored in the Wallet app on your iPhone and added to Apple Watch, you can use Apple Pay in the following ways:
- Contactless payments and apps: Use the credit, debit, and prepaid cards you add to the Wallet app to make purchases in stores that accept contactless payments, and in apps that support Apple Pay.
  Once you set up Apple Pay in the Apple Watch app on your iPhone, you're ready to make store purchases—even when you don't have your iPhone with you. (Apple Pay isn't available in all regions.)
- Person to person payments: In watchOS 4 and later you can easily and securely send and request money, right in Messages or by using Siri.
- Transit cards: You can add transit cards; they appear at the top of the collection in the Wallet app, above your passes.

Note: You can't use Apple Pay, and any cards you added to Wallet are removed, if you unpair your Apple Watch or turn off your passcode. If you turn off wrist detection, you must enter your passcode each time you use Apple Pay.

Set up Apple Pay on Apple Watch

Add a card to Apple Watch

1. Open the Apple Watch app on your iPhone.
2. Tap My Watch, then tap Wallet & Apple Pay.

3. If you have cards on your other Apple devices, or cards that you recently removed, tap Add next to a card you want to add, then enter the card's CVV.
4. For any other card, tap Add Card, then follow the onscreen instructions.

Your card issuer may require additional steps to verify your identity.

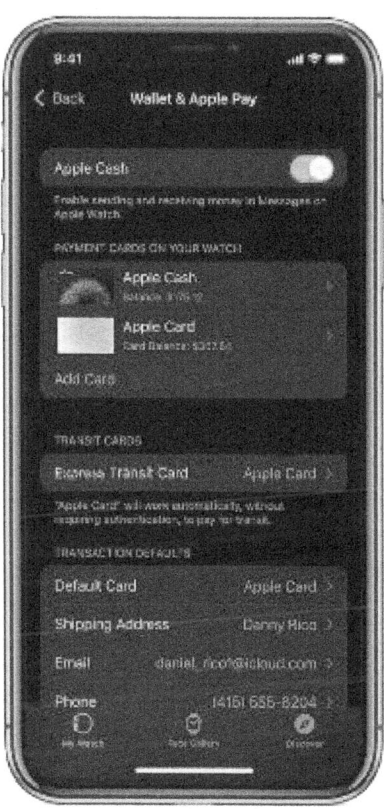

Choose your default card

1. Open the Apple Watch app on your iPhone.
2. Tap My Watch, tap Wallet & Apple Pay, tap Default Card, then select the card.

Reorder payment cards

Open the Wallet app on your Apple Watch, touch and hold a card, then drag it to a new position.
On a managed Apple Watch, you can touch and drag both payment cards and passes.

Remove a card from Apple Pay

1. Open the Wallet app on your Apple Watch.
2. Tap to select a card.
3. Scroll down, then tap Delete.

You can also open the Apple Watch app on your iPhone, tap My Watch, tap Wallet & Apple Pay, tap the card, then tap Remove This Card.

Find the Device Account Number for a card

When you make a payment with your Apple Watch, the Device Account Number of the card is sent with the payment to the merchant. To find the last four digits of this number, follow these steps:

1. Open the Wallet app on your Apple Watch.
2. Tap to select a card, then tap Card Information.

Note: If you select an Apple Card, you must enter your Apple Watch password before you can see the card details.
You can also open the Apple Watch app on your iPhone, tap My Watch, tap Wallet & Apple Pay, then tap the card.

Change your default transaction details

You can change your in-app transaction details—including default card, shipping address, email, and phone number.

1. Open the Apple Watch app on your iPhone.

2. Tap My Watch, tap Wallet & Apple Pay, then scroll down to see Transaction Defaults.
3. Tap an item to edit it.

If your Apple Watch is lost or stolen

If your Apple Watch is lost or stolen, you can:
- Put your Apple Watch in lost mode to suspend the ability to pay from your Apple Watch.
- Sign in to appleid.apple.com using your Apple ID and remove the ability to pay using your credit and debit cards in Wallet.
  In the Devices area, choose the device, then click Remove All under Apple Pay.
- Call the issuers of your cards.

Make purchases with Apple Watch

Pay for a purchase in a store with Apple Watch

1. Double-click the side button.
2. Scroll to choose a card.
3. Hold your Apple Watch within a few centimeters of the contactless card reader, with the display facing the

reader.

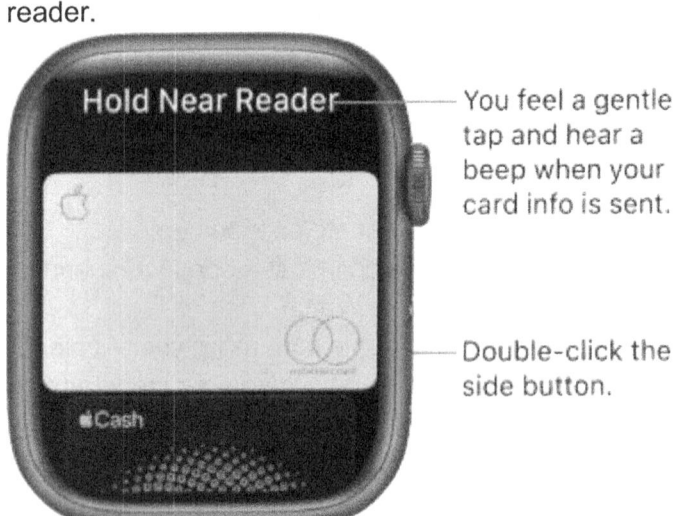

You feel a gentle tap and hear a beep when your card info is sent.

Double-click the side button.

A gentle tap and beep confirm that the payment information was sent. You receive a notification in Notification Center when the transaction is confirmed.

For cards that support it, you also receive a notification for purchases made with any card you've added to Wallet, even if you didn't make it with your Apple Watch, iPad, or an iOS device.

You can turn off notifications and history for individual cards within Wallet. Just open the Apple Watch app on your iPhone, tap My Watch, go to Wallet & Apple Pay, tap a card, tap Transactions, then turn Show History and Allow Notifications on or off.

Make a purchase within an app

1. When you're shopping in an app on your Apple Watch, choose the Apple Pay option during checkout.
2. Review the payment, shipping, and billing information, then double-click the side button to pay with your Apple Watch.

Send, receive, and request money with Apple Watch (U.S. only)

In addition to using Apple Cash to make purchases in stores, you can use it to send money to friends and family. It's as simple as sending a message or using Siri. You can request and receive money just as easily.

Note: Apple Cash isn't available in all regions.

Send a payment from Apple Watch

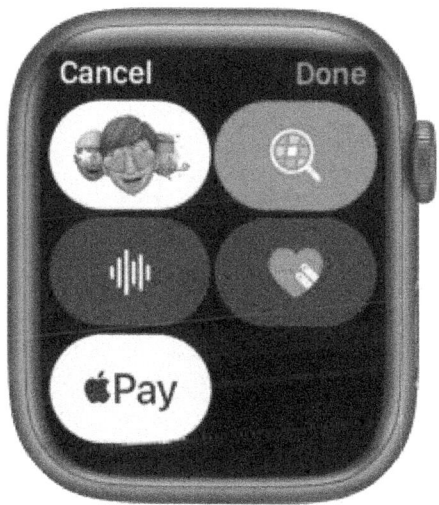

Ask Siri. Say something like "Send Claire $25." If you have more than one Claire among your contacts, you're asked to choose one.

1. Open the Messages app on your Apple Watch.
2. Start a new conversation or select an existing conversation, tap , then tap Pay .
3. Turn the Digital Crown or tap the plus or minus button to select a whole dollar amount.

   To send an amount not in whole dollars—$10.95, for

example—tap the dollar amount, tap after the decimal, then turn the Digital Crown to choose a value.
4. Tap Pay, confirm the payment, then double-click the side button to send.

When the payment is complete, a confirmation message appears. The payment first draws from your Apple Cash balance. If your Apple Cash balance is insufficient, the remaining balance is paid with a debit card.

Cancel a payment

You can cancel a payment as long as the recipient hasn't already accepted it.

1. Open the Wallet app on your Apple Watch.
2. Tap to select a card, then scroll the list of transactions.
3. Tap the unpaid transaction, then tap Cancel Payment.

You can also open the Apple Watch app on your iPhone, tap My Watch, tap Wallet & Apple Pay, then tap your Apple Cash card. Tap Transactions, tap the unpaid transaction, then tap Cancel Payment.

Request a payment from Apple Watch

You can request payment with Siri or a message.

- Use Siri: Say something like "Ask Nisha to send me $30."

- Send a message: Open Messages on your Apple Watch, start a new conversation or select an existing conversation, tap , then tap . Swipe left on the Pay button, enter an amount, then tap Request.

When you use Apple Cash for the first time, you must agree to the terms and conditions on your iPhone before accepting the payment. Subsequent payments are automatically accepted unless you choose to manually accept each payment. To change this setting, open Wallet on your iPhone, tap the Apple Cash card, tap , then tap Manually Accept Payments.

Respond to a payment request on Apple Watch

1. Tap the Pay button that appears in the payment request in Messages.
   Turn the Digital Crown or tap buttons on the screen to change the amount, if desired.
2. Tap Pay, then double-click the side button to make the payment.

See transaction details on Apple Watch

- See transactions in Messages: Open the Messages app on your Apple Watch, then tap an Apple Pay message to view a transaction summary.

- See transactions in Wallet: Open the Wallet app on your Apple Watch, tap a card, then scroll to see a list of transactions. Tap a transaction for details.

341

To view all your Apple Cash transactions on your iPhone, open the Apple Watch app on your iPhone, tap My Watch, then tap Wallet & Apple Pay. Tap your Apple Cash card, then tap Transactions. To receive a PDF statement of your Apple Cash transaction history by email, tap your Apple Cash card, tap Transactions, swipe to the bottom, then tap Request Transaction Statement.

Manage Apple Cash with Apple Watch (U.S. only)

When you receive money in Messages, it's added to your Apple Cash card in Wallet. You can use Apple Cash right away wherever you would use Apple Pay—in stores, in apps, and on the web. You can also transfer your Apple Cash balance to your bank account. If you're the organizer for your family sharing group, you can set up Apple Cash Family for family members.

Manage Apple Cash payment features

Open the Apple Watch app on your iPhone, tap My Watch, then tap Wallet & Apple Pay. There you can do the following:

- Tap the Apple Cash card to set up Apple Cash
  Tip: If you already have Apple Cash set up on another device, it will be ready to use on your Apple Watch without further setup.
- Enable or disable the Apple Cash card, and the ability to send and receive money, on this device
- See your suggested PIN
  You can also see your suggested PIN on your Apple Watch.

  Open the Wallet app , tap your Apple Cash card, scroll to the bottom, then tap Card Information.
  Apple Cash doesn't require a PIN because every payment is authenticated by Face ID, Touch ID, or a secure passcode. However, some terminals may still require you to enter a four-digit code to complete the transaction.

- View your Apple Cash balance
  Tip: To view your Apple Cash balance on your Apple Watch, open the Wallet app , then tap the Apple Cash card. Or double-click the side button, then scroll to the Apple Cash card.
- Manage Apple Cash Family for family members under 18.

Add and use passes in Wallet on Apple Watch

Use the Wallet app on your Apple Watch to keep your boarding passes, event tickets, coupons, student ID cards, and more in one place for easy access. Passes in Wallet on your iPhone automatically sync to your Apple Watch. Use a pass on your Apple Watch to check in for a flight, redeem a coupon, or get into your dorm.

Set options for your passes

1. Open the Apple Watch app on your iPhone.
2. Tap My Watch, then tap Wallet & Apple Pay.

Add a pass

To add a pass, do one of the following:
- Follow the instructions in the email sent by the issuer.
- Open the pass issuer's app, if they have one.
- Tap Add in the notification.
- Tap a pass sent to you in Messages.

Use a pass

You can use a variety of passes on your Apple Watch.
- If a notification for a pass appears on your Apple Watch: Tap the notification to display the pass. You might have to scroll to get to the barcode.

- If you have a barcode pass: Double-click the side button, scroll to your pass, then present the barcode to the scanner.

  You can also open the Wallet app on your Apple Watch, select the pass, then scan it.

If a pass changes—for example, the gate on your boarding pass—your pass updates on both iPhone and Apple Watch.

Get pass information

To get more information about a pass—a flight's departure and arrival time, for example—do the following:

1. Open the Wallet app on your Apple Watch.
2. Tap a pass, scroll down, then tap Pass Information.

Use a contactless pass or student ID card

With a contactless pass or student ID card, you can use your Apple Watch to present your pass or card at a contactless reader.

- If you have a contactless pass and a notification appears: Tap the notification. If there's no notification, double-click the side button, and hold your Apple Watch within a few centimeters of the reader, with the display facing the reader.
- If you have a student ID card: On supported campuses, hold your Apple Watch within a few centimeters of the reader, with the display facing the reader, until Apple Watch vibrates; there's no need to double-click the side button.

Reorder passes

On an Apple Watch that you set up for yourself, open the Wallet app , then touch and drag transit, access, and payment cards and passes to arrange them. The payment card you drag to the top position becomes the default payment card.

On a managed Apple Watch, you can touch and drag all pass types to reorder them.

Remove a pass you're finished with

1. Double-click the side button, then tap the pass.
2. Scroll down, then tap Delete.

You can also open the Wallet app on your iPhone, tap the pass, tap ●●●, then tap Remove Pass.

When you remove a pass from one device, it's also removed from the other.

See expired passes

To keep clutter under control, your Apple Watch hides passes that have expired. You can view expired passes by following these steps:

1. Open the Wallet app on your Apple Watch.
2. Scroll to the bottom of the screen, then tap View [number] Expired Passes.
3. Tap a pass, then view its details.
   You can also choose to unhide, share, or delete it.

To always show expired passes, open the Settings app on your Apple Watch, tap Wallet & Apple Pay, then turn off Hide Expired Passes.

Use rewards cards on Apple Watch

If you have a rewards card from a supporting merchant, you can add it to Wallet, then present it to a contactless reader as part of your transaction using your Apple Watch.

Add a rewards card to Apple Watch

You can add a rewards card from an email or website link, a message, or from a notification sent to your iPhone.

- Email or website link: Look for an "Add to Apple Wallet" link. Tap the link to add the rewards card to Wallet.

345

- Notification: After paying with Apple Pay and providing your rewards card information, you may get a notification on your iPhone that lets you add that card as a rewards card. Tap the notification, then tap Add.
- Message: Tap a card sent to you in Messages.

Use a rewards card on Apple Watch

When you're prompted to provide your rewards information (and you see the Apple Pay logo), follow these steps:
1. Double-click the side button.
2. Hold your Apple Watch within a few centimeters of the contactless reader, with the display facing the reader.

By default, Apple Watch displays the rewards card so you don't need to scroll to it.

Pay with Apple Watch on Mac

On websites that support Apple Pay, you can start a purchase in Safari on your Mac and complete the payment with your Apple Watch.

To confirm payments on your Apple Watch, you need to be signed in to iCloud with the same Apple ID on your iPhone and your Mac. Your Apple Watch and Mac need to be near each other and connected to Wi-Fi.

Shop on your Mac and pay on Apple Watch

1. When you're shopping online in Safari on your Mac, choose the Apple Pay option during checkout.
2. Review the payment, shipping, and billing information on your Mac and ensure that it displays "Confirm with Apple Watch."
3. If it does, double-click the side button to pay with your Apple Watch.
   If it doesn't, from your Mac, choose a card you use on your Apple Watch.

Turn off Apple Pay payments on Mac

By default, you can use your Apple Watch to confirm Apple Pay payments made on your Mac. If you don't want to confirm payments with your Apple Watch, follow these steps:
1. Open the Apple Watch app on your iPhone.
2. Tap My Watch, tap Wallet & Apple Pay, then turn off Allow Payments on Mac.

Use transit cards with Apple Watch

On your Apple Watch, you can use a transit card with Apple Pay where accepted to pay your fare.
Note: Apple Pay may not be available in all areas, and Apple Pay features may vary by area.
If a preferred card is not required by a transit system, you can use a payment card in Wallet to pay for transit without double-clicking the side button. To choose a card for Express Transit and use it to pay for transit, follow these steps:

1. Open the Settings app on your Apple Watch.
2. Tap Wallet & Apple Pay, then tap Express Mode.
3. Tap the card you want to use, then enter your Apple Watch passcode.
4. As you approach a fare gate or board the bus, make sure your Apple Watch is turned on (it doesn't need to be connected to a network).
5. Hold your Apple Watch display within a few centimeters of the middle of the contactless reader until you feel a vibration. You see Done and a checkmark on the display.

You can also open the Apple Watch app on your iPhone, tap My Watch, tap Wallet & Apple Pay, then tap Express Transit Card. Under Payment Cards, tap the card you want to use, then enter the Apple Watch passcode on your watch.

Unlock your car, home, and hotel room with keys in Wallet on Apple Watch

In the Wallet app on your Apple Watch, you can store keys to your car, home, and hotel room.

Unlock and start your car

Unlock, lock, and start your car just by being near a compatible car. Ultra Wideband provides precise spatial awareness, ensuring that you won't be able to lock your iPhone or Apple Watch in your car or start your vehicle when iPhone or Apple Watch isn't inside.

To add car keys to your Apple Watch, follow these steps:

1. Add the car keys to the Wallet app on the iPhone that's paired with your Apple Watch.
2. Open the Apple Watch app on your iPhone.
3. Tap My Watch, then tap Wallet & Apple Pay.
4. Tap Add next to the card for your car key.

To unlock and start your car, do one of the following:

- If you have a car that supports Ultra Wideband technology, approach your car while wearing your Apple Watch to unlock it. Press the car's start button to start the car.
  Note: If the car doesn't support Ultra Wideband technology but can use a car key stored in the Wallet app, unlock and start the car just as you would with Apple Watch.

Unlock your home

With a compatible HomeKit door lock, you can store a home key in the Wallet app on your compatible iPhone and Apple Watch. Then unlock your door by placing your iPhone or Apple Watch near the lock.

To set up a home key, follow these steps:

1. Add the lock to the Home app on your iPhone.
2. Choose an unlocking option.

- Enable Express Mode: Unlock the door just by holding your iPhone near the lock.
  To enable Express Mode on your Apple Watch, after adding the home key, open the Settings app on your Apple Watch, go to Wallet & Apple Pay > Express Mode, then turn on Express Mode for your home key.
- Require Authentication: Similar to paying for a purchase with your iPhone or Apple Watch, double-click the side button, then hold your device near the lock.

3. Choose automations such as Lock After Door Closes and Lock When Leaving Home.

Unlock your hotel room

You can add a hotel key to Wallet from the participating hotel provider's app, use it to check in without going to the lobby, and use your iPhone and Apple Watch to unlock your room. Wallet automatically archives your pass after you check out to keep passes organized as you travel.

Use vaccination cards in Wallet on Apple Watch

With iOS 15, you can securely download verifiable COVID-19 vaccination and lab records and store them in the Health app on your iPhone. Once downloaded, you can easily add the vaccination record to the Wallet app on iPhone. That vaccination record is then automatically added to your Apple Watch (iOS 15.1 and watchOS 8.1 and later; supported by certain healthcare providers and authorities). Present the card when you need to show proof of vaccination.

Show a vaccination card

On your Apple Watch, double-click the side button, scroll to the vaccination card, tap it, then present the QR code to the reader. You may be asked to verify your identity by showing a photo ID, such as your driver's license.

Note: Your vaccination card may contain sensitive information such as your birthdate. To review the information stored on your card, scroll up, then tap Pass Information.

Remove a vaccination card

1. Double-click the side button, then tap the vaccination card.
2. Tap Remove.

Note: Removing a vaccination card from Apple Watch also removes it from the Wallet app on your iPhone. However, it doesn't remove the corresponding vaccination record from the Health app on iPhone.

Check the weather on Apple Watch

Ask Siri. Say something like: "What's tomorrow's forecast for Honolulu?"

Check weather conditions

- See the current temperature and conditions for the day: Open the Weather app on your Apple Watch. Tap a city, then tap the display to cycle through hourly forecasts of rain, conditions, or temperature.

Turn to see more weather information.

Tap to see temperature or precipitation forecast.

- See air quality, UV index, and wind speed information, and a 10-day forecast: Tap a city, then scroll down. Tap < in the top-left corner to return to the list of cities.

Note: Air quality readings not available in all regions.

Add a city

1. Open the Weather app on your Apple Watch.
2. Scroll to the bottom of the list of cities, then tap Add City.

3. Type the city name, or use Scribble or dictation to enter the city name.
   To use Scribble on Apple Watch Series 7, swipe up from the bottom of the screen, then tap Scribble.
   Note: Scribble is not available in all languages.
4. Tap Done, then tap the city name in the list of results.

The Weather app on your iPhone shows the same cities, in the same order, that you add to the Weather app on your Apple Watch.

Remove a city

1. Open the Weather app on your Apple Watch.
2. In the list of cities, swipe the city you want to remove to the left, then tap X.

The city is removed from your Apple Watch and iPhone.

Choose your default city

1. Open the Settings app on your Apple Watch.
2. Tap Weather, tap Default City, then choose a city.

You can also open the Apple Watch app on your iPhone, tap My Watch, then go to Weather > Default City.

Conditions for that city are shown on the watch face, if you've added weather to the face.

See weather advisories

When a significant weather event is predicted, a notification may appear at the top of the Weather app. To learn more about the event, tap Learn More.

Workout

Work out with Apple Watch

The Workout app on your Apple Watch gives you tools to manage your individual workout sessions. You can set specific goals, such as time, distance, or calories, and your Apple Watch tracks your progress, nudges you along the way, and summarizes your results. You can also create a workout that contains multiple activities, such as a run, swim, and bike ride. You use the Fitness app on your iPhone to review your complete workout history.
Ask Siri. Say something like:
- "Start a 30-minute run"
- "Go for a 5-mile walk"
- "Start a 300-calorie bike ride"

Start a workout on Apple Watch

Start a workout

Tap to set workout goals.

Turn the Digital Crown to choose another workout.

1. Open the Workout app  on your Apple Watch.
2. Turn the Digital Crown to the workout you want to do.
   Tap Add Workout at the bottom of the screen for sessions like kickboxing or surfing.
3. To set a goal, tap ● ● ● .
4. Choose a calorie, time, distance, or open goal (meaning that you've set no particular goal but still want your Apple Watch to track your workout).
5. Turn the Digital Crown or tap + / – to set.
6. When you're ready to go, tap Start.

As you use the app and choose workouts, the order of workouts reflects your preferences.

Tip: To start a workout without setting a goal, just tap the workout type you're going for—a run, walk, or stair stepper.

Set a target pace for an outdoor run workout

Choose a target pace for an outdoor run, and your Apple Watch will tap you on the wrist to let you know if you're ahead or behind a set pace after one mile.

1. Open the Workout app on your Apple Watch.
2. Turn the Digital Crown to scroll to Outdoor Run, then tap ●●●.
3. Tap Set Alert, then tap OK.
4. Adjust the target time for running a mile—9 minutes, for example—then tap Done.
5. Choose Average or Rolling, then tap <.
   Average is your average pace for all the miles you've run.
   Rolling is your one mile pace taken at that moment.

Your Apple Watch remembers your target pace across workouts. To change it, choose Outdoor Run, tap ●●●, then tap the currently set pace to edit it.

Combine multiple activities in a single workout

1. Open the Workout app 🏃 on your Apple Watch.
2. Begin your first workout—an outdoor run, for example.
3. When you're ready to start a different activity—like an outdoor bike ride—swipe right, tap ➕ , then choose the workout.
4. When you finish all your activities, swipe right, then tap End.
5. Turn the Digital Crown to scroll through the results summary.
6. Scroll to the bottom and tap Done to save the workout.

Tip: When you do an outdoor workout, you can leave your iPhone at home—the built-in GPS gives you accurate distance measurements.

Adjust Apple Watch during a workout

Your Apple Watch can be an active partner even during your workout. While working out you can do the following:

- Check your progress: Raise your wrist to see your workout stats, including your goal completion ring, elapsed time, average pace, distance covered, calories consumed, and heart rate. (There's no goal ring if you haven't set a goal.) In watchOS 8, you can hear metrics like pace, speed, time elapsed, pause, resume, and progress against activity rings and goals. To turn Voice Feedback on or off, open the Settings app ⚙️ on your Apple Watch, tap Workouts, then tap Voice Feedback.
  Using the Apple Watch app, you can choose the metrics that appear during your workout. For example, you can choose to see your current elevation for outdoor run, outdoor walk, hiking, and outdoor cycle workouts.
- Pause and resume the workout: To pause the workout at any time, press the side button and the Digital Crown at the same time. For all workouts except swimming workouts you

can also swipe right on the workout screen, then tap Pause. To continue, tap Resume.
- Mark a segment of your workout: Double-tap the display to indicate a segment of your workout. You briefly see the stats for that segment. To see all your segment stats after the workout, open the Fitness app on your iPhone, tap Workouts, tap the workout, then scroll down.
- Rock out while you work out: During a workout, swipe left to the Now Playing screen to choose music and control the volume on your Bluetooth headphones. To choose a playlist that plays automatically when you begin a workout, open the Apple Watch app on your iPhone, then tap My Watch. Tap Workout, tap Workout Playlist, then choose a playlist.
Note: Music or other audio you're already listening to when you begin your workout continues to play.

End and review your workout on Apple Watch

End the workout on Apple Watch

When you reach your goal, you hear a tone and feel a vibration. If you're feeling good and want to continue, go ahead—your Apple Watch continues to collect data until you tell it to stop. When you're ready to end your workout:
1. Swipe right, then tap End.
2. Turn the Digital Crown to scroll through the results summary, then tap Done at the bottom.

Tip: The heart rate sensor stays active for three minutes after you end a workout to measure your heart rate recovery. After completing a workout, you can tap the heart icon on your workout summary to view your recovery in real time.

Review your workout history

1. Open the Fitness app on your iPhone.
2. Tap Summary, then tap a workout.

Tip: To see a particular type of workout—Walking or Swimming, for example—tap Show More next to Workouts, tap All Workouts, then tap a workout type. To return to all workouts, tap the workout name in the top-right corner, then tap All Workouts in the list that appears.

Review your workout route and pace

1. Open the Fitness app on your iPhone.
2. Tap Summary, tap a workout, then tap the map thumbnail that appears below Map.

Route is available for outdoor walk, hiking, run, open water swim, or cycle workouts.

The colors found in your route indicate your pace, with green the fastest pace and red, the slowest.

To see the route you must turn on route tracking. You can turn on route tracking when you set up your Apple Watch, or at any time later:

- On your Apple Watch: Open the Settings app, go to Privacy > Locations Services, tap Apple Watch Workout, then tap While Using the App.
- On your iPhone: Go to Settings > Privacy > Location Services, tap Apple Watch Workout, then tap While Using the App.

Go for a swim with Apple Watch

Start a swimming workout

1. Open the Workout app on your Apple Watch.
2. Choose Open Water Swim or Pool Swim.

To pause or resume your swim, press the Digital Crown and side button at the same time.

When you start a swimming workout, your Apple Watch automatically locks the screen with Water Lock to avoid accidental taps. When you're out of the water to rest or because you've finished your workout, turn the Digital Crown to unlock the screen and clear any water from the speaker. You hear sounds and may feel some water on your wrist.

View your swimming workout summary

Unlock your Apple Watch, then tap End.
The pool swim workout automatically tracks your sets and when you rest. The summary on your Apple Watch displays the kinds of strokes you used and the total distance you swam. You can find the pace for each set in the workout summary on your iPhone.

Manually clear water after swimming

1. Touch and hold the bottom of the screen, swipe up to open Control Center, then tap 💧 .
2. Turn the Digital Crown to unlock the screen and clear water from the speaker.

Use gym equipment with Apple Watch

Your Apple Watch can pair and sync data with compatible cardio equipment such as treadmills, ellipticals, indoor bikes, and more, providing you with more accurate information about your workout.

Pair your Apple Watch with gym equipment

1. Check if the equipment is compatible—you'll see "Connects to Apple Watch" or "Connect to Apple Watch" on the equipment.
2. Make sure your watch is set to detect gym equipment—open the Settings app on your Apple Watch, tap Workout, then turn on Detect Gym Equipment.
3. Hold your Apple Watch within a few centimeters of the contactless reader on the gym equipment, with the display facing the reader.
   A gentle tap and beep confirm that your Apple Watch is paired.

If Detect Gym Equipment is off in Settings on your Apple Watch, open the Workout app , then hold your Apple Watch near the contactless reader on the gym equipment, with the display facing the reader.

Start and end a workout

Press Start on the gym equipment to begin. Press Stop on the equipment to end the workout.

When you end your workout, data from the equipment appears in the workout summary in the Activity app on your Apple Watch and the Fitness app on iPhone.

Adjust the workout settings on Apple Watch

Update your height and weight

1. Open the Apple Watch app on your iPhone.
2. Tap My Watch, go to Health > Health Details, then tap Edit.
3. Tap Height or Weight, then adjust.

Your Apple Watch uses the information you provide about your height, weight, gender, age, and wheelchair status to calculate how many calories you burn, how far you travel, and other data. The more you run with the Workout app 🏃, the more your Apple Watch learns your fitness level—and the more accurately it can estimate the calories you burned during aerobic activity.

Your iPhone GPS allows your Apple Watch to achieve even more distance accuracy. For example, if you carry your iPhone while using the Workout app 🏃 on a run, your Apple Watch uses the iPhone GPS to calibrate your stride. Then later, if you're not carrying your iPhone, or if you're working out where GPS is unavailable (for example, indoors), your Apple Watch uses the stored information about your stride to measure distance.

Apple Watch may use the built-in GPS to calibrate your movement.

Change your workout view

1. Open the Apple Watch app on your iPhone.
2. To choose which stats are shown for each workout type—for example, if you want to see your current elevation while

you're hiking in the mountains—tap the workout type, tap Edit, then add or delete stats and drag to reorder.

During your workout, turn the Digital Crown to highlight a different metric—distance or your heart rate, for example.

Change measurement units

If you prefer meters to yards or kilojoules to calories, you can change the measurement units the Workout app uses.

1. Open the Settings app ⚙ on your Apple Watch.
2. Tap Workout, scroll to the bottom, then tap Units of Measure.

You can change units for energy, pool length, cycling workouts, and walking and running workouts.

Pause running and cycling workouts automatically

1. Open the Settings app ⚙ on your Apple Watch.
2. Tap Workout, then turn on Auto-Pause.

Your Apple Watch automatically pauses and resumes your outdoor running and cycling workouts—for example, if you stop to cross the street or get a drink of water.

Turn workout reminders on or off

For walking, running, swimming, and other workouts, your Apple Watch senses when you're moving and alerts you to start the Workout app. It even gives you credit for the exercise you've already done. It will also remind you to end your workout, in case you get distracted when you're cooling down. Follow these steps to turn workout reminders on or off.

1. Open the Settings app ⚙ on your Apple Watch.
2. Tap Workout, then change the Start Workout Reminder and End Workout Reminder settings. (Workout reminders are on by default.)

You can also open the Apple Watch app on your iPhone, tap My Watch, tap Workout, then change the workout reminder settings.

Avoid accidental taps

If the exercise you're doing or the gear you're wearing causes accidental taps on your Apple Watch, lock the screen so your workout record isn't interrupted.
- Lock the screen: Swipe right, then tap Lock.
- Dismiss a notification: Press the Digital Crown.
- Unlock the screen: Turn the Digital Crown.

Conserve power during a workout

You can extend battery life on Apple Watch during walking and running workouts.

1. Open the Settings app on your Apple Watch.
2. Tap Workout, then turn on Power Saving Mode.

During walking and running workouts, power saving mode turns off Always On display and cellular on models that support these features. The built-in heart rate sensor is also turned off until you end your workout.

Use World Clock on Apple Watch to check the time in other locations

Use the World Clock app on your Apple Watch to check the time in cities around the globe.
Ask Siri. Say something like: "What time is it in Auckland?"

Add and remove cities in World Clock

1. Open the World Clock app on your Apple Watch.
2. Tap Add City.

3. Type the city name, or use Scribble or dictation to enter the city name.

   To use Scribble on Apple Watch Series 7, swipe up from the bottom of the screen, then tap Scribble.

   Note: Scribble is not available in all languages.

4. Tap the city name to add it to World Clock.

To remove a city, swipe left on its name in the city list, then tap X. The cities you add on your iPhone also appear in World Clock on your Apple Watch.

Check the time in another city

1. Open the World Clock app on your Apple Watch.
2. Turn the Digital Crown or swipe the screen to scroll the list.
3. To see more information about a city, including time of sunrise and sunset, tap the city in the list.

   While you're viewing info about a city, you can scroll to see the next city in your list.
4. When you're finished, tap < in the top-left corner, or swipe right to return to the city list.

If there's a city whose time you'd always like to see, you can add the world clock to your watch face and choose the city to display.

Turn to scroll through cities.

Change city abbreviations

To change a city abbreviation used on your Apple Watch, follow these steps:
1. Open the Apple Watch app on your iPhone.
2. Tap My Watch, then go to Clock > City Abbreviations.
3. Tap any city to change its abbreviation.

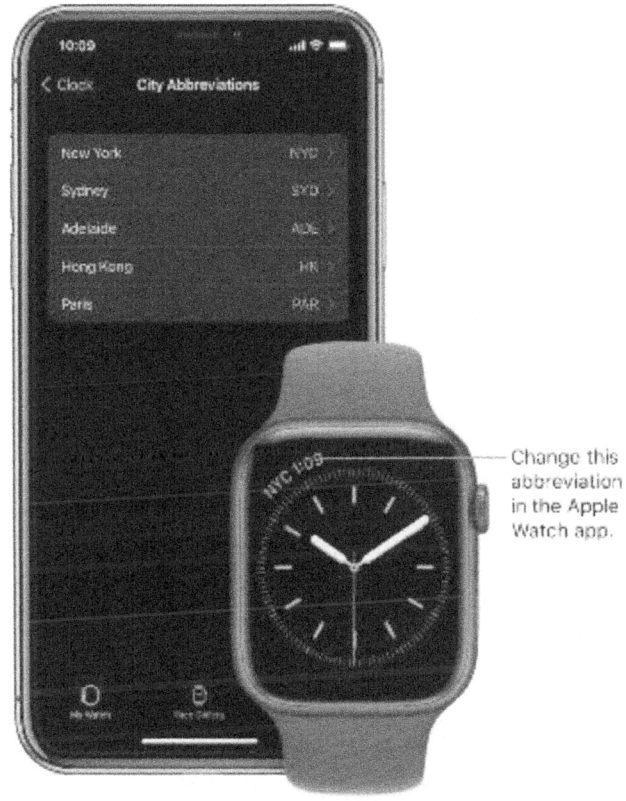
Change this abbreviation in the Apple Watch app.

Accessibility and related settings

Use VoiceOver on Apple Watch

VoiceOver helps you use your Apple Watch even if you can't see the display. Use simple gestures to move around the screen and listen as VoiceOver speaks each item you select.

Turn VoiceOver on or off

1. Open the Settings app ⚙ on your Apple Watch.
2. Go to Accessibility > VoiceOver, then turn on VoiceOver. To turn VoiceOver off, double-tap the VoiceOver button.

Ask Siri. "Turn VoiceOver on" or "Turn VoiceOver off."

You can also use your iPhone to turn on VoiceOver for your Apple Watch—open the Apple Watch app on your iPhone, tap My Watch, go to Accessibility, then tap the VoiceOver option. Or, use the Accessibility Shortcut.

Use VoiceOver for setup

VoiceOver can help you set up your Apple Watch—triple-click the Digital Crown during setup.

VoiceOver gestures

Use these gestures to control your Apple Watch with VoiceOver.
- Explore the screen: Move your finger around on the display and listen as the name of each item you touch is spoken. You can also tap with one finger to select an item, or swipe left or right with one finger to select an adjacent item. Swipe left or right, up or down with two fingers to see other pages.
- Go back: If you've gone down a path you didn't expect, do a two-finger scrub: use two fingers to trace a "z" shape on the display.

- Act on an item: With VoiceOver on, use a double tap instead of a single tap to open an app, switch an option, or perform any action that would normally be done with a tap. Select an app icon, list item, or option switch by tapping it or swiping to it, then double-tap to perform its action. For example, to turn VoiceOver off, select the VoiceOver button, then double-tap anywhere on the display.
- Perform additional actions: Some items offer several actions—listen for "actions available" when you select an item. Swipe up or down to choose an action, then double-tap to perform it.
- Pause reading: To have VoiceOver stop reading, tap the display with two fingers. Tap again with two fingers to resume.
- Adjust VoiceOver volume: Double-tap and hold with two fingers, then slide up or down. Or, open the Apple Watch app on your iPhone, tap My Watch, then go to Accessibility > VoiceOver and drag the slider.

Use the VoiceOver rotor

You can use the rotor to change VoiceOver settings and jump from one item to the next on the screen. On Apple Watch, you can use the rotor to choose Words, Characters, Actions, Headings, Volume, and Speaking Rate.

When VoiceOver is turned on, rotate two fingers on your screen as if you're turning a dial. VoiceOver speaks the rotor setting. Keep rotating your fingers to hear more settings. Stop rotating your fingers when you hear the setting you want.

Use these gestures with the rotor.

Action	Gesture
Choose a rotor setting	Rotate two fingers
Move to the previous item or increase (depending on the rotor setting)	Swipe up

Move to the next item or decrease (depending on the rotor setting)	Swipe down

Adjust VoiceOver settings

You can adjust VoiceOver behaviors from your Apple Watch. Open the Settings app on your Apple Watch, go to Accessibility > VoiceOver, then do any of the following:

- Turn off VoiceOver
- Adjust the speaking rate
- Adjust VoiceOver volume
- Turn Haptics on or off
- Use your current Siri voice for VoiceOver
- Set Braille options
  Tap Braille, then choose options for Braille output, Braille input, word wrap, alert display duration, and Braille tables.
- Turn off VoiceOver hints
- Navigate with the Digital Crown
- Hear the time when you raise your wrist
- Turn on Screen Curtain, which turns off the display for privacy when using VoiceOver
- Speak seconds
- Choose rotor languages
- Configure Hand Gestures

You can find these same options on your iPhone. Open the Apple Watch app, tap My Watch, then go to Accessibility > VoiceOver.

Set up Apple Watch using VoiceOver

VoiceOver can help you set up your Apple Watch and pair it with your iPhone. To have VoiceOver speak, touch and hold the display, then move your finger around or swipe left or right. Double-tap to activate the highlighted item.

Set up Apple Watch using VoiceOver

1. If your Apple Watch isn't on, turn it on by holding down the side button (below the Digital Crown).
2. On your Apple Watch, turn on VoiceOver by triple-clicking the Digital Crown.
3. Bring your iPhone near your Apple Watch.
4. On your iPhone, select Continue, then double-tap.
5. On your iPhone, tap Set Up Apple Watch, then double-tap.
6. To try automatic pairing, point the iPhone camera at the watch from about 6 inches away.
   When you hear the pairing confirmation, follow the spoken prompts. If you have difficulty, you can try manual pairing; follow steps 7 through 13.
7. On your iPhone, select Pair Apple Watch Manually, then double-tap.
8. On your Apple Watch, select the Info button in the bottom-right corner, then double-tap.
9. On your Apple Watch, select your Apple Watch ID near the top of the screen. You hear the unique identifier for your Apple Watch—it's something like "Apple Watch 52345".
10. On your iPhone, select this same identifier, then double-tap.
11. Select the six-digit pairing code on your Apple Watch to hear it.
12. Enter the pairing code from your Apple Watch on your iPhone using the keyboard.
    When pairing succeeds, you feel a tap from Apple Watch and you hear "Your Apple Watch is paired." If pairing fails, tap to respond to the alerts. Your Apple Watch and the Apple Watch app on your iPhone reset so you can try again.
13. On your iPhone, choose Restore from Backup or Set Up as New Apple Watch, then double-tap.
14. Follow the spoken prompts to continue setting up your Apple Watch.

When you've completed setup, Apple Watch syncs with your iPhone. This takes a few moments—tap Sync Progress on your iPhone to hear progress. When you hear "sync complete" your

Apple Watch is ready to use, displaying the watch face. Swipe left or right to explore watch face features.

Apple Watch basics with VoiceOver

With VoiceOver on your Apple Watch, you can perform many functions with a press, swipe, or turn of the Digital Crown. Try the following while viewing the current watch face.

- Change the watch face: Firmly press the display, then swipe left or right with two fingers to browse available faces. When you find one you like, double-tap to select it.
- Customize a watch face: Firmly press the display, swipe down to choose Customize, then double-tap. Swipe left or right to browse the customizable features. Turn the Digital Crown to customize the selected feature. When you finish, press the Digital Crown, then double-tap the face to save your changes.
- Check notifications from the watch face: Swipe down with two fingers.
  To check notifications from most other screens, tap the time in the top-right of the display, then swipe down with two fingers.
- Open Control Center from the watch face: Swipe up with two fingers.
  To open Control Center from most other screens, tap the time in the top-right of the display, then swipe up with two fingers.
- Open the Dock: Press the side button, then turn the Digital Crown to scroll through your favorite apps. Double-tap an app to open it.
- Open any app: Press the Digital Crown once to go to the Home Screen. Swipe left or right, tap, or drag your finger to highlight an app, then double-tap to open it. Or use Siri to open it: hold down the Digital Crown until you feel the double tap, then say "launch" followed by the app name (for example, "launch Mail").

- Read mail: Press the Digital Crown once to go to the Home Screen. Swipe to highlight the Mail app, then double-tap (or hold down the Digital Crown to use Siri, then say "launch Mail"). When the Mail app opens, swipe left or right to read messages.
- Navigate with the Digital Crown: Triple-tap with two fingers, then turn the Digital Crown to select an item. Triple-tap with two fingers to turn off Digital Crown Navigation.

Use AssistiveTouch on Apple Watch

AssistiveTouch helps you use Apple Watch if you have difficulty touching the screen or pressing the buttons. The built-in sensors on Apple Watch can help you answer calls, control an onscreen pointer, and launch a menu of actions—all through hand gestures. Using gestures with AssistiveTouch, you can perform these and other actions:

- Tap the display
- Press and turn the Digital Crown
- Swipe between screens
- Hold the side button
- Access Notification Center, Control Center, and the Dock
- Show apps

- Use Apple Pay
- Confirm double-clicks of the side button
- Activate Siri

Set up AssistiveTouch

1. Open the Settings app on your Apple Watch.
2. Go to Accessibility > AssistiveTouch, then turn on AssistiveTouch.
3. Tap Hand Gestures, then turn on Hand Gestures.
   Tip: To learn how to use hand gestures, tap "Learn more" below the Hand Gestures switch, then tap each gesture. When you tap a gesture, an interactive animation shows you how to perform and perfect the gesture.

You can also open the Apple Watch app on your iPhone, tap My Watch, go to Accessibility > AssistiveTouch, then turn on AssistiveTouch.

Use AssistiveTouch with Apple Watch

With AssistiveTouch and Hand Gestures turned on, navigate your Apple Watch using the following default gestures:

- Pinch: Forward
- Double-pinch: Back
- Clench: Tap
- Double-clench: Show the Action Menu

For example, with the Meridian watch face showing, use AssistiveTouch with the Weather app by following these steps:

1. Double-clench to activate AssistiveTouch.
   A highlight appears around the Calendar complication.
2. Pinch to move to the Temperature complication, then clench to tap it.
3. When the Weather app opens, clench once to move from temperature to weather conditions.
4. Pinch once to scroll down to Air Quality, then pinch once again to see UV Index.

5. Double-pinch to move back to Air Quality.
6. Double-clench to show the Action Menu.
   Pinch to move forward through the actions; double-pinch to move back.
7. Select the Press Crown action, then clench once to return to the watch face.

Use the Motion Pointer

In addition to pinching and clenching, with the Motion Pointer you can control your Apple Watch by tilting the watch up and down and side to side. For example, use the Motion Pointer to navigate the Activity app by following these steps:
1. With the watch face showing and Apple Watch in list view, double-clench to activate AssistiveTouch.
2. Double-clench again to show the Action Menu, pinch to move to the Press Crown action, then clench to tap it.
3. If it's not already selected, pinch or double-pinch to move forward or back to the Activity app, then clench to open it.
4. Double-clench to show the Action Menu, continue pinching until you select the Interaction action, then clench to tap it. Motion Pointer should be selected.
5. Clench to turn on the Motion Pointer.
   A cursor appears on the screen.
6. Tilt the watch to place the cursor at the bottom edge of the screen to scroll up. To swipe to the Sharing screen, place the cursor on the right edge.
7. To tap a button, just hold the cursor over it for a short time.
8. To return to the watch face, double-clench to show the Action Menu, pinch to select the Press Crown action, then clench to tap it.

Adjust AssistiveTouch settings

You can change the actions assigned to pinch, clench, and the Motion Pointer gestures, as well as adjust the sensitivity of the Motion Pointer.

Open the Settings app ⚙ on your Apple Watch, go to Accessibility > AssistiveTouch, then do any of the following:

- Customize gestures: Tap Hand Gestures, tap a gesture, then choose an action.
- Customize the Motion Pointer: Tap Motion Pointer, then adjust settings for sensitivity, activation time, movement tolerance, and hot edges.
- Scanning style: Choose between Automatic scanning, where actions are automatically highlighted one after the other, or Manual, where you use gestures to move between actions.
- Appearance: Turn on High Contrast to make the highlight bolder. Tap color to choose a different highlight color.
- Customize Menu: Choose favorite actions, the position and size of the Action Menu, and its autoscroll speed.
- Confirm with AssistiveTouch: Turn on to use AssistiveTouch to confirm payments with the passcode or any time double-clicking the side button is required.

You can also open the Apple Watch app on your iPhone, tap My Watch, then go to Accessibility > AssistiveTouch.

Use a braille display with VoiceOver on Apple Watch

Apple Watch supports many international braille tables and refreshable braille displays. You can connect a Bluetooth wireless braille display to read VoiceOver output, including contracted and uncontracted braille. When you edit text, the braille display shows the text in context, and your edits are automatically converted between braille and printed text. You can also use a braille display with input keys to control your Apple Watch when VoiceOver is turned on.

Connect a braille display

1. Turn on the braille display.

2. On Apple Watch, go to Settings ⚙ > Accessibility > VoiceOver > Braille, then choose the display.
3. To see the braille commands for controlling Apple Watch, tap More Info, then tap Braille Commands.

Change the braille display settings

1. On Apple Watch, go to Settings ⚙ > Accessibility > VoiceOver > Braille.
2. Set any of the following:

Setting	Description
Output	Set the braille display output to uncontracted six-dot, uncontracted eight-dot, or contracted braille.
Input	Choose the input method for entering braille on the display—uncontracted six-dot, uncontracted eight-dot, or contracted braille. You can also turn on Automatic Translation.
Word Wrap	Wrap words to the next line.
Alert Display Duration	Adjust the duration that an alert is visible on your braille display.
Braille Tables	Add tables to the Braille Table rotor.

Use Zoom on Apple Watch

Use Zoom to magnify what's on the Apple Watch display.

Turn on Zoom

1. Open the Settings app ⚙ on your Apple Watch.

2. Go to Accessibility > Zoom, then turn on Zoom.

You can also use your iPhone to turn on Zoom for your Apple Watch—open the Apple Watch app on your iPhone, tap My Watch, tap Accessibility, then tap Zoom. Or, use the Accessibility Shortcut.

Controlling Zoom

Once you've turned on Zoom, you can perform these actions on your Apple Watch.

- Zoom in or out: Double-tap the Apple Watch display with two fingers.
  Tip: Double-tap with two fingers while setting up your Apple Watch to get a better look.
- Move around (pan): Drag the display with two fingers. You can also turn the Digital Crown to pan over the entire page, left-right and up-down. The small Zoom button that appears shows you where you are on the page.
- Use the Digital Crown normally instead of panning: Tap the display once with two fingers to switch between using the Digital Crown to pan and using the Digital Crown the way it works without Zoom on (for example, to scroll a list or zoom a map).
  - Adjust magnification: Double-tap and hold with two fingers, then drag your fingers up or down on the display. To limit magnification, open the Apple Watch app on your iPhone, tap My Watch, go to Accessibility > Zoom, then drag the Maximum Zoom Level slider.

Tell time with haptic feedback on Apple Watch

When it's in silent mode, Apple Watch can tap out the time on your wrist with a series of distinct taps. Do the following:

1. Open the Settings app on your Apple Watch.
2. Tap Clock, scroll up, then tap Taptic Time.

3. Turn on Taptic Time, then choose a setting—Digits, Terse, or Morse Code. Hours and minutes are indicated in the following ways:
    - Digits: Apple Watch long taps for every 10 hours, short taps for each following hour, long taps for every 10 minutes, then short taps for each following minute.
    - Terse: Apple Watch long taps for every five hours, short taps for the remaining hours, then long taps for each quarter hour.
    - Morse Code: Apple Watch taps each digit of the time in Morse code.
4. To feel a haptic version of the time, touch and hold two fingers on the watch face.

You can also configure Taptic Time on iPhone. Open the Apple Watch app on iPhone, tap My Watch, go to Clock > Taptic Time, then turn it on.

Note: Taptic Time is disabled if Apple Watch is set to always speak the time. To be able to use Taptic Time, first go to Settings > Clock, then turn on Control With Silent Mode under Speak Time.

Adjust text size and other visual settings on Apple Watch

You can adjust text size and other settings to make it easier to interact with items on the screen.

Adjust text size

You can adjust the size of the text that appears in any area that supports Dynamic Type, such as the Settings app.

1. Open the Settings app on your Apple Watch.
2. Go to Display & Brightness > Text Size, then turn the Digital Crown to adjust.

Choose how text and other items appear

You can make text bold, use grayscale, and set other options to change the appearance of items on the screen. Open the Settings app on your Apple Watch, tap Accessibility, then turn the following options on or off:

- Bold text
- Labels
  Turn on button labels to see an additional position indicator. With labels on, you see a one (1) on any option that is on, and a zero (0) on options that are turned off.
- Grayscale
- Reduce transparency
  Reducing transparency increases legibility with some backgrounds.

You can also open the Apple Watch app on your iPhone, tap My Watch, tap Accessibility, then change an option.

Note: Restart your Apple Watch for changes in bold text and grayscale to take effect.

Limit animation

You can limit the motion you see on the Home Screen and when apps open and close.

1. Open the Settings app on your Apple Watch.
2. Go to Accessibility > Reduce Motion, then turn on Reduce Motion.

You can also open the Apple Watch app on your iPhone, tap My Watch, go to Accessibility > Reduce Motion, then turn on Reduce Motion.

Tip: When you turn on Reduce Motion and choose grid view for the Home Screen, all the app icons are the same size.

Adjust motor skills settings on Apple Watch

If you have trouble using the touchscreen, you can adjust settings to change how the screen responds to touches.

Set the side button speed

1. Open the Settings app ⚙ on your Apple Watch.
2. Go to Accessibility > Side Button Click Speed, then choose a speed.

You can also open the Apple Watch app on your iPhone, tap My Watch, then go to Accessibility > Side Button Click Speed.

Use Touch Accommodations

1. Open the Settings app ⚙ on your Apple Watch.
2. Go to Accessibility > Touch Accommodations to do any of the following:
    - Respond to touches of a certain duration: Turn on Hold Duration, then tap the plus or minus buttons to adjust the duration.
      To perform swipe gestures without waiting for the specified hold duration, tap Swipe Gestures, then turn on Swipe Gestures. You can choose the amount of required movement before a swipe gesture begins.
    - Ignore multiple touches: Turn on Ignore Repeat, then tap the plus or minus buttons to adjust the amount of time allowed between multiple touches. Then, if you touch the screen several times quickly, your Apple Watch treats the touches as a single touch.
    - Respond to the first or last place you touch: Choose Use Initial Touch Location or Use Final Touch Location.

If you choose Use Initial Touch Location, your Apple Watch uses the location of your first tap—when you tap an app on the Home

Screen, for example. If you choose Use Final Touch Location, your watch registers the tap where you lift your finger. Apple Watch responds to a tap when you lift your finger within a certain period of time. Tap the plus or minus buttons to adjust the timing. Your device can respond to other gestures, such as drags, if you wait longer than the gesture delay.

You can also open the Apple Watch app on your iPhone, tap My Watch, then go to Accessibility > Touch Accommodations.

Set up and use RTT on Apple Watch (cellular models only)

Real-time text (RTT) is a protocol that transmits audio as you type text. If you have hearing or speech difficulties, Apple Watch with cellular can communicate using RTT when you're away from your iPhone. Apple Watch uses built-in Software RTT that you configure in the Apple Watch app—it requires no additional devices.

Important: RTT is not supported by all carriers or in all regions. When making an emergency call in the U.S., Apple Watch sends special characters or tones to alert the operator. The operator's ability to receive or respond to these tones can vary depending on your location. Apple doesn't guarantee that the operator will be able to receive or respond to an RTT call.

Turn on RTT

1. Open the Apple Watch app on your iPhone.
2. Tap My Watch, go to Accessibility > RTT, then turn on RTT.
3. Tap Relay Number, then enter the phone number to use for relay calls using RTT.
4. Turn on Send Immediately to send each character as you type. Turn off to complete messages before sending.

Start an RTT call

1. Open the Phone app on your Apple Watch.

2. Tap Contacts, then turn the Digital Crown to scroll.
3. Tap the contact you want to call, scroll up, then tap the RTT button.
4. Scribble a message, tap a reply from the list, or send an emoji.
   Note: Scribble is not available in all languages.
   Text appears on Apple Watch, much like a Messages conversation.

Note: You're notified if the other person on the phone call doesn't have RTT enabled.

Answer an RTT call

1. When you hear or feel the call notification, raise your wrist to see who's calling.
2. Tap the Answer button, scroll up, then tap the RTT button.
3. Scribble a message, tap a reply from the list, or send an emoji.
   Note: Scribble is not available in all languages.

Edit default replies

When you make or receive an RTT call on Apple Watch, you can send a reply with just a tap. To create additional replies of your own, follow these steps:

1. Open the Apple Watch app on your iPhone.
2. Tap My Watch, go to Accessibility > RTT, then tap Default Replies.
3. Tap "Add reply," enter your reply, then tap Done.
   Tip: Typically, replies end with "GA" for go ahead, which tells the other person that you're ready for their reply.

To edit or delete existing replies, or change the order of replies, tap Edit in the Default Replies screen.

Accessibility audio settings on Apple Watch

If you prefer to hear a combined left+right audio signal out of both audio channels on speakers or headphones connected to your Apple Watch, turn on Mono Audio. You can also adjust the left-right balance of your Apple Watch audio, whether stereo or mono. And you can change AirPods settings to be more accessible.

Change mono audio and balance settings

Open the Settings app on your Apple Watch, tap Accessibility, then, under Hearing, do any of the following:
- Switch from stereo to mono audio: Turn on Mono Audio.
- Adjust the audio balance: Drag the slider below Mono Audio.

You can also open the Apple Watch app on your iPhone, tap My Watch, tap Accessibility, then turn on Mono Audio and adjust the audio balance.

Change AirPods settings

You can change press speed and press-and-hold duration settings for the AirPods you use with your Apple Watch. You can also turn on noise cancellation on AirPods Pro for when you have one of your AirPods in only one ear.

1. Open the Settings app on your Apple Watch.
2. Go to Accessibility > AirPods, then choose settings.

You can also open the Apple Watch app on your iPhone, tap My Watch, then go to Accessibility > AirPods.

The Accessibility Shortcut on Apple Watch

You can set the Digital Crown to turn VoiceOver, Zoom, or Touch Accommodations on or off with a triple-click.

Set the Accessibility Shortcut

1. Open the Settings app ⚙ on your Apple Watch.
2. Go to Accessibility > Accessibility Shortcut, then choose VoiceOver, Zoom, AssistiveTouch, or Touch Accommodations.

You can also open the Apple Watch app on your iPhone, tap My Watch, go to Accessibility > Accessibility Shortcut, then choose an option.

Use the shortcut

Press the Digital Crown quickly three times. Triple-click the Digital Crown again to turn off the accessibility feature.

Restart, reset, restore, and update

Restart Apple Watch

If something isn't working right, try restarting your Apple Watch and its paired iPhone.

Restart Apple Watch

- Turn off your Apple Watch: Press and hold the side button until the sliders appear, then drag the Power Off slider to the right.
- Turn on your Apple Watch: Hold down the side button until the Apple logo appears.

Note: You can't restart your Apple Watch while it's charging.

Restart the paired iPhone

- Turn off your iPhone: For models with Face ID, press and hold the side button and a volume button, then drag the slider to the right. For models without Face ID, press and

hold the side or top button until the slider appears, then drag the slider to the right. With any model, you can also go to Settings > General > Shut Down.
- Turn on your iPhone: Hold down the side or top button until the Apple logo appears.

Force Apple Watch to restart

If you can't turn off your Apple Watch or if the problem continues, you may need to force your Apple Watch to restart. Do this only if you're unable to restart your Apple Watch.
To force restart, hold down the side button and the Digital Crown at the same time for at least ten seconds, until the Apple logo appears.

Erase Apple Watch

In some cases, you may need to erase your Apple Watch—if you forgot your passcode, for example.

Erase Apple Watch and settings

1. Open the Settings app ⚙ on your Apple Watch.
2. Go to General > Reset, tap Erase All Content and Settings, then enter your passcode.
   If you have an Apple Watch with a cellular plan, you're offered two options—Erase All and Erase All & Keep Plan. To completely erase your Apple Watch, choose Erase All. If you want to erase and then restore it with your cellular plan in place, choose Erase All & Keep Plan.

You can also open the Apple Watch app on your iPhone, tap My Watch, go to General > Reset, then tap Erase Apple Watch Content and Settings.
If you can't access the Settings app on your Apple Watch because you've forgotten your passcode, put your Apple Watch on its charger, then press and hold the side button until you see Power Off. Press and hold the Digital Crown, then tap Reset.

After the reset finishes and your Apple Watch restarts, you need to pair your Apple Watch with your iPhone again—open the Apple Watch app on your iPhone, then follow the instructions shown on your iPhone and Apple Watch.

Remove your cellular plan

If you have an Apple Watch with cellular, you can remove the cellular plan at any time.
1. Open the Apple Watch app on your iPhone.
2. Tap My Watch, tap Cellular, then tap ⓘ next to your cellular plan.
3. Tap Remove [name of carrier] Plan, then confirm your choice.
You may need to contact your carrier to remove this Apple Watch from your cellular plan.

Restore Apple Watch from a backup

Your Apple Watch is backed up automatically to your paired iPhone, and you can restore it from a stored backup. Apple Watch backups are included when you back up your iPhone—either to iCloud, or to your Mac or PC. If your backups are stored in iCloud, you can't view the information in them.

Back up and restore Apple Watch

- Back up your Apple Watch: When paired with an iPhone, Apple Watch content is backed up continuously to the iPhone. If you unpair the devices, a backup is performed first.
- Restore your Apple Watch from a backup: If you pair your Apple Watch with the same iPhone again, or get a new Apple Watch, you can choose Restore from Backup and select a stored backup on your iPhone.

An Apple Watch that's managed for a family member backs up directly to the family member's iCloud account when the watch is connected to power and a Wi-Fi network. To disable iCloud backups for that watch, open the Settings app ⚙ on the managed Apple Watch, go to [account name] > iCloud > iCloud Backups, then turn off iCloud Backups.

Update Apple Watch software

You can update your Apple Watch software by checking for updates in the Apple Watch app on your iPhone.

Check for and install software updates

1. Open the Apple Watch app on your iPhone.
2. Tap My Watch, go to General > Software Update, then, if an update is available, tap Download and Install.

If you forget your Apple Watch passcode

If your Apple Watch is disabled because you forgot your passcode or entered an incorrect passcode too many times, you can use the Apple Watch app on your iPhone to allow you to enter the passcode again. If you still can't remember your passcode, you can reset Apple Watch, reset the passcode, then restore Apple Watch from a backup. Restoring erases the content and settings on your Apple Watch, but uses a backup to replace your data and settings.
Important: If Erase Data is turned on, the data on your Apple Watch is erased after 10 failed passcode attempts.

Made in the USA
Monee, IL
31 May 2022